LAST

PROPHECIES

The Prophecies in the First 3½ Years of the Tribulation

BILL SALUS

Author of The NOW Prophecies and The NEXT Prophecies

The LAST Prophecies: The Prophecies in the First 3 ½ Years of the Tribulation
First printing October 2019

Publisher: Prophecy Depot Publishing
Customer Service: 714-376-5487
P.O. Box 5612
La Quinta, CA 92248

www.prophecydepotministries.net

ISBN: 978-0-578-56329-9

Interior and cover by Mark Conn
Editor Karol Bankston

Printed in the United States of America

Acknowledgements

Heartfelt thanks to my wife, children, grandchildren and friends who inspired me to write this book. A further debt of gratitude is extended to Ned and Karol Bankston, Bill and Beverly Williams, Bob and Lynette Holmes, Ladd Holton, Brad Myers, Scott and Deb Bueling, Mark Conn our Prophecy Depot Ministry Partners and all those who in one way or another, through prayer, encouragement, support, research, or otherwise, genuinely blessed this book.

Contents

Introduction

Welcome to *The LAST Prophecies*, which is the third book in a series that is entirely devoted to the close examination and detailed explanations of end times biblical prophecy. If you are curious to know what the Bible has to say about your generation's future, then you will find this prophetic series relevant, informative and easy to understand.

Prophecy is a central part of the Bible, which consists of 31,102 verses. There are 23,145 verses in the Old Testament and 7,957 verses in the New Testament and over one-fourth of these verses are devoted toward predictive information.

According to *"The Encyclopedia of Biblical Prophecy"* by Dr. J. Barton Payne, there are 1,239 prophecies in the Old Testament and 578 prophecies in the New Testament for a total of 1,817. Details of these predictions are deliberately dispersed by the Lord into approximately 8,335 verses, constituting about 26.8 percent of the Bible's volume.[1]

Thousands of these predictive verses have already found final fulfillment and all of them happened precisely as written. Hundreds remain unfulfilled and are ready to roll off of their ancient parchments and pound down on the world's pavement packing a powerful global punch. They also will happen precisely as written!

However, when these foretellings finally arrive, they will not all occur at the same time, rather they will happen in a sequential order. Understanding the sequence of these foretold events enables the affected generation to prepare for them beforehand.

A case in point is the historical example of Joseph in Egypt about 3900 years ago. According to Genesis chapter 41, the Pharaoh of Egypt at the time had a prophetic dream that Joseph interpreted. Joseph's interpretation of Pharaoh's dream is quoted below.

> "Indeed seven years of great plenty will come throughout all the land of Egypt; but after them seven years of famine will arise, and all the plenty will be forgotten in the land of Egypt; and the famine will deplete the land. So the plenty will not be known in the land because of the famine following, for it *will be* very severe." (Genesis 41:29-31)

In this historical episode, God made it known to Pharaoh that his country was going to experience seven years of severe famine in the near future. What an incredible blessing it was for the Egyptians to have had their leader be given this advanced privileged information. What world leader today would not like to know the future fate of his country and countrymen?

The good news for Pharaoh was that Joseph, guided by the Spirit of God, understood the prophetic sequence of Egypt's nearby future. The helpful information that Joseph imparted was that seven years of plenty would precede the seven years of severe famine, which enabled the Egyptians ample time to prepare beforehand for the coming catastrophe, which they did.

According to Gen. 41:46-57, led by Joseph, the Egyptians wisely gathered and stored up all the available food throughout the land of Egypt during the seven years of plenty. This responsible action sustained the Egyptians through the seven years of severe famine.

Like then in Egypt's past, a future time is soon forthcoming when the world, not just Egypt, will experience seven years of severe famine and judgment. It's called the "Seven-Year Tribulation Period." The next two books in this end times series are about these rapidly approaching seven years!

The GOOD NEWS is that all world leaders today, like Pharaoh of yesteryear, have the ability to know the future. And, there are types of Joseph, Bible prophecy experts led by the living Spirit of God, who can interpret the biblical predictions that they need to know now and prepare for in advance.

The stunning reality is that, the GOD WHO informed Pharaoh of Egypt's future, is the same GOD WHO has foretold of these final seven years of severe tribulation. Fortunately, Joseph's God has provided us with the necessary advance information we need to prepare ourselves, families, friends, leaders and countrymen in advance.

The undertaking of the first two books in this series was to chronologically order the sequence of predicted events that lead up to the final seven years of tribulation. But, now it's time to line up the predictions that will find fulfillment in the Seven-Year Tribulation Period.

This book series is specifically formatted to classify three easy to understand categories of coming biblical prophecies. They are the:

1.   NOW Prophecies,

2.   NEXT Prophecies,

3.   LAST Prophecies.

It turns out that there are twice as many LAST Prophecies than there are NOW or NEXT Prophecies. Thus, in order to keep the books flowing in the same easy reading formats, I elected to split *The LAST Prophecies* book into two volumes.

This book, *The LAST Prophecies*, will focus upon the prophecies of the first three and one-half years of the final Seven-Year Tribulation Period. The following book, *The LAST Prophecies*

– *Volume 2*, will explore the predictions of the middle and second three and one-half years of the Tribulation Period.

Moreover, this book appeals to the following people groups:

1. People in general who are curious to know what epic events happen during the Seven-Year Tribulation Period.

2. Believers alive today that are concerned about the unsaved souls that will get left behind to experience the travails within the Seven-Year Tribulation Period.

3. Unbelievers alive today that need to be warned in advance about this future perilous period.

4. People who become believers during the Seven-Year Tribulation Period that need prophetic warnings and biblical instructions to guide them.

5. Unbelievers who find themselves reading this book during the Seven-Year Tribulation Period that want to get saved before it's too late.

6. Unbelievers who find themselves reading this book during the Seven-Year Tribulation Period that need to be made aware of the eternal consequences of their rebellious choices to remain unsaved.

1

Recapping the NOW and NEXT Prophecies

Before introducing *The LAST Prophecies* it is important to define what is meant by the NOW and NEXT Prophecies and then recap the biblical predictions that were presented in those first two books of this end times series.

The NOW Prophecies – Book One

The NOW Prophecies are the unfulfilled ancient biblical predictions that appear to be imminent, which means they could happen NOW! These foretellings have either minor or no remaining preconditions inhibiting them from happening.

Noah was given a NOW Prophecy about a forthcoming worldwide flood. Joseph's NOW Prophecies dealt with seven years of plenty that would be swallowed up by seven years of ensuing famine in Egypt. The prophet Jeremiah warned about seventy years of desolation in Judah and the corresponding Jewish dispersion from Judah during those years.

In these instances, it was the NOW Prophecies that were of the utmost benefit to the affected populations within their respective times. These timely predictions enabled the peoples of those times to prepare for the powerful events that directly affected them!

This present generation has several powerful NOW Prophecies racing towards their fulfillment. These predictions are the subject of the first book in this end times non-fiction series called, *"The NOW Prophecies."* The NOW Prophecies include, but are not limited to, the following globally impacting events. They are the:

- Disaster in Iran – (Jeremiah 49:34-39),

- Destruction of Damascus – (Isaiah 17, Jer. 49:23-27),

- Final Arab-Israeli War – (Psalm 83),

- Toppling of Jordan – (Jer. 49:1-6, Zephaniah 2:8-10, Ezekiel 25:14),

- Terrorization of Egypt – (Isaiah 19:1-18),

- Emergence of the exceedingly great Israeli army – (Ezekiel 37:10, 25:14, Obadiah 1:18),

- Expansion of Israel – (Obadiah 1:19-20, Jer. 49:2, Zephaniah 2:9, Isaiah 19:18),

- Vanishing of the Christians – (1 Corinthians 15:51-52, 1 Thessalonians 4:15-18),

- Emergence of a GREATER, SAFER and WEALTHIER Israel – (Ezekiel 38:8-13),

- Decline of America (Ezekiel 38:13), (*USA could be the young lions of Tarshish*).[2]

The NEXT Prophecies – Book Two

The NEXT Prophecies are those biblical predictions that seemingly follow the fulfillment of the above NOW Prophecies. The NOW Prophecies provide the necessary nexus of events that pave the path for the execution of the coming NEXT Prophecies. Although the NEXT Prophecies are rapidly racing toward fulfillment, mostly they require the completion of the NOW's for their stage to become appropriately set.

What distinguishes the NOW Prophecies from the NEXT Prophecies, is that the Next Prophecies have at least one or more significant preconditions prohibiting their final fulfillment. Although these NEXT Prophecies appear to be presently stage setting, their completion is being prevented by some other epic prophetic event, or series of events.

The NEXT Prophecies are the subject of the second book in this end time's non-fiction series called, "*The NEXT Prophecies.*" This book introduced the mysterious time-gap that exists between the Rapture of the Christian Church and the start of the Seven-Year Tribulation Period. It is called the "Post-Rapture / Pre-Tribulation time-gap." "Post-Rapture" because it happens after the Rapture, yet "Pre-Tribulation" since the time interval concludes when the Tribulation period commences.

The premise for the gap is based on the understanding that it's not the Rapture, but rather the confirmation of the covenant in Isaiah 28:15-18 and Daniel 9:27 that triggers the Tribulation Period, which is also commonly referred to as, Daniel's Seventieth Week. This time-gap is for an unspecified period of time and its existence is widely accepted by some of today's top Bible prophecy teachers, such as Dr. David Reagan, Gary Stearman, and Dr. Mark Hitchcock to name just a few.

The unique contribution that *The NEXT Prophecies* book presented to the prophetic community, was that it boldly transported the readers into this time interval to see what prophecies might fit within this period, which was a place where few to no other writers had dared to go before.

The NEXT Prophecies include, but are not limited to, the following world-changing events. They are the:

- Gog of Magog invasion – (Ezekiel 38 and 39),

- Decline of Islam, (*Allah loses his Akbar after the wars of Psalm 83 and Ezekiel 38*),

- Unrestrained supernatural satanic deception – (2 Thessalonians 2:7-12),

- Arrival of the Antichrist – (Revelation 6:1-2),

- World Wars and global famines, plagues and pestilences – (Rev. 6:3-6),

- Emergence of "Mystery Babylon," the Harlot world religion – (Rev. 17),

- Post-Rapture Christian martyrdom – (Rev. 6:9-11 and 17:6),

- True content of the False Covenant – (Isaiah 28:15-18 and Daniel 9:27),

- Two phases of the "Overflowing Scourge" – (Isaiah 28:15-18 and Rev. 6:7-8),

- Start of the third Jewish Temple's construction – (Rev. 11:1-2),

- Two Witnesses – (Rev. 11:3-12). (These Two Witnesses will be covered further in this book).

Generally speaking, the NOW Prophecies could happen before the Post-Rapture / Pre-Tribulation time-gap and the NEXT Prophecies should happen within it. This time-gap will be referred to for the remainder of this book as simply the, Post-Rapture / Pre-Trib gap.

CAVEAT: The fulfillment of some of the NOW and NEXT events could defy this basic timing rule. For instance, if the Rapture happens prior to the fulfillment of any or all of the other NOW Prophecies, which it could since it is an imminent event, then any remaining unfulfilled NOW events would slide into the Post-Rapture / Pre-Trib gap. Similarly, once the "False Covenant" gets confirmed, any remaining unfulfilled NEXT events will find fulfillment in the Seven-Year Tribulation Period.

2

Introducing the
LAST Prophecies

The *NOW* and *NEXT Prophecies* books escorted the readers through the biblical predictions that seemingly commence sometime between now and the end of the Post-Rapture / Pre-Trib gap. The *LAST Prophecies* will deal with the foretellings that find fulfillment during the Seven-Year Tribulation Period, which henceforth in this book will simply be called the "Trib-period."

The sobering reality is that the Bible clearly states that this present earth has an expiration date. It concludes with a final seven-year period that is packed with globally impacting events that are well described in the book of Revelation and elsewhere in the Scriptures.

As a result of twenty-one judgments, which include seven seals, seven trumpets and seven bowls, as well as other devastating events, the earth as we know it will become *"toast"* and in dire need of a *"facelift."*

> CAVEAT: *This book occasionally uses colloquialisms and / or slang, like the two examples of "toast" and "facelift" in the paragraph above, in an attempt to present powerful end times prophetic information in a non-doom and gloom manner. This writing method is also employed to emphasize that end times Bible prophecy is not just for the scholars, but for every man, woman and child, no matter what their level of literacy or sophistication. God wants everyone, who cares to learn, what He precisely knows is coming!*

The apostle Peter sums up the coming global destruction this way,

> "But the day of the Lord will come as a thief in the night, in which the heavens will pass away with a great noise, and the elements will melt with fervent heat; both the earth and the works that are in it will be burned up." (2 Peter 3:10)

Alluding to this dreadful period as "the day of the Lord," Peter makes it clear that life on earth will no longer be *business as usual.* The heavens will pass away, but contrarily "the earth and the works that are in it will be burned up." Although the planet will be devastated it won't "pass away," but it will be in need of a major renovation. The planetary restoration will be accomplished by Jesus Christ upon His return in the Second Coming. At that time, the earth will be restored to Eden-like conditions.

> "See, I (*Messiah*) will create   new heavens and a new earth. The former things will not be remembered, nor will they come to mind. But be glad and rejoice forever in what I will create, for I will create Jerusalem to be a delight and its people a joy. I will rejoice over Jerusalem and take delight in my people; the sound of weeping and of crying will be heard in it no more." ....."The wolf and the lamb will feed together, and the lion will eat straw like the ox, and dust will be the serpent's food. They will neither harm nor destroy on all my holy mountain," says the Lord." (Isaiah 65:17-19, 25, NKJV; emphasis added)

> "The infant will play near the cobra's den, and the young child will put its hand into the viper's nest. They will neither harm nor destroy on all my holy mountain, for the earth will be filled with the knowledge of the Lord as the waters cover the sea." (Isaiah 11:8-9)

Like the *NEXT Prophecies*, the *LAST Prophecies* have preconditions that prohibit them from happening *NOW*. The primary condition that prevents the *LAST Prophecies* from finding a present fulfillment, is the confirmation of the false covenant in Isaiah 28:15-18 and Daniel 9:27. The true content of this covenant and why its ratification starts the Trib-period clock ticking is explained in the chapter entitled, "*The False Covenant that Starts the Seven-Year Tribulation Period.*"

The *LAST Prophecies* that are the subject of the next two books in this series and are chronologically cataloged below. They are inserted within four categories of the Trib-period, which are the first-half, the midpoint, the second-half and the aftermath seventy-five-day interval. Although this list identifies the majority of the biblical predictions that occur during the earth's final years, it does not promise to address the entirety of the predicted events foretold to happen during that time.

As previously stated, the Trib-period begins with the confirmation of the false covenant. The events that follow are sequenced below.

First Half of the Trib-period – *(The first three and one-half years)* These prophecies are explored in *The LAST Prophecies.*

Tribulation Prophecies of the First Half

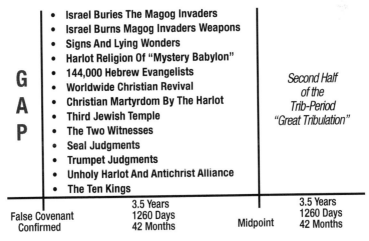

G A P

- Israel Buries The Magog Invaders
- Israel Burns Magog Invaders Weapons
- Signs And Lying Wonders
- Harlot Religion Of "Mystery Babylon"
- 144,000 Hebrew Evangelists
- Worldwide Christian Revival
- Christian Martyrdom By The Harlot
- Third Jewish Temple
- The Two Witnesses
- Seal Judgments
- Trumpet Judgments
- Unholy Harlot And Antichrist Alliance
- The Ten Kings

Second Half of the Trib-Period "Great Tribulation"

| False Covenant Confirmed | 3.5 Years 1260 Days 42 Months | Midpoint | 3.5 Years 1260 Days 42 Months |

- Israel buries the Magog invaders for seven months – (Ezekiel 39:11-16),

- Israel burns the Magog invaders weapons for seven years – (Ezekiel 39:9-10),

- Unrestrained supernatural deception, (signs and lying wonders) – (2 Thessalonians 2:7-10),

- The reign of the Harlot World Religion of "Mystery Babylon" – (Rev. 17:1-15),

- The ministry of the 144,000 Hebrew evangelists – (Rev. 7:1-8),

- The worldwide Christian revival – (Rev. 7:9-17),

- Christian martyrdom by the Harlot (Ecclesiastical Babylon) – (Rev. 17:6),

- The building of the 3rd Jewish Temple – (Rev. 11:1-2),

- The ministry of the 2 Witnesses – (Rev. 11:1-12),

- The opening of the 6th and 7th Seal Judgments – (Rev. 6:12-17 and Rev. 8:1),

(Most traditional commentaries place all of the 7-seal judgments within the first half of the Trib-period. This traditional view could be correct, but *In The NEXT Prophecies* book I present an alternative view, which explores the possibility that the first 5-seal judgments could be opened in the Post-Rapture / Pre-Tribulation gap, but that some of those will continue to operate with the first half of the Trib-period).

- The 7 Trumpet judgments (Rev. 8:7-9:21 and Rev. 11:15),

- The political alliance between the Antichrist and the Harlot – (Rev. 17:3, 7),

- The emergence of the Ten Kings – (Daniel 7:7, 20, 24 and Rev. 17:12, 16-17).

Midpoint of the Trib-period – *(Events that happen within the proximity of the middle of the Trib -period)* These prophecies are explored in *The LAST Prophecies - Volume 2.*

Prophecies at the Midpoint of Tribulation Period

First Half of the Trib-Period	• The Little Bittersweet Book • Death And Resurrection of Antichrist • Desolation Of Harlot • Death of the Two Witnesses • Abomination Of Desolation • The False Prophet • (666) Image And Mark Of The Beast • War In Heaven - Satan Cast to Earth • Persecution Of Jews • 7th Trumpet Sounds The 3rd Woe	Second Half of the Trib-Period "Great Tribulation"
3.5 Years 1260 Days 42 Months	**Midpoint**	3.5 Years 1260 Days 42 Months

- The ingestion of the little bitter-sweet book – (Rev. 10),

- Death, resurrection and establishment of worship of the Antichrist – (Rev. 13:3-18),

- The desolation of the Harlot by the Ten Kings – (Rev. 17:16-17),

- The killing and resurrection of the 2 Witnesses – (Rev. 11:1-12),

- The Abomination of Desolation – (Matthew 24:15, Daniel 9:27),

- Emergence of the False Prophet – (Rev. 13:11-17),

- (666) The Image and Mark of the Beast (Rev. 13:15-18),

- War in heaven and the casting down of Satan to the earth – (Rev. 12:7-9),

- The start of the fleeing of the Jewish remnant to the mountains – (Matt. 24:16),

- The sounding of the 7ᵗʰ Trumpet – (Rev. 11-14-19).

Second Half of the Trib-period – *(The last three and one-half years)* These prophecies are explored in *The LAST Prophecies - Volume 2.*

Tribulation Prophecies of the Second Half

First Half of the Trib-Period	Midpoint	Endpoint
	• The "Woman In The Wilderness" • The 7 Bowl Judgments • The 8 Stages Of Armageddon Campaign 1. The Antichrist Assembles His Allies 2. The Destruction Of Commercial Babylon 3. The Fall Of Jerusalem 4. The Antichrist Armies At Petra (Jordan) 5. The National Regeneration of Israel 6. The Second Coming Of Jesus Christ 7. The Battle At The Valley Of Jehoshaphat 8. Christ's Ascent Up The Mount of Olives	75 Day Interval
3.5 Years 1260 Days 42 Months	← 3.5 Years 1260 Days 42 Months →	

- The period of exile of the "Woman in the Wilderness" – (Rev. 12:6),

- The pouring out of God's wrath in the seven Bowl judgments – (Rev. 16),

- The 8-stages of the Armageddon campaign – (Joel 3:2 and elsewhere),

  1. The Antichrist and his allies assemble,

2. The destruction of commercial Babylon in one-hour,

3. The fall of Jerusalem,

4. The armies of the Antichrist at Petra (historic Bozrah),

5. The national regeneration of Israel,

6. The Second Coming of Jesus Christ,

7. The Battle at the Valley of Jehoshaphat,

8. The Victory Ascent of Christ up the Mount of Olives.

The Seventy-Five Day Interval - These prophecies are explored in *The LAST Prophecies - Volume 2.*

The Seventy Five Day Interval Period

	Midpoint	Endpoint	
First Half of the Trib-Period	*Second Half of the Trib-Period*	• Antichrist & False Prophet Cast Into Lake Of Fire • Satan Bound For 1000 Years into Bottomless Pit • Sheep And Goat Gentile Judgment • The First Resurrection • The Resurrection Of Old Testament Saints • The Resurrection Of The Tribulation Saints • The Marriage Supper Of The Lamb	
3.5 Years 1260 Days 42 Months	3.5 Years 1260 Days 42 Months	← —— 75 Day Interval ——→	

After the seven years of the Trib-period conclude there is a seventy-five-day time interval as per Daniel 12:11-12. The events that take place within those days are:

• The casting of the Antichrist and False Prophet into the Lake of Fire – (Rev. 19:20),

- The binding of Satan in the bottomless pit for 1000 years – (Rev. 20:2-3),

- The judgment of the Sheep and Goat Gentiles – (Matthew 25:31-46, Joel 3:1-3),

- The First Resurrection – (1 Corinthians 15:20-23 and Rev. 20:5-6)

- The Resurrections of the Old Testament and Tribulation Saints – (Isaiah 26:19, Daniel 12:2, Rev. 20:4),

- The Marriage Feast of the Lamb – (Rev. 19:9 and elsewhere).

Another excellent resource that identifies and explains the Trib-period prophecies and much more is the book authored by Dr. Arnold Fruchtenbaum entitled, *The Footsteps of the Messiah, A Study of the Sequence of Prophetic Events.* This book is available through Dr. Fruchtenbaum's website at www.ariel.org.

3

Daniel's Seventieth Week and The Seven-Year Tribulation Period

This chapter will discuss:

- The biblical basis for splitting the Seven-Year Tribulation Period into a first and second half,

- The distinction between the first three and one-half years of tribulation and the second three and one-half years of "Great Tribulation,"

- The connection between the Trib-period and Daniel's Seventieth Week.

The previous chapter split the 7-year Trib-period into two equal halves. This was done in accordance with the biblical basis that these two periods represent distinctive phases that go from bad to progressively worse. The first three and one-half years is a period of tribulation, but the second three and one-half years is characterized by even greater tribulation. As such, the second half of the Trib-period is commonly referred to as, "The Great Tribulation."

The scriptural support for this split is identified in three primary formats, which are:

1. *A time and times and half a time* – (time = one year, times = two years and half a time = half a year for a total of three and one-half years).

2. *Forty-two months* – (42 months divided by 12 months per year = three and one-half years).

3. *One thousand two hundred and sixty days* – (1260 days divided by 360 days of the Jewish calendar = three and one-half years).

The related verses to these three and one-half years timing categories are below.

A time and times and half a time

"He shall speak *pompous* words against the Most High, Shall persecute the saints of the Most High, And shall intend to change times and law. Then *the saints* shall be given into his hand For a time and times and half a time." (Daniel 7:25)

This three and one-half years increment occurs in the second half of the Trib-period. This is when *"He,"* alluding to the Antichrist, will be beheading *"the saints"* in Revelation 20:4 who refuse to worship him and take the mark of the beast in Revelation 13:15-18.

"Then I heard the man clothed in linen, who *was* above the waters of the river, when he held up his right hand and his left hand to heaven, and swore by Him who lives forever, that *it shall be* for a time, times, and half *a time;* and when the power of the holy people has been completely shattered, all these *things* shall be finished." (Daniel 12:7)

This three and one-half years time frame likewise occurs in the second half of the Trib-period. It describes the shattering of the power of the "holy people," referring to the Jews. The Jews will be empowered in the first half of the Trib-period while they are performing sacrifices and offerings in their third temple. However, in the second half of the Trib-period they will be fleeing for their lives as the Antichrist commences a campaign of Jewish genocide.

Zechariah 13:8 informs that two-thirds of the Jews in the land will be killed during that period. In Matthew 24:15-22, Jesus Christ warns the Jews to flee when they witness the Antichrist go into the temple and commit the "Abomination of Desolation," which happens at the midpoint of the Trib-period.

> "But the woman was given two wings of a great eagle, that she might fly into the wilderness to her place, where she is nourished for a time and times and half a time, from the presence of the serpent." (Rev. 12:7)

This event also takes place in the second half of the Trib-period. The "woman" represents Israel. A remnant of Jews will take heed to Christ's forewarning in Matthew 24:15 and flee to the wilderness area of Petra, Jordan, which is ancient Bozrah. They will seek refuge there throughout the duration of the Antichrist's genocidal campaign.

Forty-two months

> "But leave out the court which is outside the temple, and do not measure it, for it has been given to the Gentiles. And they will tread the holy city underfoot *for* forty-two months." (Rev. 11:2)

This happens in the first half of the Trib-period. It correlates with the timing of the 2 Witnesses in Revelation 11. The third Jewish temple will exist and "the Gentiles," who are primarily represented by the Harlot world religion of Revelation 17, will have access to go through the "holy city" of Jerusalem "*for* forty-two months" to get to the Temple's outer court.

> "And he was given a mouth speaking great things and blasphemies, and he was given authority to continue for forty-two months." (Rev. 13:5)

This verse correlates with Daniel 7:25, which was previously quoted. The "he" is the Antichrist and during the second half of the Trib-period he blasphemes God by using "*pompous* words against the Most High."

One thousand two hundred and sixty days

> "And I will give *power* to my two witnesses, and they will prophesy one thousand two hundred and sixty days, clothed in sackcloth." (Rev. 11:3)

These two witnesses are active during the first half of the Trib-period. They are the subject of the chapter entitled, "*The 144,002 Witnesses – Part Two: the 2 Witnesses.*"

> "Then the woman fled into the wilderness, where she has a place prepared by God, that they should feed her there one thousand two hundred and sixty days." (Rev. 12:6)

This verse supports Revelation 12:7 above. The woman represents the surviving remnant of Israel and the "wilderness" of Petra, Jordan is where "she is nourished for a time and times and half a time." In Rev. 12:6 this same time span is precisely calculated to be, "one thousand two hundred and sixty days."

Tribulation versus Great Tribulation

The Bible separates the Trib-period into two phases by calling the first half the Tribulation and the second half, the Great Tribulation. Jesus Christ makes this distinction in His Olivet Discourse. In Matthew 24:3, the disciples ask Christ the following questions, "*Tell*

*us, when will these things be? And what will be the sign of Your coming,
and of the end of the age?"*

> "And Jesus answered and said to them: "Take heed
> that no one deceives you. For many will come
> in My name, saying, 'I am the Christ,' and will
> deceive many. And you will hear of wars and
> rumors of wars. See that you are not troubled;
> for all these things must come to pass, *but the
> end is not yet.* For nation will rise against nation,
> and kingdom against kingdom. And there will be
> famines, pestilences, and earthquakes in various
> places. All these are *the beginning of sorrows.*"
> (Matthew 24:4-8; emphasis added)

In these above verses Christ says, *"the end is not yet"* and *"All
these are the beginning of sorrows."* These two statements identify
the select events that He identified will happen prior to the Trib-
period. Then, at the conclusion of the *"beginning of sorrows,"* Christ
informs that the Trib-period commences.

> "Then, (*after the beginning of sorrows and when
> the end is not yet come*), they will deliver you up
> to (*the*) tribulation (*period*) and kill you, and
> you will be hated by all nations for My name's
> sake. And then many will be offended, will betray
> one another, and will hate one another. Then
> many false prophets will rise up and deceive
> many. And because lawlessness will abound, the
> love of many will grow cold." (Matthew 24:9-12,
> NKJV; emphasis added)

At the start and throughout the Trib-period there will be
Christian martyrdom that is accompanied by an unprecedented
increase in lawlessness, which according to 1 John 3:4 is sin. This
verse reads, *"Whoever commits sin also commits lawlessness, and sin
is lawlessness."*

Matthew 24:9-12 acknowledges that true believers in the Trib-period will be hated and killed for their genuine faith in Christ. This persecution will include Jewish and Gentile believers. In the first half of the Trib-period the primary means of Christian martyrdom will be committed by the Ecclesiastical Babylon. The Harlot's hands will be stained with the blood of believers.

> "I saw the woman, drunk with the blood of the saints, (*in the past*), and, (*the same woman will be intoxicated*), with the blood of the martyrs of Jesus, (*in the first half of the Trib-period*). And when I saw her, I marveled with great amazement." (Rev. 17:6, NKJV; emphasis added)

At the midpoint of the Trib-period, the Harlot's religious system is abolished by the ten kings, who in turn submit their power and authority into the Antichrist's kingdom.

> "And the ten horns, (*kings*) which you saw on the beast, these will hate the harlot, make her desolate and naked, eat her flesh and burn her with fire. For God has put it into their hearts to fulfill His purpose, to be of one mind, and to give their kingdom to the beast, until the words of God are fulfilled." (Rev. 17:16-17; emphasis added)

The hatred and killing of believers continues into the second half of the Great Tribulation, but this period of martyrdom is executed by the Antichrist, who will behead *"the saints"* in Revelation 20:4 who refuse to worship him and take his *"mark of the beast"* in Revelation 13:15-18.

Jesus informs of the other key concern that occurs during the Trib-period. He warns that *"lawlessness will abound, the love of many will grow cold."* According to 2 Thessalonians 2:3-12, lawlessness:

- Is currently being restrained in the Church Age,

- Will be UNRESTRAINED in the Trib-period,

- Will give rise to the "lawless one," who is the Antichrist,

- Will be rooted in "the working of Satan, with all power, signs, and lying wonders, and with all unrighteous deception among those who perish."

In Matthew 24:9, Christ uses the Greek "Thlipsis" to reference the start of the Trib-period. It can be translated as tribulation, affliction, distress, or persecution. Subsequently, in Matthew 24:21-22, He enjoins the Greek words "megas-thlipsis." This is translated as "Great Tribulation." The word megas means great, greater, greatest, more important, severe or stricter.[3] Christ inserts "megas thlipsis" to differentiate from the severe tribulation of the first half of the Trib-period, to contrast the even greater tribulation that occurs within the second half.

> "For then, (*referring to the second half of the Trib-period after the Abomination of Desolation in Matthew 24:15 has occurred*), there will be great, (*megas*), tribulation, (*thlipsis*), such as has not been since the beginning of the world until this time, no, nor ever shall be. And unless those days were shortened, no flesh would be saved; but for the elect's sake those days will be shortened." (Matthew 24:21-22, NKJV; emphasis added)

Lastly, Christ uses the word tribulation a third time in this sequence of Matthew 24 passages. This final usage explains the cosmic events that happen at the end of the Trib-period that segues into His Second Coming.

> "Immediately after the tribulation of those days the sun will be darkened, and the moon will not

give its light; the stars will fall from heaven, and
the powers of the heavens will be shaken. Then
the sign of the Son of Man will appear in heaven,
and then all the tribes of the earth will mourn,
and they will see the Son of Man coming on the
clouds of heaven with power and great glory."
(Matthew 24:29-30)

The Greek words "megas thlipsis" are translated as "Great
Tribulation" in Revelation 2:22 and 7:14. Both of them appear to
allude to prophetic events that take place in the second half of the
Trib-period.

"And I gave her time to repent of her sexual
immorality, and she did not repent. Indeed I will
cast her into a sickbed, and those who commit
adultery with her into *great tribulation*, unless
they repent of their deeds." (Rev. 2:21-22, NKJV;
emphasis added)

These above verses are addressed to the Church of Thyatira,
which I point out in *The Next Prophecies* book appear to have a
prophetic correlation with the Catholic Church as the head of
end times Ecclesiastical Babylon. If my assessment is correct, the
Catholic Church will be left behind as a religious institution and
will ultimately wind up in the "Great Tribulation" period.

"And I said to him, "Sir, you know." So he said
to me, "These are the ones who come out of the
great tribulation, and washed their robes and
made them white in the blood of the Lamb."
(Rev. 7:14, NKJV; emphasis added)

This verse addresses the martyred believers of the Trib-period.
More than likely, it incorporates those martyred by the Harlot in
the first half of the tribulation period and the Antichrist in the
second half of the Great Tribulation period.

Daniel's Seventieth Week

Another name for the Trib-period is Daniel's Seventieth Week. It originates from Daniel 9:24-27, which speaks of the Jewish people receiving seventy weeks to accomplish seven monumental achievements.

> "Seventy weeks are determined For your people, (*the Jews*), and for your holy city, (*Jerusalem*), To finish the transgression, To make an end of sins, To make reconciliation for iniquity, To bring in everlasting righteousness, To seal up vision and prophecy, And to anoint the Most Holy." (Daniel 9:24; emphasis added)

The Hebrew word Daniel uses for weeks is "*shabua,*" which can be translated as: a period of seven days, weeks or years.[4] This usage is commonly interpreted as seventy seven-year periods equaling a grand total of four-hundred and ninety years.

The seven feats that will be accomplished during this period of seventy sevens are:

1. To finish the transgression,

2. To make an end of sins,

3. To make reconciliation for iniquity,

4. To bring in everlasting righteousness,

5. To seal up vision,

6. To seal up prophecy,

7. And to anoint the Most Holy.

The first significant item on the list is, "*to finish the transgression*," which deals with the generational Jewish rejection of Jesus Christ as their Messiah.[5] This is finally accomplished by the last item on the needs list, which is "*to anoint the Most Holy.*" This anointing occurs at the Second Coming of Christ, which is at the end of the Trib-period.

In the ensuing verses Daniel separates these seventy sevens into three distinct periods.

- Seven weeks =   49 years   17,640 days

- Sixty-two weeks =   434 years   156,240 days

Totals: *(Sixty-nine weeks = 483 years   173,880 days)*

- One week =   7 years   2,520 days

> "Know therefore and understand, *That* from the going forth of the command To restore and build Jerusalem Until Messiah the Prince, *There shall be* seven weeks and sixty-two weeks; The street shall be built again, and the wall, Even in troublesome times." (Daniel 9:25)

The fact that the "*seven weeks and sixty-two weeks*" are distinguished from each other, but yet located in the same verse, implies that they happen consecutively with no gap between them. It also means that two different things are accomplished during each time-period.

During the first seven weeks, (49 years), the Jews rebuilt the "holy city" of Jerusalem. Daniel 9:24 opens up with the determination that the Jews would return to their historic homeland out of the seventy years of Babylonian captivity and rebuild Jerusalem. The rebuilding process spanned the 49-year period and was immediately followed by the sixty-two weeks, which ran consecutively. Below is a quote from The Bible Knowledge Commentary: Old Testament about this.

> "*The first period of 49 years may refer to the time in which the rebuilding of the city of Jerusalem, permitted by Artaxerxes' decree, was completed (444-395 b.c.). Though Nehemiah's wall construction project took only 52 days, many years may have been needed to remove the city's debris (after being desolate for many decades), to build adequate housing, and to rebuild the streets and a trench.*" … "*The first two segments of the important time period—the 7 sevens (49 years) and the 62 sevens (434 years)—ran consecutively with no time between them. They totaled 483 years and extended from March 5, 444 b.c. to March 30, a.d. 33.*"[6]

"And after the sixty-two weeks Messiah, (*Jesus Christ*), shall be cut off, (*crucified*), but not for Himself; And the people (*the Romans*) of the prince who is to come, (*the European Antichrist*), Shall destroy the city, (*Jerusalem*), and the sanctuary, (*the second Jewish temple*). The end of it *shall be* with a flood, And till the end of the war desolations are determined." (Daniel 9:26; emphasis added)

During these sixty-two weeks the Persian Empire was overtaken by the Greek Empire, which was in turn conquered by the Romans. However, the main point of Daniel 9:26 is three-fold. *First*, it announces the timing of the first coming of the Messiah in His role as the "Suffering Servant." *Second*, it foretells of His sacrificial death. *Third*, it makes a clear timeline separation between the sixty-nine weeks from the final seventieth week.

Unlike Daniel 9:25, which included the two time-periods of seven and sixty-two weeks, Daniel 9:26 does not mention the sixty-two weeks in connection with the seventieth week. This is because it's a stand-alone week that is reserved for introduction in Daniel 9:27. This indicates that the seventieth week does not run consecutively with the first sixty-nine weeks, rather there is a break in the action. This gap turned out to be the Church Age.

Important studies, like that performed by Sir Robert Anderson,[7] have been done to prove that Jesus Christ fulfilled Daniel 9:26 by coming at the precise time that was predicted. Commencing with the decree to restore and rebuild Jerusalem by Artaxerxes Longimanus, issued on March 5, 444, the sixty-nine weeks clock started ticking. This event is recorded in Nehemiah 2:1-8. Exactly, 173,880 days later as per the Jewish calendar, Christ made his triumphal entry and was crucified shortly thereafter, *"but not for Himself,"* but as the sacrifice for the sins of mankind. Below is another quote from the Bible Knowledge Commentary.

> *"According to Daniel 9:26 the Anointed One was not "cut off" in the 70th "seven"; He was cut off after the 7 and 62 "sevens" had run their course. This means that there is an interval between the 69th and 70th "sevens." Christ's crucifixion, then, was in that interval, right after His Triumphal Entry, which concluded the 69th "seven." This interval was anticipated by Christ when He prophesied the establishing of the church (Matt. 16:18).""*[8]

> "Then he, (*the* Antichrist), shall confirm a covenant with many, (*Israel and another signatory*), for one week; (*of seven years*) But in the middle of the week He shall bring an end to sacrifice and offering. And on the wing of abominations shall be one who makes

desolate, Even until the consummation, which
is determined, Is poured out on the desolate."
(Daniel 9:27; emphasis added)

This is a cornerstone verse that connects the *Seven-Year
Tribulation Period* with *Daniel's Seventieth Week.* Daniel identifies a
similar seven-year timespan with an identical split, "*in the middle
of the week.*" The seventieth week wasn't erased, abandoned nor
forgotten; it was just postponed until the end of the Church age.
Throughout the Church age the Jews were out-of-commission
when it came to fulfilling the seven feats of Daniel 9:24. But, after
the Rapture, they are recommissioned to this calling.

Importantly, Daniel 9:27 informs what starts the Trib-period.
It's not the Rapture, rather the confirmation of the covenant
between Israel and the many. There exists a gap of unspecified time
between the two events. This gap was a central theme within *The
Next Prophecies* book.

The Terminal Generation (Part One)

The next two chapters are devoted to the topic of THE TERMINAL GENERATION. There are six important themes to cover when it comes to this subject.

Chapter four will:

1. Introduce the "THE TERMINAL GENERATION" and explain what it means,

2. Provide the biblical basis for the existence of THE TERMINAL GENERATION,

3. Explore the reasons for THE TERMINAL GENERATION.

Chapter five will:

4. Present the reasons why this could be THE TERMINAL GENERATION,

5. Address when the Final Generation started and when it will end,

6. Evidence why believers of Christ living within THE TERMINAL GENERATION must **TREMBLE AT GOD'S WORD!**

To better understand the remainder of this book, it's important to define the following terms.

- *Biblical Generation:* The Bible primarily identifies generational timespans of 40, 70, 100, and 120-year lengths.

The reference to a 120-year generation occurs during the days of Noah.

> "And the Lord said, "My Spirit shall not strive with man forever, for he is indeed flesh; yet his days shall be one hundred and twenty years.""
> (Genesis 6:3)

Beginning at the time of Joseph the Israelites served the Egyptians for 400 years and the fourth generation, representing 100 years, was the one that Moses delivered during the exodus period.

> "Then He, (*the Lord*), said to Abram: "Know certainly that your descendants, (*the Israelites*), will be strangers in a land, (*Egypt*), that is not theirs, and will serve them, (*the Egyptians*), and they will afflict them four hundred years."
> (Genesis 15:13; emphasis added)

> "But in the fourth generation they shall return here, for the iniquity of the Amorites is not yet complete." (Genesis 15:16)

Then after the 400 years in Egypt the Israelites wandered in the wilderness for 40 years in the exodus.

> "So the Lord's anger was aroused against Israel, and He made them wander in the wilderness forty years, until all the generation that had done evil in the sight of the Lord was gone." (Numbers 32:13)

Subsequently, centuries later during the period of the Babylonian conquest of Israel, the Jews went into 70 years of Babylonian captivity.

> "And this whole land shall be a desolation and an astonishment, and these nations shall serve the king of Babylon seventy years." (Jeremiah 25:11)

Psalm 90:10 below also speaks of a 70-year generation.

> "The days of our lives are seventy years; And if by reason of strength they are eighty years, Yet their boast is only labor and sorrow; For it is soon cut off, and we fly away."

- *Final Generation:* This term refers to the last generation that lives in the biblical end times. For the purposes of this book they are born within 70 years of the Second Coming of Christ, which correlates in time with the end of this present earth. This group includes Church Age believers and unbelievers.

The Church Age ends with the Pre-Tribulation Rapture, but that does not end the existence of the *Final Generation*, it only removes the believers from within that generation. Unbelievers are left behind and remain part of the *Final Generation*. Within the unbelievers left behind, some will become believers, but they become Post Church Age believers.

- *Terminal Generation:* also referred to as the "Tribulation Generation," alludes to the people alive during the Seven-Year Tribulation Period. They are part of the "*Final Generation,*" but they are a distinct subset within it because they experience the Tribulation period. This grouping includes people that were left behind from, or born after, the Rapture. It includes both believers and unbelievers.

Not everyone in the Final Generation becomes members of the Terminal Generation. Some are believers who are removed prior via the Rapture and some are Post-Rapture believers who are martyred in the gap between the Rapture and the start of the Tribulation period, which means they are not alive when the Tribulation period starts.

1. Introduce the "THE TERMINAL GENERATION" and explain what it means

Living inside of the seven-year tribulation timespan will be "THE TERMINAL GENERATION." According to the Merriam-Webster dictionary the word terminal is defined as; "extremely or hopelessly severe, occurring at or constituting the end of a period."[9] For this generation conditions existing on the earth will indeed be extremely and hopelessly severe.

Hopeless is the appurtenant word because during this concluding period mankind will have no ability to redirect the course of its history. Predetermined proceedings that culminate in the end of this present earth will happen exactly as prophesied. Although hope in eternal salvation through Jesus Christ will still exist, there will be no hope that the world will survive the coming judgments, get a temporary extension date, or receive a stay of execution.

The good news between now and the dreaded end is that the Bible informs us that many people will be saved by receiving Jesus Christ as their Lord and Savior. However, unprecedented Christian persecution and martyrdom awaits those who receive Christ during the Trib-period.

2. Provide the biblical basis for the existence of THE TERMINAL GENERATION

Prophesying about this terminal time-period, Jesus said,

> "For then there will be great tribulation, such as has not been since the beginning of the world

until this time, no, nor ever shall be. And unless those days were shortened, no flesh would be saved; but for the elect's sake those days will be shortened." (Matthew 24:21-22)

The Holman Christian Standard Bible (HCSB) translates these same verses to say,

"For at that time there will be great tribulation, the kind that hasn't taken place from the beginning of the world until now and never will again! Unless those days were limited, no one would survive. But those days will be limited because of the elect."

It was pointed out in a prior chapter that Christ's reference to "Great Tribulation" was dealing with the last three and one-half years of the Trib-period. In this verse Jesus foretells that global events will get so chaotic and catastrophic in the end that, given ample time, all human and animal flesh would be terminated. As such, those days will be limited to the final three and one-half years of Great Tribulation.

The absence of all flesh would make God a promise breaker because He made an unconditional covenant with Abraham that he would have descendants forever.[10] As such, the elect, who represent a remnant of Abraham's Jewish descendants, will survive this perilous period. The days are limited to prevent the extinction of mankind on their behalf.

Referring to them as, "the children of Israel," in Isaiah 66:20, we find that this elect group will spend part of their lives in the Trib-period, but the remainder of their futures in the restored earth during the millennial reign of Christ.

"For as the new heavens and the new earth Which I will make shall remain before Me," says the Lord, "So shall your descendants and your name remain." (Isaiah 66:22)

This faithful remnant will be identified more thoroughly later in this chapter.

Concerning the topic of "the elect," some commentaries teach that this term refers to Gentiles and Jewish believers living during and surviving through the Great Tribulation period. However, contextually Matthew 24 in general, and especially Matthew 24:15-22, deals with Israel and Jewish centered events. The elect are those Jews who witness the Abomination of Desolation in Matthew 24:15 and take heed to Christ's instructions in Matthew 24:16-20. These Jews flee to the mountains to avoid the coming period of Great Tribulation warned about in Matthew 24:21-22. Ultimately, those that survive fulfill the biblical role of the faithful Jewish remnant.

People who become believers after the Rapture, which concludes the Church Age, are called "the saints," rather than "the elect." They are specifically referenced in the two Revelation verses below.

> "If anyone has an ear, let him hear. He who leads into captivity shall go into captivity; he who kills with the sword must be killed with the sword. Here is the patience and the faith of the saints." (Rev. 13:9-10)

> "Here is the patience of the saints; here *are* those who keep the commandments of God and the faith of Jesus. Then I heard a voice from heaven saying to me, "Write: 'Blessed *are* the dead who die in the Lord from now on.' " "Yes," says the Spirit, "that they may rest from their labors, and their works follow them."" (Rev. 14:12-13)

Whereas "the elect" survive through the Trib-period, many believers, Jew and Gentile, do not. The days are not shortened so that they can survive, rather they are martyred as "the saints" and these two verses are provided to inform and console them. They are to be comforted in the knowledge that their deaths are not in vain, but that they *"die in the Lord"* and that their reward is, *"rest from their labors, and their works follow them."*

3. Explore the reasons for THE TERMINAL GENERATION

At this point it's time to ask the logical question, *"but why must it come to this?*" Globally devastating judgments that threaten the survival of humankind and climax in a final three and one-half years time span of Great Tribulation certainly makes for a good apocalyptic movie, but this is not about a thrilling Hollywood blockbuster. This is destined to become REAL LIFE *for* THE TERMINAL GENERATION!

To explain why events happening within the final seven years are so severe, it is important to identify the core purposes for the existence of this Trib-period. The general consensus among some of today's top Bible prophecy teachers is that the Trib-period exists to accomplish the following things:

- To make an end of wickedness and wicked ones,

- To evict Satan,

- To bring about a worldwide revival,

- To break the power of the holy people,

- To convert Israel.

To make an end of wickedness and wicked ones and to evict Satan

A purging of the wicked ones and their perpetration of wickedness must take place on the planet prior to the establishment of the millennial reign of Jesus Christ. Those privileged to reside upon the restored earth during this Messianic Age will be given a clean slate from which to write the new pages of history.

1 John 5:19 informs that presently, "*the whole world lies under the sway of* the wicked one." This WICKED ONE is Satan and he cunningly sways WICKED ONES to execute WICKEDNESS upon the earth. However, the devil is about to get his due. Satan is going to be imprisoned, without the possibility of parole, during the Millennium. The serpent of old will be confined to the bottomless pit for a thousand years and unable to further promote wickedness upon the earth.

> "Then I saw an angel coming down from heaven, having the key to the bottomless pit and a great chain in his hand. He laid hold of the dragon, that serpent of old, who is *the* Devil and Satan, and bound him for a thousand years; and he cast him into the bottomless pit, and shut him up, and set a seal on him, so that he should deceive the nations no more till the thousand years were finished. But after these things he must be released for a little while." (Revelation 20:1-3)

On an interesting side note, observe that a single angel is able to overpower, handcuff and cast the mighty devil into the bottomless pit. This point was brought to my attention by prophecy expert Pastor Billy Crone while we were on a speaking tour together in Australia in 2018.

The once upon a time anointed cherub of Ezekiel 28:14, who rebelled against God and proceeded to weaken the nations in Isaiah 14:12, in the end can't even fend off a single angel. Satan's dramatic slide downward begins with his future defeat in the war of heaven by Michael the archangel.

> "And war broke out in heaven: Michael and his angels fought with the dragon; and the dragon and his angels fought, but they did not prevail, nor was

a place found for them in heaven any longer. So the great dragon was cast out, that serpent of old, called the Devil and Satan, who deceives the whole world; he was cast to the earth, and his angels were cast out with him." (Rev. 12:7-9)

This war happens around the midpoint of the Trib-period and results in the permanent eviction of Satan from heaven. This devil deceiver is then exiled to the earth and greatly displeased with these turn of events! This timing corresponds with the Great Tribulation period, which complicates matters even more for the TERMINAL GENERATION.

> "Therefore rejoice, O heavens, and you who dwell in them! Woe to the inhabitants of the earth and the sea! For the devil has come down to you, having great wrath, because he knows that he has a short time." (Rev. 12:12)

When it comes to ending wickedness and wicked ones in the Trib-period, Dr. Arnold Fruchtenbaum provides sound scriptural support. Concerning these two points, he writes,

> "*There are two key passages that express this purpose. The first is found in Isaiah 13:9:*
>
> > *Behold, the day of Jehovah comes, cruel, with wrath and fierce anger; to make the land a desolation, and to destroy the sinners thereof out of it.*
>
> *This passage uses the term the Day of Jehovah as a reference to the Great Tribulation and gives its goal in the phrase, to destroy the sinners thereof out of it. The purpose, then, is to destroy wicked ones out of the land. This is further described in Isaiah 24:19-20:*

> *The earth is utterly broken, the earth is rent asunder, the earth is shaken violently. The earth shall stagger like a drunken man and shall sway to and fro like a hammock; and the transgression thereof shall be heavy upon it, and it shall fall, and not rise again.*

> *The closing words of this verse state that the basic reason for the judgments of the Tribulation is that the transgression worldwide shall fall and not rise again. Its purpose is to make an end of wickedness."[11]*

To bring about a worldwide revival

> *"And this gospel of the kingdom will be preached in all the world as a witness to all the nations, and then the end will come."* (Matthew 24:14)

During the Trib-period, which is the time context of Matthew 24:14, the GOOD NEWS GOSPEL of JESUS CHRIST will be preached worldwide. According to Revelation 7:9-17, this leads to the salvation of an innumerable multitude of people from *"all nations, tribes, peoples, and tongues."*

The primary means through which these future believers get saved are:

- Through independent study, (After the instant disappearances of millions of believers, it can be anticipated that some inquiring minds will search the scriptures, as well as some of the left behind prophetic resources, to see if the Rapture theory is credible. In the process they will discover that the Rapture was predicted and some of them will eventually be convinced that Jesus Christ is the Messiah),

- The preaching of the 144,000 Jewish Witnesses of Revelation 7:1-8,

- The teachings of the Two Witnesses of Revelation 11:3-13,

- The angel having the everlasting gospel of Revelation 14.

> *"Then I saw another angel flying in the midst of heaven, having the everlasting gospel to preach to those who dwell on the earth—to every nation, tribe, tongue, and people— saying with a loud voice, "Fear God and give glory to Him, for the hour of His judgment has come; and worship Him who made heaven and earth, the sea and springs of water.""* (Rev. 14:6-7)

The fantastic news is that there will be a worldwide revival during the Trib-period. The bad news is that receiving Christ will be a difficult decision for someone to make at that time. *First,* according to 2 Thessalonians 2:9-12, supernatural deception will influence many to believe in what the Bible calls, "THE LIE." This will be the more popular alternative choice, which will contradict the biblical narrative about THE TRUTH of Jesus Christ, which is:

> "Jesus said to him, "I am the way, the truth, and the life. No one comes to the Father except through Me." (John 14:6)

Second, Christian martyrdom will be rampant during that period, rendering it as the less popular and much more costly choice. In *The NEXT Prophecies* book, I identify three different groups of believers from Revelation 6:9-11 who are martyred for their faith through two Christian killing crusades.

These three groups are the:

- *The Fifth Seal Saints,* who are killed by the Harlot world religion during the Post-Rapture / Pre-Trib gap,

- *The Fellow Servants of the Fifth Seal Saints*, who are martyred by the Harlot in the first three and one-half years of the Trib-period,

- *The Brethren of the Fellow Servants of the Fifth Seal Saints*, who are executed (beheaded) by the Antichrist in the Great Tribulation period.

(These are uniquely my teachings above, so search the scriptures to see if my interpretations are correct).

The two Christian killing crusades during the Trib-period are the Harlot world religion during the gap and first half of the Trib-period, and the Antichrist during the Great Tribulation period. Read Revelation 17:6 for the proof text about the Harlot and Revelation 20:4 in relationship to Revelation 13:15-18 for the scriptural support of the Antichrist's killings. This topic is also covered in the later chapter of this book entitled, *"Believers in the Tribulation Period."*

To break the power of the holy people

After the Pre-Trib fulfillment of several *NOW* and *NEXT* prophecies, Israel will become greater in size, safer in security and wealthier economically. They will be highly esteemed as a result. The prophet Ezekiel informs us that this future Israel will gain world renown.

> "Indeed all the people of the land will be burying, (*the dead Ezekiel 38:1-6 invaders*), and they will gain renown for it on the day that I am glorified," says the Lord God." (Ezek. 39:13)

However, this coming highly empowered Jewish state will still reject Jesus Christ as the Messiah. Instead, the leadership of Israel will build the third temple, resurrect the antiquated Mosaic Law, reinstate their animal sacrificial system and believe that these activities will induce the Jewish Messiah to come. This misguided mentality must change in order for the national conversion of Israel to occur, which is the final purpose for the Trib-period.

Daniel the prophet clearly states that during the last three and one-half years of the Trib-period the power of the holy people, alluding to the Jews, will be completely shattered.

> "Then I heard the man clothed in linen, who *was* above the waters of the river, when he held up his right hand and his left hand to heaven, and swore by Him who lives forever, that *it shall be* for a time, times, and half *a time; (time = one year, times = two years and half a time = half a year for a total of three and one-half years)*; and when the power of the holy people has been completely shattered, all these *things* shall be finished." (Daniel 12:7; emphasis added)

Stripping the chosen people of their falsely held sense of power happens in the Great Tribulation period and paves the way for the emergence of the "Faithful Jewish Remnant," which ultimately leads to the national conversion of Israel.

Dr. Fruchtenbaum puts it this way:

> "*God intends to break the power of the holy people in order to bring about a national regeneration. The means by which God will perform this is given in Ezekiel 20:33-38.*
>
> "*As I live, says the Lord Jehovah, surely with a mighty hand, and with an outstretched arm, and with wrath poured out, will I be king over you. And I will bring you out from the peoples and will gather you out of the countries wherein ye are scattered , with a mighty hand, and with an*

*outstretched arm, and with wrath poured out; and
I will bring you into the wilderness of the peoples
and there will I enter into judgment with you face
to face. Like as I entered into judgment with your
fathers in the wilderness of the land of Egypt, so
will I enter into judgment with you, says the Lord
Jehovah. And I will cause you to pass under the
rod, and I will bring your into the bond of the
covenant; and I will purge out from among you
the rebels, and them that transgress against me; I
will bring them forth out of the land where they
sojourn, but they shall not enter into the land of
Israel and ye shall know that I am Jehovah."*

*What is important to note here is that after God
gathers the Jews from around the world, He will
enter into a period of judgment (the Tribulation)
with them. The rebels among the Jewish people will
be purged out by this judgment. Only then will the
whole new nation, a regenerate nation, be allowed
to enter the Promised Land under King Messiah."*[12]

To convert Israel

"And so all Israel will be saved, as it is
written: "The Deliverer will come out of Zion,
And He will turn away ungodliness from Jacob."
(Romans 11:26)

After the shattering of the power of the holy people, the Messiah
"will turn away ungodliness from Jacob" and *"all Israel will be saved."*
Jacob is Israel according to Genesis 32:28 and *all Israel* alludes to
every surviving Jew alive at the Second Coming of Jesus Christ.

The scriptures below introduce the flow of Trib-period events
that lead to the national conversion of Israel.

"Alas! For that day *is* great, So that none *is* like it; And it *is* the time of Jacob's trouble, But he shall be saved out of it." (Jeremiah 30:7)

The *"time of Jacob's trouble"* occurs during the Trib-period. Jeremiah declares that the events transpiring within this period are unprecedented. Yet, out from this Great Tribulation, Jacob (Israel) will be saved. However, the Zechariah verses below inform that millions of Jews will be killed during this period in a genocidal campaign.

"And it shall come to pass in all the land, (*of Israel*)," Says the Lord, "*That* two-thirds, (*of the Jews*), in it shall be cut off *and* die, But *one*-third, (*of the Jews*), shall be left in it: I will bring the *one*-third, (*the faithful Jewish remnant*) through the fire, Will refine them as silver is refined, And test them as gold is tested. They will call on My name, And I will answer them. I will say, 'This *is* My people'; And each one, (*representing all Israel of Romans 11:26*), will say, 'The Lord *is* my God.' " (Zechariah 13:8-9; emphasis added)

The national conversion of Israel involves the one-third of the Jewish population that survives the final genocidal onslaught of the Jews by the Antichrist. This is not referring to the six million Jews exterminated by Hitler during the Holocaust because those Jews were not killed in the land of Israel. Hitler's campaign occurred between 1933-1938, which was prior to the reestablishment of the nation of Israel on May 14, 1948.

The faithful remnant will recognize that Jesus Christ is the Messiah in their affliction and call out for Him to come to the earth a second time to rescue them from the killing campaign of the Antichrist.

"I, (*Jesus the Messiah*), will return again to My place, (*according to Acts 1:9-11, Jesus ascended to heaven*), Till they, (*the Jews*), acknowledge their offense, (*which is the generational rejection*

of Christ as the Messiah). Then they will seek My
face; (*the person of Jesus Christ*), In their affliction,
(*the Great Tribulation period*), they will earnestly
seek Me." (Hosea 5:15; emphasis added)

This remnant of Jews will realize that Jesus Christ, by His own
mandate, won't return in His Second Coming until they petition
Him to do so. Matthew 23:39 is the key verse that must be fulfilled
by the Jews in order for Christ to return.

> "O Jerusalem, Jerusalem, the one who kills the
> prophets and stones those who are sent to her! How
> often I wanted to gather your children together,
> as a hen gathers her chicks under *her* wings, but
> you were not willing! See! Your house is left to
> you desolate; for I say to you, you shall see Me no
> more till you say, 'Blessed *is* He who comes in the
> name of the Lord!' " (Matthew 23:37-39)

The Hebrew translation that the remnant will cry out for
"Blessed is He who comes in the name of the Lord" is, "baruch haba
beshem adonai." These words, which will be uttered by the Jewish
remnant, will prompt Jesus to return in His Second Coming. This
has nothing to do with the coming of Jesus to Rapture the Church.
These are two separate events.

When Christ comes to rescue the faithful remnant of Israel he
subsequently fulfills the Zechariah verse below, which involves the
conversion of Israel spoken about above in Romans 11:26, "*And
so all Israel will be saved.*"

> "And I will pour on the house of David and on the
> inhabitants of Jerusalem the Spirit of grace and
> supplication; then they will look on Me whom
> they pierced. Yes, they will mourn for Him as one
> mourns for *his* only *son,* and grieve for Him as
> one grieves for a firstborn." (Zechariah 12:10)

The Terminal Generation (Part Two)

Recapping, chapter four covered topics #1, #2 and #3 below. This chapter will address #4, #5 and #6.

1. Introduce the "THE TERMINAL GENERATION" and explain what it means,
2. Provide the biblical basis for the existence of THE TERMINAL GENERATION,
3. Explore the reasons for THE TERMINAL GENERATION,
4. Present the reasons why this could be THE TERMINAL GENERATION,
5. Address when the Final Generation started and when it will end,
6. Evidence why believers of Christ living within THE TERMINAL GENERATION must **TREMBLE AT GOD'S WORD!**

4. Present the reasons why this could be THE TERMINAL GENERATION

What a daunting prospect that there will be a TERMINAL GENERATION. Even more unnerving is the legitimate possibility that this might be that generation! Listed below are a few tell-tale indicators that support the strong possibility that this IS IT! For further research, the detailed explanations of these events are provided in either the *NOW, NEXT* or *LAST* Prophecies books of this end times series.

- *The Third Jewish Temple:* The Jews are preparing to build the Tribulation Temple. (Rev. 11:1-2, Matt. 24:15, 2 Thess. 2:4 and elsewhere). (*The LAST Prophecies*).

- *The Prophecy of Elam:* The nuclear disaster in Iran, (ancient Elam), is poised to occur. Jeremiah 49:39 calls this a "latter days" prophecy. (Jer. 49:34-39). (*The NOW Prophecies*).

- *The Destruction of Damascus:* This prediction could happen at any time and it will probably happen in close proximity to the fulfillment of the latter days prophecy of Elam. (Isaiah 17 and Jer. 49:23-25). (*The NOW Prophecies*).

- *The IDF in Bible Prophecy:* The Israeli Defense Forces (IDF) are prepared to become "an exceedingly great army" in fulfillment of Bible prophecy. (Ezek. 25:14, 37:10, Obadiah 1:18, Zechariah 12:6, Isaiah 11:13-14 and 17:9, Jer. 49:2, Zephaniah 2:9, Psalm 83:9-12 and elsewhere). (*The NOW Prophecies*).

- *The Formation of the Gog of Magog Coalition:* Russia, Turkey, Iran and others are beginning to align in potential fulfillment of the Magog invasion of Israel foretold in Ezekiel 38 and 39. Ezekiel 38:8 calls this a "latter years" prophecy. (Ezekiel 38:1-6). (*The NEXT Prophecies*).

- *The Satellite TV Technologies:* Technological equipment and Internet sites now exist, like YouTube, smart TV's and smart cell phones that will enable the whole world to watch:

    THE TWO WITNESSES: The "Two Witnesses" will be killed by the Antichrist, lie dead in the streets of Jerusalem for three-and-a-half days and then resurrect and ascend to heaven afterward. This happens during the first three and one-half years of the Trib-period.

About a century ago, before the advent of today's advanced TV technologies, critics would discredit the Bible because of this prophecy. They asked the question, *"How can the whole world watch two dead guys lie in the streets of Jerusalem?"* However, today's technologies render that question no longer valid. (Rev. 11:3-13). (*The LAST Prophecies*).

On a side note; about these two witnesses, Rev. 11:8 says,

"And their dead bodies *will lie* in the street of the great city which spiritually is called Sodom and Egypt, where also our Lord was crucified."

Jesus was crucified in Jerusalem, but this verse compares Jerusalem to "Sodom and Egypt" at the time these two witnesses are killed. In biblical typologies, Sodom symbolizes sexual sin with a heavy emphasis on homosexuality and Egypt embodies sin in general.[13] The use of these name comparisons could imply that during the Trib-period Israel, with its capital of Jerusalem, is a sinful place characterized by rampant homosexuality.

Presently, Tel Aviv proudly promotes itself as the gayest city on earth. Check out this Boston Globe headline from March 17, 2016. *"Welcome to Tel Aviv, the gayest city on earth."*[14] Is modern-day Tel Aviv foreshadowing what will be happening in Jerusalem at the time of the two witnesses? Is this another indicator that this could be the TERMINAL GENERATION?

- *The Artificial Intelligence and Biometric Technologies*: The expertise and technologies currently exist and are continually being improved to set up the global cashless economic system of the Antichrist and to track the whereabouts of every human being. This system exists throughout the Great Tribulation period. (Rev. 13:16-18). (*The LAST Prophecies*).

- *The Nuclear and Military Technologies*: The current advanced weapons already exist:

1. "To take peace from the earth, and that *people* should kill one another," as per the fiery red horseman of the apocalypse. This happens sometime after the Rapture. (Rev. 6:3-4). (*The LAST Prophecies*).

2. To threaten the extinction of the human race, which is partially why the days are limited to the three and one-half years of the Great Tribulation. (Matt. 24:21-22). (*The LAST Prophecies*).

- *The Revived Roman Empire:* The dominant last days empire has reemerged as the European Union. The Antichrist will arise out of this Revived Roman Empire. The Antichrist is revealed after the Rapture and is active throughout the Trib-period. (Daniel 7, and 9:26, Rev. 13:1-2) (*The LAST Prophecies*).

These are just a few of the stage-setting signs that indicate we could be living in the final generation. For more information on this subject, I recommend watching Jan Markell's DVD entitled, "*Why We May be the Terminal Generation: 15 Signs of His Imminent Return.*" The DVD is available at: www.olivetreeviews.org. Jan Markell says in an article,

> *"Jesus chastised the Pharisees for not being able to discern the signs of His first coming. So why would God not want us to be watching for indicators of His soon return? Sure, many of the signs manifest during the Tribulation, but they are casting a giant shadow now. To the Christian, they are a herald of His coming and to the unbeliever, they are a warning that they are running out of time. But there are specific signs for the Church Age that we should be keeping an eye on! Nations are aligning as predicted. There is a great apostasy taking place. Israel and all activity surrounding her are the super-signs. The convergence* of many events is also a super-sign forming now."[15]

5. Address when the Final Generation started and when it will end

If this is the Final Generation, the important questions are; when did it start and when will it end? I believe these answers must be given in the hypothetical, but not all would agree. Some teach that the start and stop date of the final generation to live on this present earth can be calculated. Moreover, they believe that we are living in that generation.

This teaching primarily advocates that the final generation began on May 14, 1948 when Israel was restored as a nation. This start date is connected with their interpretation of the Parable of the Fig Tree in Matthew 24, Mark 13 and Luke 21. Matthew's version is quoted below.

> *The Parable of the Fig Tree* -"Now learn this parable from the fig tree: When its branch has already become tender and puts forth leaves, you know that summer *is* near. So you also, when you see ALL THESE THINGS, know that it is near—at the doors! Assuredly, I say to you, this generation will by no means pass away till ALL THESE THINGS take place. Heaven and earth will pass away, but My words will by no means pass away." (Matt. 24:32-35; emphasis added)

The theory behind this teaching is that the Parable of the Fig Tree finds a prophetic application through the country of Israel. They correlate the uses of "figs" in Jeremiah 24 and "fig tree" in Hosea 9 as examples for Israel. Thus, when Israel was reborn as a nation in 1948, they believe the Final Generation began.

> "I found Israel Like grapes in the wilderness; I saw your fathers As the firstfruits on the fig tree in its first season. *But* they went to Baal Peor,

And separated themselves *to that* shame; They became an abomination like the thing they loved." (Hosea 9:10)

Generally, those who teach this theory tag seventy, eighty or one hundred years, whichever they believe biblically supports the timespan of a generation, on to May of 1948 when Israel was rebirthed. Some even use the start date of June 7, 1967, which was when East Jerusalem was recaptured by the IDF. They suggest at the end of that generational time-period is when this present world ends.

Unwittingly, this type of teaching date sets a Pre-Tribulation Rapture, which is an imminent event that will happen at an unknown time. For instance, adding seventy years to May 14, 1948 means that May 14, 2018 would have to be the end of this world. But herein is the problem with this idea; this world can't end until the Rapture occurs, and is sometime thereafter followed by seven years of Tribulation.

If May 14, 2018 was the drop-dead date for the end of this present world, then the Rapture should have occurred on or before May 14, 2011, which was seven years prior, and the Tribulation should have already commenced. Obviously that didn't happen or you wouldn't be reading this book today because I wouldn't have been left behind to author it.

This same example applies in every instance whether 1948 or 1967 is used as a start date. Pick any date by adding a biblical generation to 1948 or 1967 and move backward from that date seven years. If there is a Pre-Tribulation Rapture it must occur on or before that hypothesized date. This clearly amounts to a form of date setting.

Revelation 3:3 and Matthew 24:44 informs that Christ is coming at an unspecified time and warns people to repent and become believers before He comes.

"Remember therefore how you have received and heard; hold fast and repent. Therefore if you will not watch, I will come upon you as a thief, and you will not know what hour I will come upon you." (Rev. 3:3)

"Therefore you also be ready, for the Son of Man is coming at an hour you do not expect." (Matt. 24:44)

I do believe that the Parable of the Fig Tree is intended to draw our attention toward the rebirth of Israel on May 14, 1948, but I don't believe these Matthew passages date set when a final generation exists; rather they simply inform us that a final generation will exist.

After introducing Israel as the super-sign of the end times in Matthew 24:32, Christ says in verse 34, "Assuredly, I say to you, this generation will by no means pass away till ALL THESE THINGS take place." The inference is that there is a generation that will pass away, but not until certain predicted things all take place.

This beckons the question of, "What THINGS was the Messiah alluding to?" Certainly the main THING Christ alluded to was the restoration of the nation of Israel as the fig tree, but the Lord didn't say "When you see that sole thing, the final generation exists." Christ alluded to EVERYTHING that He had predicted throughout Matthew 24:2-44.

The point I believe the Lord was making, is that some generation will be able to say, "Yes, EVERYTHING that Jesus Christ predicted in the Olivet Discourse has found fulfillment with 100% accuracy." That generation will be the Tribulation Generation that can say ALL THESE prophesied THINGS can be read about in the history books.

The final generation will be able to declare that:

- The Jewish temple was destroyed in 70 AD fulfilling Matt. 24:2,

- The Temple was rebuilt by the Jews, but subsequently desecrated by the Antichrist, which was foretold in Matt. 24:15,

- There came false Christ's, rumors of war, World Wars, (nation against nation), Mideast wars, (kingdom against kingdom), and earthquakes, as predicted in Matt. 24:4-8,

- The rebirth of Israel became a reality as per the Parable of the Fig Tree in Matt.24:32,

- The Rapture of the Church has taken place in Matt. 24:36-44,

- Then the Trib-period began as per Matt. 24:9,

- The Jewish remnant fled to the mountains in exile, according to Matt. 24:16,

- The final three and one-half years of Great Tribulation commenced, as spoken in Matt. 24:21.

The generation that can testify to the fulfillment of ALL THESE above THINGS will be the TERMINAL GENERATION. For them, the only THING left to be looking for is the BEST THING, which is the SECOND COMING of CHRIST to establish HIS MESSIANIC KINGDOM THING!

So then, the TERMINAL GENERATION is the one that lives through the Seven-Year Tribulation Period. In my estimation, the knowledge of who lives in this generation can only be known when the Trib-period starts, which happens with the ratification of the seven-year covenant of Isaiah 28:15-18 and Daniel 9:27.

When this monumental event happens, the start of the Final Generation and the end of the TERMINAL GENERATION can be calculated. It then becomes a knowable mathematical equation. The endpoint is seven years after the execution of the false covenant, but the start date for the Final Generation precedes the enactment of this covenant by the length of a biblical generation, which is more than seven years.

6. Evidence why believers of Christ living within THE TERMINAL GENERATION must TREMBLE AT GOD'S WORD!

> "To everything *there is* a season, A time for every purpose under heaven:... A time to weep, *And...* A time to mourn..." (Ecclesiastes 3:1,4; abbreviated)

Throughout history there have been generations that were forced to endure tremendously grievous events. Noah had to reside at a time when, "the wickedness of man *was* great in the earth, and *that* every intent of the thoughts of his heart *was* only evil continually." (Genesis 6:5). Ultimately, he and his immediate family survived the worldwide flood, but must have deeply mourned over the drowning of humanity that resulted.

In modern history, the Jewish generation that lived in the early to mid-Twentieth Century had to lament over the Nazi-led extermination of six-million people of their ethnicity. THE TERMINAL GENERATION will also have much to grieve about. Read what the prophet Isaiah says about the final season, which will indeed be a *"time to weep, And... A time to mourn."*

> "Wail, for the day of the Lord, (*the Trib-period*), is at hand! It will come as destruction from the Almighty.

Therefore all hands will be limp, Every man's heart will melt, And they will be afraid. Pangs and sorrows will take hold of them; They will be in pain as a woman in childbirth; They will be amazed at one another; Their faces will be like flames. Behold, the day of the Lord comes, Cruel, with both wrath and fierce anger, To lay the land desolate; And He will destroy its sinners from it. For the stars of heaven and their constellations Will not give their light; The sun will be darkened in its going forth, And the moon will not cause its light to shine. "I will punish the world for its evil, And the wicked for their iniquity; I will halt the arrogance of the proud, And will lay low the haughtiness of the terrible. I will make a mortal more rare than fine gold, A man more than the golden wedge of Ophir. Therefore I will shake the heavens, And the earth will move out of her place, In the wrath of the Lord of hosts And in the day of His fierce anger."" (Isaiah 13:6-13; emphasis added)

There are five stages of grief that the final generation will have to face, which are denial, anger, bargaining, depression and acceptance. If we are that generation, then it is us that must graduate through these grievous phases and come to grips with the reality of our predicament.

But how? We are to take consolation in God's Word. There is more written about the final generation generally, and the TERMINAL GENERATION specifically, in the Bible than any other generation, even the one that existed at the time of Christ's first coming.

The following is a personal story that I feel compelled to share with the final generation. On a sunny summer day in 2017, I was driving in my car and stopped at a red light. I began to reflect upon the final generation and I asked the Lord,

"Lord, I know there will be a final generation. I know there has to be because you are a just God, Who must judge a Christ rejecting mankind. But, really, I mean is it really this generation? I mean, must it be this generation?"

My thoughts took into consideration a strong understanding of the perilous events that are predicted to happen to the final generation. Also, I was concerned for some loved ones, who I believe might be left behind to face the coming tribulations.

Still stopped at the red light and steeped in deep thought, I peered into my rear-view mirror. I saw a man, probably in his mid-forties, enjoying the summer day in his car with his convertible top down. In that instant, I thought, *"Lord, this poor soul probably has no idea about what could happen in the world, if this is really it, if this is the final generation."* Before the light turned green, the Lord comforted me with these words,

….."*Bill, I gave them the information they need to know."*….

Notice that the words I received were not, *"Relax; this is not the final generation."* The inference from this profound one-liner that I believe came from the Lord, is that *"I gave them,"* alluding to the gentleman in my rear-view mirror as a representative of this present generation, *"the information they need to know."*

Brothers and sisters, this is what I impart to you. The Lord has given us the Bible and inside of its pages is the comprehensive and full proof information that we all need to know. God loves us and informs us about the future so that we can prepare for what's coming. Our volitional response is to thank God for caring and to receive Jesus Christ as our Savior.

Sadly today, many pastors are not preaching the prophetic words of the Bible. They are not providing the people with *"the information they need to know."* Regardless, it's not God's fault if people don't get the memo. The Lord provided an abundance of information for the Final Generation and everyone has a personal responsibility to learn and benefit from it. This information is His gift to end times humanity.

> "Thus says the Lord: "Heaven is My throne, And earth is My footstool. Where is the house that you will build Me? And where is the place of My rest? For all those things My hand has made, And all those things exist," Says the Lord. "But on this one will I look: On him who is poor and of a contrite spirit, And who trembles at My word." (Isaiah 66:1-2; emphasis added)

The context of these Isaiah verses is in the Final Generation when the Jews are preparing to build their third temple. This will be more thoroughly explained in the later chapter entitled, "*The Coming Jewish Temple*," that deals with this future temple. The Lord says that at that future time He will look upon, "*him who is poor and of a contrite spirit, And who trembles at My word.*"

Those within the TERMINAL GENERATION who take heed to God's word will certainly be overwhelmed at the magnitude of global events taking place, but consoled in the fact that God is looking upon them as they tremble at His word. These Isaiah verses imply that people within the TERMINAL GENERATION will be trembling at His word.

Why wait to see if this really is the Final Generation that concludes with the TERMINAL GENERATION? Tremble at God's word now with a poor and contrite spirit and rest assured that the Lord will be looking favorably upon you.

> "Since it is a righteous thing with God to repay with tribulation those who trouble you, and to give you who are troubled rest with us when

the Lord Jesus is revealed from heaven with His mighty angels, in flaming fire taking vengeance on those who do not know God, and on those who do not obey the gospel of our Lord Jesus Christ. These shall be punished with everlasting destruction from the presence of the Lord and from the glory of His power, when He comes, in that Day, to be glorified in His saints and to be admired among all those who believe, because our testimony among you was believed." (2 Thess. 1:6-10)

6

How to Escape the Terminal Generation

Before presenting the coming chapters that lay out the horrendous tribulation events that the TERMINAL GENERATION must undergo, it's important to acknowledge that there is a way to escape all of them. The wrath of God gets poured out in the Trib-period, but believers are not going to experience this wrath and are removed from the earth prior via the Rapture. Church Age believers:

- Are not appointed to the wrath of God poured out in the Trib-period. (1 Thess. 5:9-10),

- Are saved from the wrath of God during the Trib-period. (Romans 5:9),

- Will be delivered from the wrath of God by Jesus in the Rapture. (1 Thess. 1:10),

- Are kept from that, "*hour of trial which shall come upon the whole world, to test those who dwell on the earth.*" (Rev. 3:10),

- Have a way of escaping the terrible things that will happen in the Trib-period. (Luke 21:36),

- Are to comfort one another with all these facts above. (1 Thess. 4:18).

These verses below explain how we are saved, delivered and kept from wrath and why we are comforted to know this.

We become citizens of heaven and get new heavenly homes

> "Let not *your* heart be troubled; *you* believe in God, believe also in Me (*Jesus Christ*). In My (*Heavenly*) Father's house are many mansions; if it were not so, I would have told *you*. I go to prepare a place for *you*; (*if you are a believer insert your name here*). And if I go and prepare a place for *you*, I will come again and receive *you* to Myself; that where I am, there *you* may be also. And where I go *you* know, and the way *you* know." Thomas said to Him, "Lord, we do not know where You are going, and how can we know the way?" Jesus said to him, "I am the way, the truth, and the life. No one comes to the Father except through Me."" (John 14:1-6; emphasis added)

Jesus uses the pronoun *your* or *you* nine times in these verses in reference to His believers. This is a very personal promise to **you** from **HIM**; if you are a believer! These verses above explain why we are comforted and the verses below explain how we are saved, delivered and kept from the wrath of God during the Trib-period.

We leave the earth and will always be with the Lord throughout eternity

> "For this we say to you by the word of the Lord (*Jesus Christ*), that we who are alive and remain until the coming of the Lord will by no means precede those who are asleep (*those who die as true Christian believers before the Rapture*). For the Lord Himself will descend from heaven with a shout, with the voice of an archangel, and with

the trumpet of God. And the dead in Christ will rise first. Then we who are alive and remain shall be caught up together with them in the clouds to meet the Lord in the air. And thus we shall always be with the Lord. Therefore comfort one another with these words." (1 Thess. 4:15-18; emphasis added)

We receive new immortal bodies

"Behold, I tell you a mystery: We (*true Christian believers*) shall not all sleep, but we shall all be changed (*receive new immortal bodies*)— in a moment, in the twinkling of an eye, at the last trumpet. For the trumpet will sound, and the dead will be raised incorruptible, and we shall be changed. For this corruptible must put on incorruption, and this mortal must put on immortality." (1 Corinthians 15:50-53; emphasis added)

We have a way of escape and are enabled to stand before Jesus Christ

"Watch therefore, and pray always that you may be counted worthy to escape all these things that will come to pass, and to stand before the Son of Man." (Luke 21:36)

Observe the following from this verse:

- Believers are to be watchful for the coming of the Lord in the Rapture because we don't know the precise time that He will come for us,

- We are to be in constant prayer,

- We must be counted worthy to escape. Worthiness results from becoming a true believer in Jesus Christ as your Lord and Savior. We don't earn this worthiness, because Christ paid the full pardon price for our sins on the Cross. Ephesians 2:8-9 clarifies this by saying, "For by grace you have been saved through faith, and that not of yourselves; it is the gift of God, not of works, lest anyone should boast."

- We escape, rather than endure, all the bad things that occur in the Trib-period,

- We get to stand before Jesus Christ.

If you are reading this book and the Rapture has not yet happened then you can receive Christ as your personal Lord and Savior. In so doing, you not only eliminate any possibility of being part of the TERMINAL GENERATION, but you receive abundant life now, as per John 10:10, and eternal life in the hereafter according to John 10:28.

If you are ready to make that decision now, or at any time throughout the reading of this book you want to accept Jesus Christ as your personal Lord and Savior, then skip ahead to the appendix entitled, "The Sinner's Salvation Prayer."

7

The False Covenant that Starts the Seven-Year Tribulation Period

This chapter will cover the following topics:

1. Explain why and how this covenant triggers the Seven-Year Tribulation Period,
2. Identify the parties of this covenant,
3. Expose the myths about this covenant,
4. Explore the true content of the false covenant.

1. Explain why and how this covenant triggers the Seven-Year Tribulation Period

The Trib-period is also called Daniel's Seventieth Week. Daniel 9:24-27 explained that the Jews and their holy city of Jerusalem were going to be allotted seventy weeks of years to accomplish seven feats. In the prior chapter entitled, *Daniel's Seventieth Week and The Seven-Year Tribulation Period,* the seven feats were identified and sixty-nine of those weeks were historically accounted for. However, the Seventieth Week was reserved for a future fulfillment at an unspecified time.

The interruption between the sixty-ninth and seventieth week includes the Church Age and the mysterious Post-Rapture / Pre-Trib time gap. The Church Age ends with the Rapture event, which then ushers in the Pre-Trib time gap period. This gap of unknown time exists because it's not the Rapture that starts the seventieth week, rather it's the confirmation of the false covenant between Israel and another signatory by the Antichrist. These two significant end times events are not likely to happen simultaneously.

> "Then he, (*the Antichrist*), shall confirm a covenant with *many*, (*Israel and the other party*), for one week; But in the middle of the week He shall bring an end to sacrifice and offering. And on the wing of abominations shall be one who makes desolate, Even until the consummation, which is determined, Is poured out on the desolate." (Daniel 9:27; *emphasis added*)

Speaking of interruptions, the seventy weeks of Daniel presented a pause in his prophetic thinking. Nearing the end of seventy years of Babylonian captivity, Daniel began a prayer for Israel's national repentance that included a petition for the establishment of the Messianic Kingdom, which was the high point of Old Testament prophecy. The selected verses below put you into the mind of Daniel at that time.

> "In the first year of his reign I, Daniel, understood by the books the number of the years specified by the word of the Lord through Jeremiah the prophet, that He would accomplish seventy years in the desolations of Jerusalem, (*Jer. 25:11-12 and 29:10*). Then I set my face toward the Lord God to make request by prayer and supplications, with fasting, sackcloth, and ashes. And I prayed to the Lord my God, and made confession, and said, "O Lord, great and awesome God, who keeps His covenant and mercy with those who love Him, and with those who keep His commandments, we have sinned and committed iniquity, we have done wickedly and rebelled, even by departing from Your precepts and Your judgments."" (Daniel 9:2-6; *emphasis added*)

"Now therefore, our God, hear the prayer of Your servant, and his supplications, and for the Lord's sake cause Your face to shine on Your sanctuary, (*the Temple*), which is desolate, (*the Babylonians destroyed the 1ˢᵗ Jewish Temple*). O my God, incline Your ear and hear; open Your eyes and see our desolations, and the city, (*Jerusalem*), which is called by Your name; for we do not present our supplications before You because of our righteous deeds, but because of Your great mercies. O Lord, hear! O Lord, forgive! O Lord, listen and act! Do not delay for Your own sake, my God, for Your city and Your people are called by Your name." (Daniel 9:17-19; *emphasis added*)

Unaware at that time the Lord had seven feats yet to accomplish through the Jews and Jerusalem, Daniel was inclined to think that the next phase in Jewish history would be the Messianic Age. Terms like, "*cause Your face to shine on Your sanctuary,*" and "*Lord, listen and act! Do not delay for Your own sake,*" are anticipatory for the establishment of the long-awaited Messianic Kingdom era.

According to Daniel 9:20-23, it was the angel Gabriel that informed Daniel that the Lord still had seven major endeavors that needed to be accomplished prior to the establishment of the Kingdom. After these duties are accomplished the Messianic Kingdom, which we know from Revelation 20:4 will span one-thousand years, will be established. This is when Daniel's requests of, "*cause Your face to shine on Your sanctuary,*" and "*Lord, listen and act! Do not delay for Your own sake,*" will be affirmatively answered.

Assisting with the final fulfillment of the seven feats are the *LAST Prophecies* of the Trib-period. These powerful predictions run parallel in time with the Lord's innerworkings through the Jews and Jerusalem to complete the last of these tasks.

Daniel's Seventieth week begins with the nation of Israel living in denial as to the Messiahship of Jesus Christ, but it ends by a believing Jewish remnant accomplishing the final seventh feat, which is "*to anoint the Most Holy.*" Once this is done the mission will be accomplished and the Millennial Messianic Kingdom will be established.

2. Identify the parties of this covenant

> "Then he, (*the Antichrist*), shall confirm a covenant with many, (*Israel and the other party*), for one week;…" (Daniel 9:27a; *emphasis added*)

When it comes to understanding some of the details of the false covenant, there are three insightful verses to consider. Daniel 9:27 is one of them and Isaiah 28:15 and 18 are the others. Isaiah, whose ministry spanned between 740-701 BC, was the first of the two prophets to mention this covenant.[16]

Daniel 9:27, which was previously quoted in this chapter, informs of the following features of the covenant:

- It has a seven-year term,

- It is confirmed by the Antichrist,

- It appears to enable the Jews to reinstate their Temple sacrifices and offerings,

- The Antichrist voids out the covenant in the middle of the seven-year term.

As important as these above details are, they don't explain several other important things about the covenant. Fortunately, Isaiah does.

> "Because you, (*Israel*), have said, "We have made a covenant with death, And with Sheol we are in agreement. When the overflowing scourge

passes through, It will not come to us, For we have made lies our refuge, And under falsehood we have hidden ourselves.""" (Isaiah 28:15; *emphasis added*)

"Your covenant with death will be annulled, And your agreement with Sheol will not stand; When the overflowing scourge passes through, Then you will be trampled down by it." (Isaiah 28:18)

Isaiah 28:15 and 18 provides the following information:

- That the other signatories of the covenant are "Death" and "Sheol,"

- Israel becomes a signatory to avoid an overflowing scourge,

- Israel's participation in the pact involves deceit; "lies" and "falsehood." This suggests that Israel becomes a signatory for politically expedient purposes. Israel's apparent motives are thoroughly explained in book two of this series entitled, *The NEXT Prophecies*,

- The covenant will be annulled.

Daniel tells us that the Antichrist confirms a seven-year pact *"with many."* It's easy to determine that Israel is among the *many* because Daniel 9:24-27 is specially related to the Jewish people and Jerusalem. However, unless Israel undergoes a massive population explosion, the nation will only represent a few within the overall *many*.

The Hebrew word Daniel uses for *many* is *"rab."* Most Bible translations interpret this word to mean *many*. According to the *New American Standard Hebrew and Greek Dictionaries*, it can also mean; great, mighty, numerous, powerful, prevalent, plentiful and populous. It appears to represent a great and mightily powerful prevailing populous that is ruling over the earth at the time of the ratification of the false covenant.

It's interesting that Daniel doesn't identify the other signatory within the *many* as a specific nation. In his twelve chapters he identifies numerous peoples, territories and nations. Daniel writes about Babylon, Elam (modern-day Iran), Greece , Cyprus, Media, Persia (Iran), Egypt, Ethiopia, Libya, and Jordan as (Ammon, Moab and Edom).

In modern history Israel has made treaties with other countries, namely Egypt in 1979 and Jordan in 1994. However, when it comes to the other party of the false covenant, Daniel provides no nation's name. This is likely because the other party to the covenant is a powerful global force rather than a national power.

According to Isaiah this *many* is a formidable force that is perpetrating an overflowing scourge that threatens Israel's national security. Isaiah identifies Israel's motive as, "*We have made a covenant with death, And with Sheol we are in agreement. When the overflowing scourge passes through, It will not come to us.*"

Israel is concerned about threatening events that are taking place throughout the world, which are being perpetrated by whoever death and Sheol represent. The connection between Isaiah 28:15 and Daniel 9:27 is that "*death and Sheol*" are the "*many.*"

Whatever this scourge is, it must be occurring sometime prior to the start of the Trib-period. Otherwise, Israel wouldn't need to worry about it, nor covenant with *death and Sheol* to prevent it.

Therefore, we turn our attention to the book of Revelation to see if a threatening scourge is being perpetrated by Death and Sheol leading up to the start of the Trib-period.

"When he opened the fourth seal, I heard the voice of the fourth living creature call out, "Come!" I

> looked and there was a pale green horse! Its rider's
> name was **Death, and Hades**, (*Hades is the Greek
> translation for the Hebrew word Sheol*), followed
> with him; they were **given authority over a
> fourth of the earth**, to kill with sword, famine,
> and pestilence, and by the wild animals of the
> earth." (Rev. 6:7-8; *emphasis added*)

Could the pale green horse and its horsemen called, Death
and Hades, be a valid candidate for the *many* of the false covenant?
They have the same exact symbolic names as in Isaiah 28:15 and
possess "*authority over a fourth of the earth*," which some estimate at
that time could be about a billion or more people. This multitude
could also qualify as the "*many*" in Daniel 9:27.

They are also perpetrating an overflowing scourge of sorts, in
that they are killing people through the multiple means of wars
(*sword*), famines, pestilences and apparently blood sport (*the wild
animals of the earth*).

Some would argue that this fourth horse of the apocalypse
rides onto the world scene after the Trib-period has already started.
If they are correct, then these two horsemen can't qualify as the
many. However, it's most of these same Bible teachers that say
Death and Hades are *killing over a fourth of the earth*, and frankly
that doesn't appear to be what Revelation 6:8 says.

Read the various Bible translations of Rev. 6:8 below and
determine if that's what the verse clearly states. Beforehand,
compare these translations to what happens in the sixth trumpet
judgment that clearly kills one-third of mankind.

> "By these three *plagues* **a third of mankind
> was killed**—by the fire and the smoke and the
> brimstone which came out of their mouths."
> (Rev. 9:18; **emphasis added**)

Does the pale green horse kill a fourth of mankind or simply have authority over that many people? There is a big difference between killing about one-fourth of the earth's population and having power over one-fourth of the earth to kill an untold multitude.

KJV, NKJV, NRSV, ESV: *they were given authority over a fourth of the earth, to kill...*

ASV: *And there was given unto them authority over the fourth part of the earth, to kill...*

GNV: *and power was given unto them over the fourth part of the earth, to kill...*

NIV: *They were given power over a fourth of the earth to kill...*

Moreover, if the fourth horse of the apocalypse is conducting a globalized killing campaign during the Trib-period, then why does a large group of their victims, called the Fifth Seal Saints, not seem to know that they have been martyred during the Trib-period? These saints ask the telling question below.

> "When He opened the fifth seal, I saw under the altar the souls of those who had been slain for the word of God and for the testimony which they held. And they cried with a loud voice, saying, "**How long, O Lord, holy and true**, until You judge and avenge our blood on those who dwell on the earth?"" (Rev. 6:9-10; emphasis added)

These people become believers after the Rapture, when prophetic awareness should be at an all-time high. Yet, they apparently don't know that the Trib-period lasts for seven years. If these saints died during the Trib-period they would know exactly how long until the Lord would judge and avenge their blood on the earth-dwellers. Their blood would be avenged seven years after the ratification of the false covenant.

In my estimation they ask this question because they die in the Post-Rapture / Pre-Trib gap period, which precedes the confirmation of the false covenant. Therefore, their question is genuinely legitimate, rather than prophetically ignorant.

In *The NEXT Prophecies* book I go into great length to argue this point in the chapter entitled, "The Alternative View of the Seal Judgments of Revelation 6." In that book I also make the connection between the Harlot world religion of Revelation 17 and the fourth horsemen of Death and Hades.

Revelation 17:6 informs that the Harlot is drunk with the blood of the martyrs of Jesus, and that would likely include the Fifth Seal Saints of Revelation 6:9-11. Thus, Death and Hades, which symbolizes the Harlot world religion, is drunk with the blood of the Fifth Seal Saints.

To summarize this above section, it is my teaching that the three primary parties involved in the confirmation and implementation of the false covenant are as follows:

1. *The Confirmer of the Covenant*   – is the Antichrist,

2. *Signatory #1 of the Covenant*   – is the nation of Israel,

3. *Signatory #2 of the Covenant*   – is the Harlot religion of Revelation 17, who is also represented in the fourth seal judgment of Revelation 6:7-8 as the pale green horse with its riders called, Death and Hades.

The logical question is, who is the Harlot of Revelation 17? I believe this whore of end times ecclesiastical Babylon is the Catholic Church. This is the topic of a future chapter in this book and it has also been explained exhaustively in *The NEXT Prophecies* book.

3. Expose the myths about this covenant

Many of today's Bible prophecy experts teach that the false covenant ends the Arab-Israeli conflict. Or, they sometimes refer to it as resolving the Palestinian-Israeli problem. Some of them don't actually state this directly, but they infer this indirectly when they say that the false covenant creates the peaceful people of Israel that dwell securely without walls, bars nor gates in Ezekiel 38.

> "You, (*alluding to Gog, the Russian leader of the Ezekiel 38 invading coalition*), will say, 'I will go up against a land of unwalled villages, (*Israel*); I will go to a peaceful people, (*the Israelis*), who dwell safely, all of them dwelling without walls, and having neither bars nor gates'" (Ezekiel 38:11; *emphasis added*)

These Bible expositors teach that the safe-dwelling Israel described in this Ezekiel verse is the direct result of the enactment of the false covenant of Daniel 9:27. This reasoning forces these teachers to put the start of Ezekiel 38 in the first half of the Trib-period, which is when Israel is enjoying a period of pseudo-peace. This timing goes against the teaching of, Dr. Arnold Fructhenbaum, Dr. Ron Rhodes, Dr. David Reagan, Gary Stearman, me and many others that teach that Ezekiel 38 happens prior to the Trib-period.

Is it likely that Ezekiel 38 will happen in the first half of the Trib-period? Why would Israel sign a covenant with Death and Sheol, when lurking in the not so distant shadows is the coming massive Gog of Magog invasion? This would show no foresight and amount to a significant miscalculation on Israel's part. It would also promptly put Israel in a major war at a time when they are experiencing a period of peace.

On the surface this theory that the false covenant fulfills the requirements of Ezekiel 38:11 seems logical. The rationale within this teaching is that Israel signs onto a treaty with the "*many*" of

Daniel 9:27. The covenant is politically brokered by the Antichrist between Israel and the Palestinians and / or *"many"* of their Arab neighbors. This covenant then:

- Ends the Arab-Israeli conflict,

- Settles the Palestinian Refugee issues,

- Brings about peace in the Middle East,

- And, enables the Jews to tear down all of their border barrier walls, eliminate their internal partition wall and network of security checkpoints and perhaps even eliminate all of their bomb shelters.

Oh; that it could be that simple and Oh; if it were only biblical, but OH NO, IT'S NOT! This thinking is entirely current event driven. When Isaiah and Daniel prophesied about this infamous covenant they were not concerned with the Arab-Israeli conflict, nor did they issue any clues about this specific conflict in their covenant related prophecies.

When Daniel 9:27 was written, the Jews were not having Arab-Israeli issues. The Arabs were not contesting the state of Israel's right to exist, nor did the Palestinian refugees even exist. Just the opposite was taking place. Around 538 BC, King Cyrus of the dominant Persian Empire was fully endorsing the Jewish State. As per Ezra 1:1-4, Cyrus authorized the Jews to return to their homeland, restore the nation of Israel and to rebuild their historic temple.

During Isaiah's time, the Jewish state existed without Arab contest and so did the first Jewish Temple. Also, there was no Palestinian refugee crisis to contend with.

Therefore, from the historical-grammatical context, which attempts to interpret Scripture through the lens of the existing peoples of the time, neither the Jews during Isaiah's nor Daniel's time would be under the impression that this covenant was about a future Palestinian refugee crisis or a coming Arab-Israeli conflict.

From the historical-grammatical-position, Daniel 9:26-27 was dealing with the dreadful fourth beast of Daniel 7:19-25. Thus, the people of Daniel's time would be less concerned about their Arab neighbors and more concerned about the coming fourth empire, which turned out to be the Roman Empire headquartered in the great city of Rome.

Sadly, most of these advocates have entirely ignored or dismissed the Psalm 83 prophecy as the viable means for Israel's ability to achieve peace in the Mideast. This prophecy is one of the subjects covered in *The NOW Prophecies* book. This Psalm predicts that the Arab-Israeli conflict ends in a war that Israel wins.

Related to Psalm 83 there are many other related NOW Prophecies that foretell of Israel winning wars against their Arab neighbors. Taking the position that the false covenant resolves the Arab-Israeli conflict peacefully, either totally ignores these unfulfilled war prophecies or pushes their fulfillment into the Trib-period or Messianic age, which are both scriptural impossibilities.

Below is a list of verses that predict the IDF will wage and win wars with their Arab neighbors and then capture additional territory as a result. The list is taken from a quote in my book entitled, *"Psalm 83, The Missing Prophecy Revealed, How Israel Becomes the Next Mideast Superpower."*

As you take the time to open your Bibles and read these following prophetic verses, remember that in the first half of the Trib-period Israel is living in a pseudo-peace and not fighting wars. Then, in the second half of the Trib-period, the Jews are fleeing into exile from the genocidal campaign of the Antichrist and not fighting the Arab states in the process.

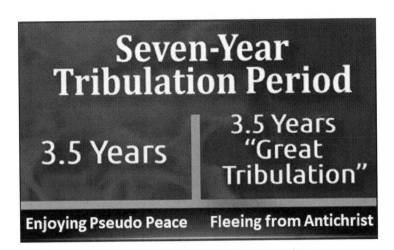

Below is the quote concerning this subject from my *Psalm 83* book:

> "*This book identifies nearly 150 verses that appear to apply to the Psalm 83 prophecy. These include prophecies from the Major Prophets including Jeremiah, Ezekiel, and Isaiah, as well as the Minor Prophets consisting of Obadiah, Zephaniah, and Zechariah. Remember that Asaph, the author of Psalm 83, is also a prophet as per 2 Chronicles 29:30. Below are just a few examples of the many passages relating to the Psalm 83 prophecy. This extensive list doesn't include the prophecies in Amos 1:1-15, which might also find application with Psalm 83.*"

- Psalm 83:1-18 . . . . (18 verses)

- Jeremiah 49:1-29, 12:14-17 . . . . (32 verses)

- Ezekiel 25:12-17, 28:24-26, 35:1-36:7, 37:10 (32 verses)

- Isaiah 17:1-14, 19:1-18, 11:14 . . . . (35 verses)

- Obadiah 1:1-21 . . . . (21 verses)

- Zephaniah 2:4-11 . . . . (8 verses)

- *Zechariah 12:2, 5-6* . . . . *(3verses)*."[17]

These prophecies above await a Pre-Trib final fulfillment. They predict that Mideast peace is achieved militarily, rather than politically. The false covenant is a political means for Israel to avoid an overflowing scourge that is happening globally. It is not a political mechanism to resolve the Arab-Israeli conflict that is happening regionally.

Summarizing this section, if someone teaches that the false covenant is the reason that Israel dwells securely without walls, bars nor gates fulfilling the requirements of Ezekiel 38:11, then they are:

- Teaching that the false covenant resolves the Arab-Israeli conflict and Palestinian problem diplomatically,

- Dismissing Psalm 83 and the related unfulfilled Arab-Israeli war peripheral prophecies as the means for Israel's ability to dwell securely as per Ezekiel 38:11,

- Overlooking the fact that this theory is not biblically endorsed, but is current event driven,

- Placing the start of Ezekiel 38 within the Trib-period,

- Advocating that the Antichrist is revealed as the confirmer of the false covenant before Ezekiel 38 finds fulfillment,

- And, teaching that the seven-year process of weapons burning in Ezekiel 39:9-10 occurs throughout the first and second halves of the Trib-period and into the early years of the Millennium.

Additionally, there are biblical clues that the true content of the false covenant has something to do with the Jews ability to build their third temple. These clues also mitigate against the teaching that the false covenant resolves the Arab-Israeli conflict.

4. Explore the true content of the false covenant

Whereas there is no biblical basis to connect the false covenant with the resolution of the Arab-Israeli conflict, there is scriptural support to correlate the false covenant with the rebuilding of the third Jewish Temple. These clues are deposited in Isaiah 28:16-17, Revelation 11:1-3 and Daniel 9:27 and explained below.

Before revealing the temple content within the false covenant, it's important to identify the three proof text verses about the covenant and to explain why the covenant is a false covenant.

> "Because you, (*Israel*), have said, "We have made a covenant with death, And with Sheol we are in agreement, (*the other parties to the covenant*).When the overflowing scourge passes through, It will not come to us, For we have made lies our refuge, And under falsehood we have hidden ourselves."" (Isaiah 28:15, NKJV, *emphasis added*)

> "Your, (*Israel's*) covenant with death will be annulled, And your agreement with Sheol will not stand; When the overflowing scourge passes through, Then you will be trampled down by it." (Isaiah 28:18, NKJV; *emphasis added*)

> "Then he, (*the Antichrist*) shall confirm a covenant with many, (*between Israel and Death and Sheol*) for one week, (*of seven years*); But in the middle of the week He shall bring an end to sacrifice and offering. And on the wing of abominations

shall be one who makes desolate, Even until the consummation, which is determined, Is poured out on the desolate." (Daniel 9:27, NKJV; *emphasis added*)

These are the verses that identify the covenant. The reason it is called the false covenant is because it does not bring a genuine peace, but only a false sense of peace. This is because:

- Isaiah 28:15 informs that it is made in lies under falsehood on Israel's part,

- Isaiah 28:18 points out that it won't stand, but will be annulled,

- Daniel 9:27 states that it will be annulled by the Antichrist at the midpoint of the designated seven-year term, which makes it a short-lived pseudo-peace.

Clue Number One – Isaiah 28:16-17

"Therefore thus says the Lord God: "Behold, I lay in Zion a stone for a foundation, A tried stone, a precious cornerstone, a sure foundation; Whoever believes will not act hastily. Also I will make justice the measuring line, And righteousness the plummet; The hail will sweep away the refuge of lies, And the waters will overflow the hiding place." (Isaiah 28:16-17)

The first clue is contained in the two Isaiah 28 verses above. These two verses are sandwiched in between Isaiah 28:15 and 18, which are the verses referring to the false covenant. These passages use terms like a "tried stone," a "precious cornerstone," a "sure foundation," a "measuring line" and a "plummet." These are terms that can find association with constructing a Jewish Temple.

To build the Temple, you start with a *tried stone* that becomes the *precious cornerstone*. This *cornerstone* has a *sure foundation* built around it. The length and width dimensions of a building need to be calculated with a *measuring line*, and the vertical accuracy of a structure is determined with a *plummet*, (plumb-line).

I interpret Isaiah 28:16-17 as a warning to the scornful rulers of Jerusalem in Isaiah 28:14 to not drag Israel into being a signatory of this dreadful covenant. These leaders seem to think that they are going to build a Temple and hasten the coming of the Messiah. Among religious Jews today, this is considered one of the main motivators for rebuilding the temple.

Isaiah cautions them to not hastily enter this covenant, because the Messiah, Jesus Christ, has already come as the, *Tried Stone* (1 Peter 2:4-8), *Precious Cornerstone* (Matthew 21:42, Ephesians 2:19-22) and *Sure Foundation* (1 Corinthians 3:11).

The scornful rulers of Jerusalem believe that the false covenant will permit them to build their temple. They believe that this pact will enable them to lay down the precious cornerstone for the sure foundation of the third temple. However, Isaiah contradicts their thinking by saying,

> "Therefore thus says the Lord God: "Behold, I, (*not the scornful leaders of Jerusalem*), lay in Zion a stone for a foundation, A tried stone, a precious cornerstone, a sure foundation; Whoever believes, (*that I accomplished this over 2000 years ago through Jesus Christ*), will not act hastily."" (Isaiah 28:16; *emphasis added*)

Clue Number Two – Revelation 11:1-3

A second interesting clue is in the book of Revelation. Several important details are provided in these passages below concerning the benefits to both parties of the covenant. These verses describe what happens in the immediate aftermath of the ratification of the false covenant.

> "Then there was given me a measuring rod like a staff; and someone said, "Get up and measure the temple of God and the altar, and those who worship in it. Leave out the court which is outside the temple and do not measure it, for it has been given to the nations; and they will tread under foot the holy city for forty-two months. And I will grant *authority* to my two witnesses, and they will prophesy for twelve hundred and sixty days, clothed in sackcloth."" (Rev. 11:1-3, NASB)

The time frame of "*forty-two months*" is associated with one-half of the seven years of tribulation. The same increment of time is used in the ensuing verse but worded differently as, "*twelve hundred and sixty days.*" It is commonly taught that both usages in these verses allude to the first half of the Trib-period.

Thus, the very first thing that appears to happen as part of the implementation of the covenant, is that the Temple gets measured for its construction. The apostle John is given a measuring rod and instructed to measure the Temple of God, alluding to the third temple. So, if the covenant called for the construction of the Temple, then this would be one of the first order of events. Measure it so that it can be built.

Notice that there are some significant restrictions placed upon John's measuring of the Temple that benefit the other covenanting party. The other party are Gentiles who must have some claims to the Temple's outer court and Jerusalem because they are given authority over the outer court, and access to trample through the holy city of Jerusalem. In order for the leaders to build their Temple they will need to negotiate with these Gentiles. This will be a first for them. Historically, the Jews did not negotiate with any Gentiles when they built their first and second temples.

The Greek word used for "Gentiles" in Rev. 11:2 is "*ethnos*." It is used over 150 times in the New Testament and can be translated as Gentiles, nations, pagans or people.[18] The Greek word in that same verse used for "trample," is "*pateo*," which can also be translated as "tread under foot."[19]

Thus, another possible way to translate this verse is, *the pagans will tread under foot, the holy city of Jerusalem.* They will need this access to make their way to the outer court of the Temple Mount, which is given over to these pagan Gentiles. This is an important concession for these pagans. It implies that whoever they are, that they have valid claims to these sacred areas. Presently, the Old City of Jerusalem is divided into four quarters: Christian, Armenian, Jewish and Muslim. The Christian category includes Roman Catholicism.

When the covenant gets confirmed and the Gentiles get awarded access to Jerusalem and authority over the outer court, several Bible prophecies will have likely happened. Two important ones will be Psalm 83 and the Rapture, not necessarily in that order. After Psalm 83, the Muslims will probably lose substantial control over their quarter in the Old City and after the Rapture some Christian and Armenian sections will be vacated by many true believers that resided there. This leaves the Jews and probably a strong Vatican contingency.

On a side note, the Catholics are amillennial and not looking for a Pre-Trib Rapture. Below is a quote from the respected Catholic apologist, Tim Drake, about the Catholic Church's view of the Pre-Trib Rapture.

> *"The Catholic Church is "amillennial," meaning that it believes that Christ's second coming and the last judgment will happen at the same time.*

> *According to Colin Donovan, theologian at EWTN,
> the Church "teaches that Christ already reigns in
> eternity (1 Cor 15:24-27) and that in this world
> his reign ... is found already in the Church.".*...
> *Therefore, we believe "He will come again in glory
> to judge the living and the dead." Our belief is that
> the rapture will take place at the end of the world,
> and not until then."[20]*

In *The Next Prophecies* book I provide the biblical basis for the Catholic Church being left behind and becoming the head of ecclesiastical Babylon of Revelation 17. The Catholic Church has a prophetic application to the letter to the Church of Thyatira in Revelation. The Church of Thyatira will be left behind and cast into the sickbed of the Great Tribulation period.

> "Indeed I will cast her, (*the Catholic Church as
> prophetic Thyatira*), into a sickbed, and those who
> commit adultery with her, (*the kings of the earth
> commit fornication with the harlot in Rev. 17:2*)
> into, (*the*) great tribulation, (*period*), unless they
> repent of their deeds." (Rev. 2:22, *emphasis added*)

This does not mean that all Catholics are unsaved, hopefully many of them are born again and will either be Raptured or become true believers afterward. It simply means that the institution of the Catholic Church still exists after the Rapture.

Clue Number Three

The next clue is found in Daniel 9:27, which also serves as a proof text verse in regard to the false covenant.

> "Then he, (*the Antichrist*), shall confirm a
> covenant with many, (*Israel and Death and
> Sheol*), for one week; (*of seven years*), But in the
> middle of the week, (*after three and one-half*

years), He shall bring an end to sacrifice and offering, (*taking place in the Temple*). And on the wing of abominations shall be one who makes desolate, Even until the consummation, which is determined, Is poured out on the desolate." (Daniel 9:27; emphasis added)

Jesus Christ foretells that this event predicted by Daniel happens in the holy place, which represents the Third Jewish Temple at the time.

"Therefore when you see the 'abomination of desolation,' spoken of by Daniel the prophet, standing in the holy place" (whoever reads, let him understand), "then let those who are in Judea flee to the mountains." (Matthew 24:15-16)

The intimations in these related verses above, are that by the middle of the Trib-period the Third Jewish Temple will exist. The Antichrist will make a bold statement by entering this Temple and stopping the priestly sacrifice and offering occurring therein. This is in fulfillment of Isaiah 28:18, which says the false covenant will be annulled.

"Your covenant with death will be annulled, And your agreement with Sheol will not stand; When the overflowing scourge passes through, Then you will be trampled down by it." (Isaiah 28)

What better way to annul a covenant than to void out its terms? If the true content of the false covenant allowed the Jews to build their Temple and perform sacrifices and offerings inside of it, then the action taken by the Antichrist to go into the Temple and stop the sacrifice and offering terminates the contract.

These three clues above seem to suggest that the true content of the false covenant has something to do with the building of the Third Jewish Temple. Rev. 11:1-3 points out that when the covenant is enacted the Jews will promptly rebuild their Temple. Isaiah 28:16-17 explains that the Jews will believe that this Temple will invoke the coming of their Messiah. Daniel 9:27 points out that the opposite will happen. It won't be the Messiah that enters the temple to bless it, rather it will be the Antichrist who intrudes into the temple to curse it and annul the false covenant.

8

The First-Half of the Seven-Year Tribulation Period

This chapter will outline and set the stage for the events that are predicted to take place in the first three and one-half years of the Trib-period. These prophecies will be explained in greater detail in the chapters that follow.

As the Trib-period begins, the three main parties of the false covenant take center stage in their new and highly acclaimed roles. Israel and the Harlot world religion, as the signatories of the covenant, and the Antichrist, as the confirmer of the covenant, will have received plenty of mainstream media attention for accomplishing a monumental seven-year pact.

This will be a much more epic event than the Israeli peace treaties of the past between Israel and Egypt that was mediated by US President Jimmy Carter in 1979 and Jordan, which was brokered by President Bill Clinton in 1994. The stakes are so much higher than mere peace between warring nations, this future treaty has international political and spiritual implications.

As a result of his role as the confirmer of the false covenant, the Antichrist will ascend to the heights of being the world's charismatic leader. This scarlet beast of Revelation 17:3 will hoist this triumph up to the top of his political resume. Yet, his prime time in the spotlight is still postponed until the second half of the Great Tribulation period.

As a result of the ratification of the covenant, world inhabitants will think that a time of "Peace and Safety" will ensue. Unfortunately, for unsuspecting humanity this euphoric feeling will be extremely short lived.

> "For when they say, "Peace and safety!" then sudden destruction comes upon them, as labor pains upon a pregnant woman. And they shall not escape." (1 Thessalonians 5:3)

As mankind faces the disruptive events described below, they will applaud the confirmation of the Daniel 9:27 covenant, which they hope will restore some sort of normalcy again in the world.

1. *The Christian Church will have vanished:* All true believers in Christ that are alive and remaining within the Church Age will have recently disappeared in a split-second without any advanced warning. Presently, there are an estimated 2.19 billion Christians around the world. This number includes Catholics, Protestants, Orthodox, and Evangelicals.[21] Not all of them are true believers, but some estimate that millions of these Christians will be caught up into the clouds in the Pre-Tribulation Rapture of 1 Thess. 4:15-18 and 1 Corinthians 15:51-53. Many friends, family, neighbors and countrymen will be taken from the earth disrupting societal functions and creating economic instability throughout much of the world. This event will also create a concern within those left behind about the destiny of their uncertain futures.

2. *Unrestrained lawlessness will be abounding:* Sinful behavior, including lying, looting, killing, sexual perversion, terrorism and more will be overtaking the earth as per 2 Thessalonians 2:6-9.

3. *The Pre-Tribulation fulfillment of Ezekiel 38 will have happened:* The world will still be in shock from witnessing

the fulfillment of the devastating Ezekiel 38 Middle East war. Global audiences will have watched Israel's God single-handedly and supernaturally destroy the armies of the Gog of Magog coalition comprised of Russia and some of the break-away Soviet Union countries, Turkey, Iran, Libya, Tunisia, Ethiopia, Sudan, Somalia and perhaps Morocco and Germany, if Gomer indeed represents Germany.

4. *Supernatural deception will delude people:* According to 2 Thessalonians 2:9-12, in a masterful attempt to steer the masses from the truth about Jesus Christ, Satan will be perpetrating a great lie throughout the earth via the use of all power, signs and lying wonders. The Devil's deceptive strategies could employ more Marian Apparitions, Eucharistic Miracles and UFO occurrences.

5. *Some Pre-Tribulation Seal Judgments will likely be occurring:* If my interpretation that the first five Seal Judgments of Revelation 6 are opened in the Post-Rapture / Pre-Trib time-gap, then the world will be reeling from the world wars of the second seal and the scarcities, famines and pestilences of the third seal. For more information on this subject read my chapter in *The Next Prophecies* book entitled, "The Alternative View of the Seal Judgments."

6. *The "Overflowing Scourge" will be sweeping throughout the world:* Death and Hades of the fourth seal judgment will be killing multitudes of political and religious dissidents around the world, or at least over a fourth-part of the earth according to Rev. 6:7-8. This will include the believers of the Fifth Seal Saints of Rev. 6:9-11.

These globally impacting events will characterize what the world will look like on day one of the start of the Trib-period. It will be a time when the supernatural is the natural and the paranormal is the new normal. There will no longer be scientific explanations for what will have happened in the Rapture and

Ezekiel 38, nor for the satanically inspired power, signs and lying wonders that will be taking place. WELCOME TO DAY ONE OF THE TRIB-PERIOD!

Although there will be a spillover from some of these above events into the first half of the Trib-period, there are additional peoples, places and events that will line the pages of this first three and one-half years period. They are listed below:

1.   Israel buries the Magog invaders and burns their weapons (Ezek. 39:9-16),

2.   The Third Jewish Temple will be built (Rev. 11:1-2),

3.   The Two Witnesses preach in Jerusalem (Rev. 11:3-6),

4.   The 144,000 Jews evangelize (Rev. 7:1-8), and spark a global revival (Rev. 7:9-17),

5.   The Harlot religion reigns (Rev. 17:1-6), from the great city of Rome (Rev. 17:9, 18),

6.   The unholy church and state alliance forms between the Harlot and the Antichrist (Rev. 17:3-7),

7.   Christian martyrdom occurs at the hands of Ecclesiastical Babylon (Rev. 17:6),

8.   The rise of the Ten Kings (Rev. 17:12-17),

9.   The judgments of the Sixth Seal (Rev. 6:12-17), and Seventh Seal (Rev. 8:1-6),
      Most Bible prophecy teachers incorporate all of the seven Seal Judgments into the first half of the Trib-period. This is the traditional view of the timing of the Seal Judgments. I present this view and my alternative view to the timing of these Seal Judgments in The NEXT Prophecies book.

10. The first Six of the Seven Trumpet Judgments sound:

    1.   The First Trumpet (Rev. 8:7), one-third of the world's vegetation is struck,

    2.   The Second Trumpet (Rev. 8:8-9), one-third of the seas become blood,

    3.   The Third Trumpet (Rev. 8:10-11), one-third of the waters become bitter,

    4.   The Fourth Trumpet (Rev. 8:12), one-third of the heavens are struck,

    5.   The Fifth Trumpet (Rev.9:1-12), a locust invasion plagues the earth for five-months,

    6.   The Sixth Trumpet (Rev. 9:13-21), a two-hundred million strong army kills one-third of mankind.

WHAT A TIME NOT TO BE ALIVE! Remember that there is a way of escape up until the Rapture occurs. It was presented in the chapter entitled, *"How to Escape the Terminal Generation."*

9

Israel in the First Half of the Tribulation

As the victor of the Pre-Trib Psalm 83 and Ezekiel 38 wars and a main signatory to the false covenant, Israel will be a front-page news-getter going into the first half of the Trib-period. On day one of the Trib-period Israel will be:

1. Continuing to settle into its enlarged borders as a result of their victories in Psalm 83 and the related peripheral prophecies of:

    *   Obadiah 1:19-20 – Israel annexes Southern Jordan, the Gaza, the West Bank, the Golan, the Sinai and portions of Southern Lebanon,

    *   Jeremiah 49:2 – Israel captures Northern Jordan,

    *   Zephaniah 2:9 – Israel plunders and possesses Central and Northern Jordan,

    *   Isaiah 19:18 – Israel inhabits five cities in Egypt.

2. Burning the weapons of the Magog invaders. Ezekiel 39:9-10 states that Israel will burn these weapons for seven years. This campaign should be well underway, likely beginning at least three and one-half years, before the Trib-period begins.

3. Burying the corpses of the Magog invaders in the future city of "Hamonah," that will be established in a yet to be named valley called "Hamon Gog." Ezekiel 39:11-16 says that Israel will be burying these hordes of Gog for a period of seven months, which is a time frame that may be completed prior to the start of the Trib-period, or it may spill over a bit into the start of this period. The seven-month process will begin in the immediate aftermath of the fulfillment of Ezekiel 38. The name and location of the valley of Hamon Gog is an interesting prophetic subject, especially since this name and place doesn't exist yet. Additionally fascinating, is that this valley will probably be designated in a territory not yet possessed by Israel. This topic is explained in more detail at the end of this chapter.

4. Gaining world renown for the events described in numbers 2 and 3 above, as per Ezek. 39:13.

5. Constructing the third temple, beginning the process of sacrifices and offerings and reinstating the ancient Mosaic Law.

6. Fending off the messages of the 144,000 Jewish Witnesses of Rev. 7:1-8 and the powers and plagues of the Two Witnesses of Rev. 11:3-6. The 144,000 Witnesses will have a worldwide ministry, whereas the Two Witnesses appear to be primarily centered in Israel, especially in and around Jerusalem, as per Rev. 11:8. All of these 144,002 Witnesses will be preaching that Jesus Christ is the Messiah, but many Jews will reject their claims.

All of the above should facilitate a massive wave of immigration (Aliyah) from world Jewry into the greater and safer Jewish state. Increased tourism could also become a reality at that time, because Revelation 11:2 predicts that Gentiles will tread through Jerusalem and into the third temple's outer court.

Another event to factor into this end times Israel equation is in Ezekiel 39:17-20, which speaks about a sacrificial meal of the dead Magog invaders by the birds of prey and beasts of the earth. This will be another amazing spectacle for the world to watch.

The Israel of today will be a different country geo-politically, socio-economically and spiritually when the Trib-period starts. The Jews will be riding high on the coat tails of their IDF military victory over the Arabs in Psalm 83 and their subsequent God orchestrated supernatural victory over the Magog invaders of Ezekiel 38.

Israel's religious outlook will be on building the third temple, reinstating the Mosaic Law with its animal sacrifices and invoking the coming of their Messiah. It will be full speed ahead for the Jewish mindset with their next prophetic stop being the establishment of the Messianic Kingdom.

What the Jewish leaders won't realize is that the Messiah Jesus Christ has already come, fulfilled the Mosaic Law and in so doing already rendered the Law inoperative with His sacrificial death on the cross as the Lamb of God. According to Psalm 50:7-15 and Isaiah 66:1-3, the sacrifices and offerings that the Jews will perform in their third temple will not be blessed, but will be considered abominable acts performed in futility.

> "He who kills a bull is as if he slays a man; "He who sacrifices a lamb, as if he breaks a dog's neck; He who offers a grain offering, as if he offers swine's blood; He who burns incense, as if he blesses an idol. Just as they have chosen their own ways, And their soul delights in their abominations." (Isaiah 66:3)

The Law was established to be mankind's temporary tutor. It was intended to bring us to recognition through faith that Christ is the Lord and Savior. These verses below explain and qualify these truths.

"The next day John saw Jesus coming toward him, and said, "Behold! The Lamb of God who takes away the sin of the world!" (John 1:29)

"Do not think that I, (*Jesus Christ*), came to destroy the Law or the Prophets. I did not come to destroy but to fulfill." (Matthew 5:17; *emphasis added*)

"But the Scripture has confined all under sin, that the promise by faith in Jesus Christ might be given to those who believe. But before faith came, we were kept under guard by the law, kept for the faith which would afterward be revealed. Therefore the law was our tutor *to bring us* to Christ, that we might be justified by faith. But after faith has come, we are no longer under a tutor." (Galatians 3:22-25)

"After this, Jesus, knowing that all things were now accomplished, that the Scripture might be fulfilled, said, "I thirst!" Now a vessel full of sour wine was sitting there; and they filled a sponge with sour wine, put *it* on hyssop, and put *it* to His mouth. So when Jesus had received the sour wine, He said, "It is finished!" And bowing His head, He gave up His spirit." (John 19:28-30)

Where is the Valley of Hamon Gog?

The city of Hamonah in the Valley of Hamon Gog was identified earlier in this chapter as the location of the mass graveyard for the killed Magog invaders. Israel will be burying these dead corpses for seven months in this location. The verses below explain this process.

"It will come to pass in that day *that* I will give Gog a burial place there *in Israel*, the valley of those who pass by *east of the sea*; and it *will obstruct travelers*, because there they will bury *Gog and all his multitude.* Therefore they will call *it* the Valley of Hamon Gog. For seven months the house of Israel will be burying them, in order *to cleanse the land.* Indeed all the people of the land will be burying, and they will gain renown for it on the day that I am glorified," says the Lord God. "*They will set apart men regularly employed, with the help of a search party*, to pass through the land and bury those bodies remaining on the ground, in order *to cleanse it.* At the end of seven months they will make a search. The search party will pass through the land; and *when anyone* sees a man's bone, he shall set up a marker by it, till the buriers have buried it in the Valley of Hamon Gog. *The* name of *the* city *will* also *be* Hamonah. Thus *they shall cleanse the land.*" ' (Ezekiel 39:11-16; *emphasis added*)

Presently, there is no city of Hamonah nor any Valley of Hamon Gog in existence, but they will get their names and locations in the immediate aftermath of the defeat of the Magog invaders. This can be determined by the name Hamon Gog, which means "multitudes of Gog," and Hamonah that means "hordes." Thus, the city of Hamonah in the valley of Hamon Gog is where Israel will designate the burial grounds for the hordes or multitudes of dead corpses from the Magog coalition.

It would make no sense for Israel to name a city and valley by these names prior to the need of a cemetery location for the dead hordes of Gog's armies. When the dead multitudes of Gog exist, Israel will be forced to promptly allocate an appropriate city and valley location for their massive burial grounds. But where is the Valley of Hamon Gog going to be located?

Ezekiel 39:7 provides the clues to the future whereabouts of this valley. The prophet says that Gog will be given a burial place *in Israel* in the valley of those who pass by *east of the sea*; and it *will obstruct travelers*, because there they will bury *Gog and all his multitude*. Additionally, Ezekiel 39:14-15 points out that trained professionals will work closely with a *search party to cleanse the land*. These clean up details sound like the dead corpses are biologically or chemically contaminated, much worse than simply natural decay.

The clues tell us the following facts:

1.   The valley will be located inside of the nation of Israel,

2.   The valley must be big enough to bury Gog and his multitude,

3.   The valley must be chosen apart from commercial and tourist centers in Israel because it will obstruct travelers,

4.   The valley must be east of some sea,

5.   The valley must be located where the contaminated corpses won't pose a problem for the Israeli citizens.

The fact that the valley must be separated from Israel proper so as not to obstruct travel and will be east of some sea, narrows down the options for its location. What sea could the prophet be alluding to, that has a large enough valley on its east side to accommodate the burial of potentially millions of dead contaminated soldiers? There are only four primary choices to choose from: the Mediterranean, the Sea of Galilee, the Red Sea, or the Dead Sea.

The Mediterranean Sea

The Mediterranean Sea can probably be ruled out for a couple of reasons. *First,* east of the Mediterranean is the heartland of Israel's commercial and tourism centers. The Jews will not want travel obstructed inside of Israel proper.

Second, the candidate valleys in Israel, like the Jezreel, Kidron, Hula, Beit Netofa, Beracah, and Valley of the Cross are inside of modern-day Israel. Logically, since Ezekiel 39:14 declares the Jews are "cleansing the land," it doesn't make sense that they would contaminate their own fertile Israeli soil, given other options.

Contamination is an appropriate term in this instance, considering Ezekiel 39:14-15 appears to involve the resemblance of a hazmat (hazardous materials) team. Additionally, some of us believe the Jews are cleansing the land in compliance with requirements specified in the Mosaic Law. (Numbers 19:11-22; Deuteronomy 21:1-9). If so, this implies the supernatural defeat of the Magog invaders inclines the Jews to revert to orthodoxy, and results in their seeking to rebuild their temple, reinstate Levitical Law, and resume their animal sacrifices.

The Sea of Galilee

The Sea of Galilee is likewise unlikely, because candidate valleys to the east are located primarily in southern Syria or northern Jordan. Occasional southwesterly wind patterns blow through these areas into Israel, which could cause the contamination referenced above to spread into the world's most heavily populated Jewish area of Gush Dan, which encompasses Tel Aviv and some surrounding metropolitan areas.

Another negative is that presently both Syria and Jordan are under Arab rule. The Syrians and Jordanians would prohibit Israel from burying the multitudes of Gog under their sovereign soil. However, if Israel captured these valleys during Psalm 83 prior, perhaps they would gain the option of someday burying the dead in one of their valleys.

But, what about Damascus, the capital city of Syria, which is approximately sixty miles northeast of the Sea of Galilee? Isaiah 17:1, 9, 14 predicts that the city will someday be destroyed overnight by the IDF. Damascus may be a desolate and potentially contaminated place, due to the possible nuclear nature of its prior destruction. This could also dissuade the use of some valley east of the Sea of Galilee.

For these above reasons the Sea of Galilee drops low on the list of choices. However, even if it is the referenced Sea, eastward Arab valleys can only be used by Israel for mass burial purposes if Israel negotiates either politically or militarily, the use of the land. Politically, this is improbable, but as a result of an IDF military victory in Psalm 83, it becomes possible.

The Red Sea

The Red Sea option is unfeasible due to the logistics of transporting multitudes of dead and probably contaminated soldiers so far southward. Remember that Ezekiel 38:15 informs us that the Magog invaders attack from the north. The Red Sea is over 400 miles to the south of Israel's city of Tel Aviv. Valleys east of the Red Sea are currently under Saudi sovereignty, inhibiting Israel's ability to bury the dead there, as well. Additionally, Saharan winds that could potentially blow contaminants into Israel should be considered.

The Dead Sea

The Dead Sea presents the best option for the creation of a place called the Valley of Hamon Gog. Satellite topography shots of the Middle East picture central Jordan as the perfect location for the mass burial site of the multitudes of Gog. Unlike northern Jordan, where most Jordanians live, and portions of southern Jordan that are mountainous, much of central Jordan is flat, barren, and home to Bedouins.

Regional wind patterns favor this location as well. For instance, the hot, dry, dusty desert wind called a "Sirocco," an Arab word for "easterly," often blows in the eastward direction of Europe. Sirocco is also known as the Sharkiye in Jordan, Sharav in Israel, and Simoom in Arabia. Easterly winds would blow the corpses contamination in the opposite direction of Israel proper, which is to the west of Jordan.

Moab, which was historically located in Central Jordan, is one of the ten members listed in the Psalm 83 Arab confederacy. If Moab gets defeated and becomes captured by the IDF during Psalm 83, then Israel would possess the unrestricted ability to establish the Valley of Hamon Gog there. According to Jeremiah 49:2 and Zephaniah 2:8-10, Israel annexes Jordan after defeating this Arab state in a future war.

In this Pre-Ezekiel 38 and 39 prophetic scenario Central Jordan would become part of Israel's eastern border and would meet the Valley of Hamon Gog requirements of being, "*in Israel, the valley of those who pass by east of the* (Dead) *sea.*" Thus, when the hordes of Gog need a burial location, one already exists, requiring Israel to simply use it and rename it.

Israel possessing Jordan in advance of the Trib-period explains why Jesus Christ instructs the Jews in Judea to flee to the mountains in Matthew 24.

> "Therefore when you, (*Jews in Judea*), see the 'abomination of desolation,' (*which happens at the midpoint of the Trib-period*), spoken of by Daniel the prophet, standing in the holy place" (whoever reads, let him understand), "then let those who are in Judea flee to the mountains." (Matthew 24:15-16; *emphasis added*)

Jesus instructs the Jews to flee to the mountains, alluding to the mountains in Southern Jordan, which is where Petra exists. This location is in ancient Edom, which historically encompassed what is today modern-day Southern Jordan. The mountainous areas of Edom are sometimes referred to in the

Bible as "the mountains of Esau." According to Genesis 36:1, 9, Esau fathered the Edomites, henceforth came the Esau / Edom connection.

Obadiah 1:19 points out that the Jews will someday possess these "mountains of Esau." One of the reasons we determine the "mountains of Esau" in Edom are the ones Christ speaks of in Matthew 24:16 is because this is where Christ comes for the faithful Jewish remnant according to Isaiah 63:1-8.

If Israel captures and annexes Jordan prior to the Abomination of Desolation, then Jesus provides brilliant advice to the Jews at that time. It demonstrates His ability to know the future. However, if Israel does not annex Southern Jordan prior to the Abomination of Desolation, then this specific advice of Jesus Christ, "*to flee to the mountains*," would be dangerous, because the Jordanians would likely attempt to prevent the exodus of Jews from Judea into Jordan.

10

The 144,002 Witnesses – Part One: the 144,000 Witnesses

The previous chapter pointed out that Israel will be in the primetime spotlight during the first half of the Trib-period. By then, the Jewish state will be a highly revered nation according to Ezekiel 39:13. The supernatural defeat by God of Gog and the Magog invaders will make the parting of the Red Sea during the Hebrew exodus from Egypt pale in comparison.

Yet, even with all of its coming renown, Israel's spiritual blindness of Jesus as the Messiah will continue. It will be a religious mindset that is reminiscent of when the Romans destroyed Jerusalem and the Second Jewish Temple in 70 AD. The nearly nineteen-hundred years of dispersion in the Diaspora that followed did not change the unmistakable fact that the Jewish religious leaders did then, and still do, reject Jesus Christ as the Jewish Messiah.

However, there will be 144,002 Jewish Witnesses and a faithful remnant of Jews that will recognize and receive Jesus Christ as their Messiah. These next two chapters will pick up their stories, namely the 144,000 Witnesses of Revelation 7:1-8, 14:1-5 and the 2 Witnesses of Revelation 11:3-13. The faithful remnant will be explored in a future chapter.

The Timing of the 144,000 Jewish Witnesses

> *"After these things* I saw four angels standing at the four corners of the earth, holding the four winds of the earth, that the wind should not blow on the earth, on the sea, or on any tree. Then I saw another angel ascending from the east, having the seal of the living God. And he cried with a loud voice to the four angels to whom it was granted to harm the earth and the sea, saying, "Do not harm the earth, the sea, or the trees till we have sealed the servants of our God on their foreheads." And I heard the number of those who were sealed. One hundred *and* forty-four thousand of all the tribes of the children of Israel *were* sealed."* (Rev. 7:1-4; *emphasis added*)

There are two timing clues in these above verses that inform when the 144,000 Witnesses come on the scene. The first is that the harming of the earth, sea and trees is prevented until after the sealing of the 144,000 Witnesses. According to Revelation 8:7-11, the earth, sea and trees are struck hard by the First, Second and Third Trumpet Judgments. Thus the 144,000 Witnesses must arrive prior to the start of the sounding of the Seven Trumpet Judgments.

Second, the introduction of the 144,000 Witnesses begins the telling timing words of, *"After these things."* Revelation 7 begins with the two Greek words *"meta tauta,"* which *means hereafter, afterward, after this,* or *after these things.*[22] The logical question is, "After what things?"

The answer can be understood by following the sequence separations that occur in between the usages of these two words throughout the book of Revelation. These two Greek words, *"meta tauta,"* are paired in tandem a total of ten times in Revelation. Study this section carefully because understanding the uses of *meta tauta* in the book of Revelation will serve useful purposes throughout this and several upcoming chapters.

The first use of meta tauta (Rev. 1:19)

> "Write the things which you have seen, and the things which are, and the things which will take place after (*meta*) this (*tauta*)." (Rev. 1:19; *emphasis added*)

In this first use of *meta tauta*, the apostle John was instructed to write what he had "seen," which was the vision described in Rev. 1:12-18. Then, John was to write about the "things which are," which was the Church Age taking place when John was alive, and John accomplished this task through the seven letters to the seven churches Revelation 2 and 3.

Revelation 2 and 3 issued seven letters to seven churches. These seven letters had multiple applications. First, they were instructional for the seven actual churches existing at the time. Second, similarities of these types of churches could be found throughout the Church Age. Third, these letters had a prophetic application. They were intended to chronologically order the seven stages of church development throughout its earthly existence.

Thus, due to the prophetic aspects of these seven letters, they represent the Church on earth during the Church Age. More information on these multiple applications is available in my book entitled, *The Next Prophecies*.

Lastly in Revelation 1:19, John was to write about the things that "will take place after (*meta*) this (*tauta*)." The things that follow the Church Age are described in Revelation 4 through 22.

The second and third uses of meta tauta (Rev. 4:1)

> "After (*meta*) these things (*tauta*) I looked, and behold, a door *standing* open in heaven. And the first voice which I heard *was* like a trumpet

speaking with me, saying, "Come up here, and I will show you things which must take place after (*meta*) this (*tauta*)." (Rev. 4:1; *emphasis added*)

John uses *meta tauta* two times in this verse. The first use in Rev. 4:1a acknowledges that the Rapture concludes "*the things that are*," which dealt with the Church Age. John sees a door standing open and hears a voice like a trumpet speaking the words "Come up here." This scene parallels what's described in the Rapture-related verses below.

> " For the Lord Himself will descend from heaven, (*through a door standing open in heaven. The door is not closed because the Lord will be swiftly returning through it with His Bride*), with a shout, (*saying come up here*), with the voice of an archangel, and with the trumpet of God. And the dead in Christ will rise first. Then we who are alive *and* remain shall be caught up together with them in the clouds to meet the Lord in the air. And thus we shall always be with the Lord." (1 Thess. 4:16-17; *emphasis added*)

In Rev. 4:1b, John uses these two Greek words again when he writes, "Come up here, and I will show you things which must take place after (*meta*) this (*tauta*)." This usage is not dealing with the conclusion of the Church Age, that was already addressed in Rev. 4:1a in the Rapture, rather this use is about what "must take place after" the Rapture.

Yes, the Rapture described in Rev. 4:1a concluded the Church Age that John covered as, "*the things that are*," in Revelation 2 and 3, but John's second usage in Rev. 4:1b is specifically intended to draw our attention to the Pre-Trib Rapture event. In essence John is saying the events that follow the Church Age in Rev. 2 and 3, and the Pre-Trib Rapture in Rev. 4;1a will be written about in the remainder of the book of Revelation 4 through 22.

The fourth use of meta tauta (Rev. 7:1)

> "After (*meta*) these things (*tauta*) I saw four angels standing at the four corners of the earth, holding the four winds of the earth, that the wind should not blow on the earth, on the sea, or on any tree."
> (Rev. 7:1; *emphasis added*)

This fourth use of *meta tauta* introduces the 144,000 Witnesses of Revelation 7:1-8. Now we can answer the question about the timing of the arrival of these witnesses on the world's scene. These individuals are sealed for Godly service after the second and third uses of *meta tauta* above.

The second use in Rev. 4:1a concluded the Church Age via the Rapture and the third use in Rev. 4:1b started the events that follow the amazing Rapture event itself. Thus, the timing of the 144,000 Witnesses begins after the Church Age, but more specifically, after the Rapture of the Church in Rev. 4:1b.

The other 6 uses of *meta tauta* will be revealed at the appropriate time throughout the remainder of this book and the next book entitled, *The LAST Prophecies (Volume 2)*. They will serve to outline the timing of certain Trib-period events. These other usages are in Rev. 7:9, 9:12, 15:5, 18:1, 19:1 and 20:3.

Revealing the Ministry of the 144,000 Witnesses through the Mystery of the Mis-ordering of Their Names

What are the ethnicities and purposes of these 144,000 Witnesses? Are these witnesses' preachers, prophets and / or evangelists as is commonly taught? Below is an interesting related quote from the book entitled, The Bible Knowledge Commentary: New Testament by John Walvoord and Roy B. Zuck.

> *"Some people believe that the 144,000 will be evangelists in the Great Tribulation. But there is no indication that the 144,000 were preachers or prophets; their testimony was largely from their moral purity and the fact that they were not martyred like many others."*

Below are three reasons why I conclude that these 144,000 Witnesses are Jewish preachers and evangelists.

1.   Their ministerial labors appear to produce a worldwide revival. (Rev. 7:9-17),

2.   Their tribal names have Hebrew origins. (Rev. 7:4-8),

3.   The mysterious mis-ordering of their names reveals their ministerial mission statement.

1. Their ministerial labors appear to produce a worldwide revival. (Rev. 7:9-17),

In Revelation 17:1 John says, *"I saw four angels standing at the four corners of the earth, holding the four winds of the earth."* This indicates that the 144,000 Witnesses come from many nations and not just Israel. They come directionally from every corner of the earth where the four winds blow, North, South, East and West.

Revelation 7:3 says that these witnesses are sealed as servants of God. Sealing serves two purposes, for service and protection. They are sealed to be protected from the judgments from God that come upon the earth, which keeps them safe and enables them to be fruitful servants of God.

The fact that the 144,000 come from the nations means that they speak different languages. This enables them to administer to audiences worldwide. The fruits of their labors appear to spark a global revival of believers in Christ.

Revelation 7:9 identifies *"a great multitude which no one could number, of all nations, tribes, peoples, and tongues, standing before the throne and before the Lamb, clothed with white robes."* This implies that a worldwide revival has resulted from the preaching of the 144,000 witnesses. The *"white robes,"* symbolizes their saved condition. This innumerable multitude of saved individuals come out from the Great Tribulation period as per Revelation 7:14.

2. Their tribal names have Hebrew origins. (Rev. 7:4-8),

There is very little dispute among the prophecy experts that these 144,000 Witnesses are Jewish. These Revelation 7:4-8 verses below are quite specific about the tribal names being described. They are all sons or grandsons of Jacob, who was later renamed Israel in Genesis 32:28.

"And I heard the number of those who were sealed. One hundred and forty-four thousand of all the tribes of the children of Israel were sealed:
of the tribe of Judah twelve thousand were sealed;
of the tribe of Reuben twelve thousand were sealed;
of the tribe of Gad twelve thousand were sealed;
of the tribe of Asher twelve thousand were sealed;
of the tribe of Naphtali twelve thousand were sealed;
of the tribe of Manasseh twelve thousand were sealed;
of the tribe of Simeon twelve thousand were sealed;
of the tribe of Levi twelve thousand were sealed;
of the tribe of Issachar twelve thousand were sealed;
of the tribe of Zebulun twelve thousand were sealed;
of the tribe of Joseph twelve thousand were sealed;
of the tribe of Benjamin twelve thousand were sealed."

3. The mysterious mis-ordering of their names reveals their ministerial mission statement.

This following section reveals the potential mystery hidden within the mis-ordering of the twelve tribal names. The names above are not listed in chronological order. This is unusual because normally, the Bible lists descendants in the sequential order of their birth. However, the apostle John lists these tribes out of their customary order, apparently giving us insights into the ministry of these witnesses.

As an example, the tribe of Judah is listed first in Revelation 7:5 however, in birth order Judah was the fourth son. An astute student of the Word watches for these abnormalities within the scriptures and is encouraged to dig deeper in order to discover what the Holy Spirit intends for him or her to understand relative to the text.

Below, the mis-order of names in Rev. 7:5-8 is correlated to the actual birth order alongside the corresponding meaning of their individual names.

Judah (*4th son*) . . . . Praise God,
Reuben (*1st son*) . . . . Behold a Son,
Gad (*7th son*) . . . . Good Fortune,
Asher (*8th son*) . . . . Happiness,
Naphtali (*6th son.* . . . . My Wrestling,
Manasseh (*a son of Joseph replaces Dan the 5th son*)
. . . . God has Caused me to Forget,
Simeon (*2nd son*) . . . . Hearing,
Levi (*3rd son*) . . . . Joining or Adhesion,
Issachar (*9th son*) . . . . . God Hath Given me Hire Or, Man
. . . . of Hire,
Zebulun (*10th son*) . . . . Elevated or, Elevated Dwelling,
Joseph (*11th son*) . . . . Adding or, Increaser,
Benjamin (*12th son*) . . . . Son of the Right Hand.

The Hidden Message within the Names:

Praise God! Behold! a son of good fortune and happiness. My wrestling God has caused me to forget. Hearing of our joining, God hath given me my hire and elevated dwelling increased by the son of the right hand.

Inherent in these oddly ordered names, appears to be the ministerial message of the 144,000 witnesses. Their "Mission Statement" should read as follows:

> "Praise God for the gospel of Christ. Behold, a Son of good fortune and happiness. My struggle with sin and the Mosaic Law, God has caused me to forget. Hearing of the mystery of our grafting in with the Gentiles,[23] God has reinstated me into an elevated position of ministry once again, and is increasing those being saved through Christ, the Son of the right hand."

It is interesting that the tribe of Manasseh is substituted in place of the tribe of Dan in Rev.7:6. Below are a couple of quotes from respected Bible prophecy teachers that address this conspicuous omission.

> *"Some have wondered why the Old Testament tribes of Dan and Ephraim are omitted from this list of Jewish tribes. ... Most scholars agree that Dan's tribe was omitted because the tribe was guilty of idolatry on many occasions and, as a result was largely obliterated (Leviticus 24:11; Judges 18:1,30; see also 1 Kings 12:28-29). To engage in unrepentant idolatry is be cut off from God's blessing. The tribe of Ephraim was also involved in idolatry and paganized worship (Judges 17; Hosea 4:17). This is probably why both tribes were omitted from Revelation 7."* (Dr. Ron Rhodes).[24]

> *"In the listing in Revelation 7, the tribes of Dan and Ephraim are dropped and replaced by Levi and Joseph to keep the list at twelve. Why? Well, no one knows for sure. My guess is that Dan and Ephraim were dropped because they were the ones that led the children of Israel into idolatry (Deuteronomy*

> *29:18-21 and 1 Kings 12:25ff). It thus appears that the two tribes responsible for luring others into idolatry will not be entrusted with sharing the Gospel with others during the Tribulation."* (Dr. David Reagan).[25]

It's interesting to note that Dan's name means "Judge." Imagine what the mission statement would read if Dan, rather than Manasseh was listed. You would add "Judge" in place of "God has caused me to forget." The revised mission statement would be:

> Praise God! Behold the judge of my wrestling. Hearing of our joining, God hath given me my hire and elevated dwelling increased by the son of the right hand.

This revision would emphasize God in His role as Divine Judge, and deemphasize Christ as the only begotten son of God in His role as Merciful Forgiver. If the intended purpose of misordering the names was to reveal the Gospel through the names of the 144,000 witnesses, then adding Dan in place of Manasseh confuses the message and defeats the purpose.

The 144,002 Witnesses – Part Two: the Two Witnesses

This chapter will explore the identities and timing of the Two Witnesses of Revelation 11:3-13. The sound reasons for placing the timing of the Two Witnesses in the first half of the Trib-period are presented in the middle of this chapter. The chapter concludes with the problems one encounters by placing the timing of the Two Witnesses in the second half of the Trib-period.

The Two Witnesses Prophesy and Possess Powers

"And I will give power to my two witnesses, and they will prophesy one thousand two hundred and sixty days, clothed in sackcloth." These are the two olive trees and the two lampstands standing before the God of the earth. And if anyone wants to harm them, fire proceeds from their mouth and devours their enemies. And if anyone wants to harm them, he must be killed in this manner. These have power to shut heaven, so that no rain falls in the days of their prophecy; and they have power over waters to turn them to blood, and to strike the earth with all plagues, as often as they desire." (Rev. 11:3-6)

The Two Witnesses are Killed

"When they finish their testimony, the beast, (*the Antichrist*), that ascends out of the bottomless pit will make war against them, overcome them, and kill them. And their dead bodies will lie in the street of the great city which spiritually is called Sodom and Egypt, where also our Lord was crucified (*in Jerusalem*). Then those from the peoples, tribes, tongues, and nations will see their dead bodies three-and-a-half days, and not allow their dead bodies to be put into graves. And those who dwell on the earth will rejoice over them, make merry, and send gifts to one another, because these two prophets tormented those who dwell on the earth." (Rev. 11:7-10; *emphasis added*)

The Two Witnesses are Resurrected

"Now after the three-and-a-half days the breath of life from God entered them, and they stood on their feet, and great fear fell on those who saw them. And they heard a loud voice from heaven saying to them, "Come up here." And they ascended to heaven in a cloud, and their enemies saw them. In the same hour there was a great earthquake, and a tenth of the city (*of Jerusalem*) fell. In the earthquake seven thousand people were killed, and the rest (*of those in Jerusalem*) were afraid and gave glory to the God of heaven." (Rev. 11:11-13; *emphasis added*)

Some standout points about the Two Witnesses from these verses are that they will:

1. Have power to prevent rainfall, turn waters to blood and create plagues (v3, 6),

2. Prophesy for one thousand two hundred and sixty days clothed in sackcloth (v3),
3. Live constantly in harm's way (v5),
4. Kill those who attempt to harm them (v5),
5. Successfully profess their testimonies (v7),
6. Be killed by the Antichrist (v7),
7. Lie dead in the streets of Jerusalem for three-and-a-half days (v8-9),
8. Torment those (unbelievers) who dwell on the earth (v10),
9. Resurrect from the dead (v11),
10. Ascend to heaven (v12),
11. Be instrumental in causing (some) Jews to recognize God (v13).

Like the 144,000 Witnesses of Rev. 7:1-8, these Two Witnesses also have a global impact. Below are a couple of interesting comparisons between the activities of these two groups of Witnesses:

- The 144,000 seemingly have no powers, but the Two Witnesses definitely do,

- The 144,000 are redeemed from among men as per Rev. 14:4, but we're uninformed if this is the case with the Two Witnesses. We are told the Two Witnesses are, "*the two olive trees and the two lampstands standing before the God of the earth.*" (Rev. 11:4),

- The 144,000 seem to escape death, but the Two Witnesses are killed,

- The 144,000 evangelize throughout the world, but the Two Witnesses prophesy in Israel, and probably predominately in Jerusalem, which is where the third Jewish Temple will be located. This implies that these two are primarily impacting the Jews and the Gentiles that will "*tread the holy city underfoot for forty-two months,*" as per Rev. 11:2.

The Identity of the Two Witnesses?

It is possible, from the clues provided in Revelation 11:3-13, to make an educated guess as to who the Two Witnesses are? Some believe that they are Moses and Elijah. Others suggest they are Elijah and Enoch. Some have posited that they could be none of the above, but might be two entirely new faces. I don't favor the "new faces" possibility for the following two reasons.

First, Revelation 11:4 says, "*These are the two olive trees and the two lampstands standing before the God of the earth.*" This seems to correlate directly with a vision described in Zechariah 4 of the Old Testament. The same two olive trees show up three times in Zechariah's verses, (Zechariah 4:3,11-12). Referring to the identity of the two olive trees, Zechariah 4:14 says, "So he said, "*These are* the two anointed ones, who stand beside the Lord of the whole earth." If these are the two anointed ones, then it is highly doubtful that they are new faces on the earth in the end times, who serve the Lord for only three and one-half years.

Second, there are clues identified below that support Moses and Elijah are these two witnesses.

1. Moses and Elijah appeared together on the mount of transfiguration. (Matthew 17:3-4). If they appeared together in a significant event of the past, they will likely appear together in the future as well.

2. Moses and Elijah possessed in the past the similar supernatural powers that the Two Witnesses possess in the future. These powers include:

    •   Fire that proceeds from the mouth and devours their enemies (v5),

    •   Power to shut heaven so that no rain falls in the day of their prophecy (6),

- Power over waters to turn them to blood (v6),

- The ability to strike the earth with ALL PLAGUES, as often as they desire (6).

Elijah's former powers concerning *rain* are documented in 1 Kings 17:1, 1 Kings 18:1, 45, James 5:17-18. Elijah also called down *fire* from heaven in 1 Kings 18:38, and 2 Kings 1:10. Moses turned the *waters to blood* in Exodus 7:20-21. Concerning Moses and his ability to strike the earth will all plagues, he struck Egypt with ten plagues, which led to the Exodus of the Hebrews out of Egyptian bondage. The plagues were:[26]

- *First Plague*: Water turned to blood, (Exodus 7:20-21),

- *Second Plague*: Frog infestation throughout Egypt, (Exodus 8:2-4),

- *Third Plague*: Gnats or lice infestation throughout Egypt, (Exodus 8:16-17),

- *Fourth Plague*: Swarms of flies on the people and in their houses, (Exodus 18:21),

- *Fifth Plague*: Livestock diseased, (Exodus 9:3),

- *Sixth Plague*: Boil infections upon the Egyptians, (Exodus 9:8-11),

- *Seventh Plague*: Hailstones rain down upon Egypt, (Exodus 9:18),

- *Eighth Plague*: Locusts cover the face of the earth, (Exodus 10:4-5),

- *Ninth Plague*: Thick blanket of darkness over Egypt, (Exodus 10:21-22),

- *Tenth Plague*: Deaths of the firstborn in Egypt, (Exodus 11:4-5).

It's worthy to note, that some of these plagues seem to be repeated in some variation within some of the trumpet judgments detailed in Revelation 8-9. The first trumpet involves hail and fire mingled with blood (Rev. 8:7). The second trumpet predicts that one-third of the seas will turn into blood (Rev. 8:8). The fourth trumpet says that one-third of the sun, moon and stars become darkened (Rev. 8:12). The fifth trumpet involves a plague of locusts (Rev. 9:3).

It is probable that the trumpet judgments are occurring within the same time-period that the Two Witnesses are ministering on the earth. Although, the trumpet judgments are cast upon the earth via the means of seven angels, and not the two witnesses, the affected populations will not likely be cognizant of that distinction. The verse below points out that the Two Witnesses are tormenting those who dwell on the earth.

> "And those who dwell on the earth will rejoice over them, make merry, and send gifts to one another, because these two prophets tormented those who dwell on the earth." (Rev. 11:10)

It can be assumed that the tormenting is primarily the result of the Two Witnesses executing their powers, which includes the ability to strike the earth with ALL PLAGUES in Rev. 11:6. When these Two Witnesses lie dead in the streets of Jerusalem, *"those who dwell on the earth will rejoice, make merry and send gifts to one another."* This merriment is likely because the gift-givers could be under the impression that ALL the PLAGUES end with their deaths. It wouldn't be surprising if at that time the Antichrist, who kills these Two Witnesses, comes out publicly and declares that the plagues have ended. However, the plagues will continue to happen as the bowl judgments are poured out in the Great Tribulation period.

More reasons to favor Moses and Elijah as the Two Witnesses continues below.

3.   Elijah was caught up in a whirlwind to heaven and never experienced death, (2 Kings 2:11-12). This fact implies that Elijah is alive, available and ready to return to the earth as one of the Two Witnesses. Enoch was also caught up to heaven, which is why some believe that he could also return as one of the Two Witnesses, (Genesis 5:24, Hebrews 11:5).

4.   The Old Testament prophet Malachi predicts the return of Elijah.

> "Behold, I will send you Elijah the prophet Before the coming of the great and dreadful day of the Lord. And he will turn The hearts of the fathers to the children, And the hearts of the children to their fathers, Lest I come and strike the earth with a curse." (Malachi 4:5-6)

Some scholars suggest that John the Baptist may have been the fulfillment of this Malachi prophecy according to the communication exchange between Jesus and His disciples in Matthew 17:10-13. However, below is a quote from Dr. Henry M. Morris negating this possibility.

> "Some assume that this prophecy was fulfilled in John the Baptist, but John the Baptist himself denied it. *"And they asked him, What then? Art thou Elias* (Elijah)? *And he saith, I am not"* (John 1:21). John did indeed come *"in the spirit and power of Elias"* (Luke 1:17), but he was not Elias, and his coming did not fulfill Malachi's prophecy. Jesus Himself confirmed this. *"Elias truly shall first come, and restore all things"* (Matthew 17:11)[27]

Although John did come before the *"great and dreadful day of the Lord,"* the prophetic implication is just prior to this period, rather than over two thousand years beforehand when John existed. Also, John did not *"turn the hearts of the fathers to the children, and the hearts of the children to their fathers."*

5. Moses represents the Law and Elijah the Prophets. When the Two Witnesses are on the earth, the Jews are reinstating the Mosaic Law and its animal sacrificial system. Moses and Elijah would be prime candidates to rebuke this effort. Both know that Jesus Christ is the Messiah. This was evidenced clearly to them at the mount of Transfiguration when the Lord said, *"This is My beloved Son, in whom I am well pleased. Hear Him!"* (Matthew 17:5). Jesus Christ fulfilled the Law, (Matthew 5:17), and in so doing, He rendered it inoperative. Galatians 3:24 clarifies the purpose of the law. It reads, "Therefore the law was our tutor *to bring us* to Christ, that we might be justified by faith."

6. There was a dispute between Satan and Michael the archangel over the body of Moses. This could imply that Satan is concerned about Moses returning to the earth again as one of the Two Witnesses, (Jude 1:9).

The Timing of the Two Witnesses

There is a debate about whether these Two Witnesses prophesy in the first or second half of the Trib-period. Below are some quotes from some of today's most respected Bible prophecy experts on this timing topic. Dr. Ron Rhodes writes the following in his book entitled, *The End Times In Chronological Order.*

> *"Scholars debate whether the ministry of the two witnesses belongs in the first half or the second half of the tribulation. Their ministry will last 1260 days, which measures out to precisely three and a*

*half years.".... "Most prophecy scholars conclude
that the two witnesses do their miraculous work
during the first three and a half years."*[28]

In his book on page 127, Dr. Rhodes places the death and
resurrection of the two witnesses at the midpoint of the Trib-
period just before the Antichrist annuls the false covenant in
Daniel 9:27 through the Abomination of Desolation spoken by
Jesus in Matthew 24:15-22. Thus, Rhodes places the timing of the
Two Witnesses in the first half of the Trib-period.

So does Tim LaHaye. In his book entitled, *Revelation Unveiled*,
LaHaye says,

> *"As a result of the shocking treatment of these two
> faithful witnesses of God by the inhabitants of
> the city of Jerusalem, the Lord will send a great
> earthquake, destroying a tenth part of the city and
> slaying seven thousand people. This cataclysmic
> judgment of God on the city of Jerusalem may be the
> event that triggers a revival that will sweep across
> Israel during the latter half of the Tribulation, for
> the passage reads, "and the survivors were terrified
> and gave glory to the God of heaven." This remnant
> may refer to the Jewish inhabitants of the city who,
> after seeing the judging hand of God slay seven
> thousand of their residents and destroy a tenth
> part of their city, will turn in faith to embrace the
> message of the two witnesses so recently resurrected.
> All of these events take place before the third woe
> is sounded in verse 14, which identifies these two
> witnesses who live, preach, die, and are resurrected
> during the first half of the Tribulation period. In
> addition to closing this second parenthetical passage,
> it also sets the stage for the events of the latter half of
> the Tribulation period."*[29]

Tim LaHaye places the death and resurrection of the Two Witnesses before the third woe judgment in Rev. 11:14, which reads, "The second woe is past. Behold, the third woe is coming quickly." The three woe judgments of the fifth, sixth and seventh trumpets will be explained later in the chapter dealing with the seven trumpet judgments. That chapter will demonstrate how the three woes provide evidence that the first six trumpet judgments happen in the first half of the Trib-period and that the seventh trumpet judgment happens around the middle of the Trib-period.

Whereas Rhodes and LaHaye place the timing of the Two Witnesses in the first half of the Trib-period, others such as Dr. John Walvoord and Dr. Mark Hitchcock favor the possibility that they prophesy in the second half. At the end of this chapter I will present this timing position and lay out the various problems with it.

A few of the clues that lead me to reason the Two Witnesses exist in the first half are below.

• The Counting the Worshippers in the Temple Clue

> "Then I was given a measuring stick, and I was told, "Go and measure the Temple of God and the altar, and count the number of worshipers. But do not measure the outer courtyard, for it has been turned over to the nations. They will trample the holy city for 42 months." (Rev. 11:1, NLT)

This verse pictures the apostle John measuring the third temple, the altar and counting the number of worshippers therein. This measuring and counting is taking place in the first half of the Trib-period. Then, Rev. 11:3 introduces the Two Witnesses in that same three and one-half year time frame.

> "And I will give power to my two witnesses, and they will be clothed in burlap and will prophesy during those 1,260 days." (Rev. 11:3, NLT)

Counting the number of worshippers in the temple won't happen in the second half of the Trib-period, because the temple worship will have ceased by then as a result of the Antichrist abominating the temple and stopping the sacrifices and offerings as per Daniel 9:27. Any Jew attempting to worship inside the temple during the second half of the Trib-period will be killed on his way through the door as part of the genocidal campaign of the Antichrist.

Therefore, the Jewish religious leaders are counting the number of the worshippers inside the temple during the first half of the Trib-Period, at the same time that the Two Witnesses are prophesying outside in the streets of Jerusalem.

Is it possible that one of the reasons the rabbis are taking a headcount of the worshippers is to keep track of the potential impact that the Two Witnesses are having on overall temple attendance? It is plausible to consider that the prophesying and supernatural powers being performed by this incredible tag team may be causing temple worshippers to rethink their religious beliefs. Will temple traffic increase or decrease as time passes with these Two Witnesses preaching from their pulpits in the streets of Jerusalem?

Inside the temple the rabbis will be performing sacrifices and offerings as per the Levitical Law, but outside on the streets the Two Witnesses will be preaching about Jesus Christ as the Messiah and prophesying about forthcoming tribulation events. Below are three of the prophecies that these Two Witnesses might be warning the Jews about.

1. Matthew 24:15-16, whereby Jesus Christ warns of the coming Abomination of Desolation in the temple. Jesus instructs the Jews to flee immediately when they see this happen.

Many Jews living inside Israel, perhaps millions, are going to follow the instructions of Jesus from these Matthew 24 verses and flee to the mountains. They become the faithful remnant of Israel of Zechariah 13:9 and elsewhere. A few pertinent questions concerning this are:

- How does the Faithful Jewish Remnant discover these life-saving instructions from Jesus in advance?

- How do these Jews know when and where to flee?

- When the Antichrist stops the sacrifices and offerings in the Temple and then initiates his Jewish genocidal campaign, are these Jews going to be surprised, slap their foreheads and say, "*Oy Vey*," what do we do now?

- In the heat of that moment, are they all going to frantically search for New Testament Bibles to see what Jesus said for lack of having any better ideas?

NO! NOT LIKELY! These Jews will probably not be surprised, but will have already become very familiar with the warning and instructions within Matthew 24:15-16, largely because of the Two Witnesses. Many of them will have likely already left Jerusalem ahead of the Abomination of Desolation. The remaining stragglers that will flee when this abominable act occurs, which are the ones Christ is speaking to directly, are likely those Jews that were waiting to see if what these Two Witnesses were prophesying about would actually happen.

2. Zechariah 13:8, which predicts that the Antichrist will kill two-thirds of the Jews living in Israel. The Two Witnesses will probably be pleading feverishly for their Jewish brethren to not become numbered among these millions of Jews that will be killed.

3. Revelation 11:7-13, that foretells that the Antichrist will kill them, leave their two dead corpses on public display in the streets of Jerusalem, then they will resurrect and

ascend to heaven and at that time there will be a great earthquake that kills 7000 people and destroys one-tenth of the city. Forecasting their own deaths, resurrections and ascensions would have a profound impact on those Jews playing the wait and see game.

- ## The Malachi 4:5-6 Clues About the Coming of Elijah Before the Day of the Lord

> "Behold, I will send you Elijah the prophet Before the coming of the great and dreadful day of the Lord. And he will turn The hearts of the fathers to the children,
>
> And the hearts of the children to their fathers, Lest I come and strike the earth with a curse." (Malachi 4:5-6)

Malachi prophesies that Elijah will come before the GREAT and DREADFUL DAY of the LORD, which is commonly taught to be the Trib-period. This prophet of old will be sent in advance to make a spiritual impact on the Jewish people.

Elijah will influence Jewish fathers to be mindful of what their children's near future holds. He will also turn the children's hearts toward their fathers. This could refer to their biological fathers and / or their patriarchal fathers of Abraham, Isaac and Jacob, through whom God gave the Abrahamic Covenant.

The point is that the testimonies of Elijah and the other second witness will likely contribute toward the conversions of Jews who ultimately become members of the "Faithful Jewish Remnant." This scenario could segue into the reasoning from the Tim LaHaye quote above. When the earthquake kills 7,000 people and destroys one-tenth of Jerusalem as per Rev. 11:13, the survivors, *"will turn in faith to embrace the message of the two witnesses so recently resurrected."*

Remember, unlike the 144,000 Witnesses within the four winds spread throughout the world, the Two Witnesses appear to be centrally located in Jerusalem in Israel where the strong concentration of Jews are.

• A Few Other Clues

In addition to the clues above, some other considerations about the timing are:

1. According to Rev. 11:10, *"those who dwell on the earth will rejoice over them, make merry, and send gifts to one another,"* when they rejoice over the sight of their dead bodies in Rev. 11:9. Some sort of a worldwide celebration on this scale is not likely going to happen at the end of the Trib-period, which would be when these Two Witnesses would be killed if they ministered in the second half of the Trib-period.

Why? Because by then the wrath of God will have been poured out in the seven bowl judgments of Revelation 16. It will be far from a time of merriment, as this wrath includes:

*   Loathsome sores will cover those who took the Mark of the Beast (Rev. 16:2),

*   Seas and Waters will be turned to blood (Rev. 16:3-7),

*   Multitudes will be scorched from intense heat (Rev. 16:8-9),

*   Great darkness intensifying the painful stress (Rev. 16:10-11),

*   The greatest earthquake in world history will strike and every island will be adversely affected and many mountains will collapse (Rev. 16:18-20),

- There will be a heavy barrage of hailstones falling upon many (Rev. 16:20-21).

Moreover, multitudes among mankind will be gathering in the valley of decision in Joel 3:14, which is the valley of Jehoshaphat in Joel 3:3. They will be preparing for the final war of Armageddon and not likely sipping wine and wrapping up gifts.

The Problems with Placing the Two Witnesses in the Last Half of the Trib-Period

This concluding section will present the primary reasons that some teach the Two Witnesses prophesy in the second half of the Trib-period. It will also include the refutations to this possibility. These refutations are outlined below and elaborated upon throughout this section.

The REFUTATIONS: The Two Witnesses will not likely be prophesying in the second half of the Trib-period because:

1. DISOBEDIENCE OF GOD: They would be disobeying God as per Matthew 24:15-16,

2. RELIGIOUS TOLERANCE: It would mean the Antichrist tolerates the preaching of Jesus in Jerusalem for three and one-half years, after he had gone into the third temple and exalted himself above all that is called God as per 2 Thess. 2:4. This implies that the Antichrist is religiously tolerant,

3. GENOCIDAL EXCEPTION: It would mean the Antichrist gives an exception to two out of an estimated 15 million plus Jews, to not be killed immediately as part of his Jewish genocidal campaign in Zec. 13:8,

4. THE BOWL JUDGMENTS: The seven bowl judgments, which complete the wrath of God as per Rev. 15:1, would

either be crammed into the seventy-five-day interval period of Daniel 12:12, or even less likely, find final fulfillment during the beginning of the Millennium.

5. THE TIMING RESTRICTIONS: The timing of the deaths of the Two Witnesses potentially exceeds the allotted 1260 days, between the Abomination of Desolation and the killing of the Antichrist by Jesus Christ.

6. CHAOTIC GLOBAL CONDITIONS: At the time of the deaths of the Two Witnesses, the world environment is not filled with the rejoicing and merriment that facilitates the gift-giving requirement of Rev. 11:10.

Dr. Mark Hitchcock is among those who teach that the Two Witnesses prophesy in the second half of the Trib-period. In his book entitled, *The Second Coming of Babylon*, he provides a proposed chronology of the end times on pages 174-175. He proposes that at the midpoint of the Trib-period the following events take place:

*   Gog and his allies invade Israel,

*   The Antichrist breaks his covenant with Israel,

*   The Antichrist sets up the Abomination of Desolation in the rebuilt temple,

*   The faithful Jewish remnant flees to Petra,

*   The Antichrist is miraculously raised from the dead,

*   The Two Witnesses begin their three and one-half years ministry,

*   The Antichrist and the 10 kings destroy the religious system of Babylon.

In addition to this outline of events above by Dr. Hitchcock, I am including below a personal email correspondence that he gave me on May 15, 2019. I had asked Mark if he would kindly provide me with some of the reasons he favored the second half timing perspective. Mark has approved my use of this email in this publication. The reason I am quoting Mark Hitchcock, is because he presents some of the more convincing arguments for this view and, as you will see from his email below, he does so humbly and non-dogmatically.

Hitchcock's email: on 5/15/19

"The timing of the 2 witnesses is difficult and could go either way. There are strong arguments for both views. The last half of the tribulation was Dr. Walvoord's view.

4 main reasons for putting them in the last half.

1. *The 42 months in 11:2 and the 1,260 days in Rev. 11:3 seem to cover the same time-period since they aren't distinguished. The 42 months when the temple is trodden down is clearly the last half in v. 2.*

2. *I put the trumpet judgments in the last half, and since the 2 witnesses (Rev 11) are placed within the trumpet judgments it makes sense that they're also in the second half. Also, the 7th trumpet sounds in Rev. 11:15 at the end of the tribulation right in the immediate context. Rev 11 is between the second and third woes (the 6th and 7th trumpets).*

3. *The persecution of the witnesses by the beast seems to fit better when he's ruling the world.*

4. *V. 8 seems to fit better during the second half.
    Jerusalem is called Sodom (which speaks
    of perversion) and Egypt (which speaks of
    bondage). These titles don't fit as well with
    the first half when the Jews will be living
    under the security of their agreement with
    the beast.*

    *There are arguments against my view, that I'm well
    aware of, but I like the 2nd half view better. I think
    it has more in its favor."*

In addition to Hitchcock's reasons above, another prevalent
argument presented for the second half timing view, is that the
logical time frame for the Antichrist to kill the Two Witnesses in
Rev. 11:7 is when the Antichrist is at his high point of power in
Revelation 13. His high point of power is during the second half
of the Trib-period. Below is a related quote from the *J. Hampton
Keathley's Commentary on Revelation.*

> *"The hideous acts of Revelation 11:9-10 also seem
> to fit better with the character of the last half
> of the Tribulation with the lawlessness of the
> beast and his system and the worship of Satan
> (Revelation 13:4)."*[30]

NOW FOR THE REFUTATIONS

The REFUTATIONS: The Two Witnesses will not likely be
prophesying in the second half of the Trib-period because:

1. DISOBEDIENCE OF GOD: In Matthew 24:15-16.
    Jesus tells the Jews to flee to the mountains immediately
    when they witness the "Abomination of Desolation." This
    happens at the midpoint of the Seven-Year Tribulation
    Period. If the Two Jewish Witnesses decided to remain
    in Jerusalem after the "Abomination of Desolation,"

instead of fleeing to the mountains with their Jewish brethren, then they would be guilty of disobeying the instructions of Jesus Christ.

2.   RELIGIOUS TOLERANCE: 2 Thess. 2:4 says that the Antichrist will enter the Temple of God, which is when he performs the "Abomination of Desolation," and that he will exalt himself above all that is called God or that is worshiped. Moreover, the Antichrist will sit in the Temple of God at that time showing off that he is God.

If the Two Witnesses begin their ministry at this time, which is the threshold of the beginning point of the second half of the Trib-period, that implies that the Antichrist is religiously tolerant. One could preclude that the Antichrist, after declaring himself as god, is giving two Jews a hall pass to stand on their pulpits in Jerusalem and preach about Jesus Christ as the Messiah. Not only the Messiah, but the only begotten Son of God as per John 3:16.

This flies in the face of the prophetic facts. The Antichrist will be anything but spiritually fair and balanced.

Firstly, by the time the Antichrist goes on his "I'm god" tirade, he will have the ten kings desolate the Harlot world religion and bestow the entirety of its wealth and all of their power to him as per Rev. 17:16-17. Eliminating a global religion is not exactly a religiously tolerant move.

Secondly, he stops the religion of Judaism when he goes into the temple and stops the sacrifices and offerings as per Daniel 9:27. This isn't a display of religious tolerance.

Thirdly, after he stomps out Judaism, he proceeds to implement a killing campaign of Jewish genocide as per Zec. 13:8. This will prevent the possible return of Judaism in the future.

Fourthly, the Antichrist begins beheading Christian believers who refuse to take his "Mark of the Beast" as per Rev. 20:4. This is a religiously intolerant attempt to eliminate and remove all vestiges of Christianity from the earth.

Therefore, there is no possible reason to believe that the Antichrist will stand by idly for three and one-half years and let two Jews preach Jesus in Jerusalem!

3. GENOCIDAL EXCEPTION: Along these same lines, it would make no sense for the Antichrist to make an exception that allows these two Jews to live, when at the time he is commanding a Jewish genocidal campaign. Revelation 11:7 says that the Antichrist, *"will make war against them, overcome them, and kill them."* If the Antichrist is going to do these three things, then why would he wait for three and one-half years to do this? Why would he allow them to counter his religious objectives throughout the entire second half of the Trib-period? This makes no sense to me!

4. THE BOWL JUDGMENTS: In his email to me, Mark Hitchcock is absolutely correct to connect the timing of the trumpet judgments with the timing of the Two Witnesses. These two scenarios are inseparable, which I will point out in the chapter entitled, "The Seven Trumpet Judgments."

Revelation 11:14 makes it clear that the deaths, resurrections and ascensions of the Two Witnesses happen between the sounding of the sixth and seventh trumpets. However, there is a potential problem with placing these events at the end of the Trib-period. This is because the sounding of the seventh trumpet in Rev. 11:15, which sounds after the Two Witnesses ascend to heaven, triggers the prophetic events within the seven bowl judgments.

Revelation 15:1 points out that the wrath of God is completed through the fulfillments of these seven bowl judgments. These judgments are described in Revelation 16 and involve the:

- Inflicting of loathsome sores (1st bowl),

- Sea turning to blood and killing all the sea creatures therein (2nd bowl),

- Rivers and Springs turning to blood (3rd bowl),

- Scorching of mankind with fires and great heat (4th bowl),

- Widespread of darkness and the gnawing of tongues from the pain of the sores (5th bowl),

- Drying of the Euphrates, enabling the world armies to gather for Armageddon (6th bowl),

- Great Earthquake that destroys end times Babylon (7th bowl).

These things will take some time to find fulfillment. If the ascensions of the Two Witnesses precedes these seven bowl events, which they do, and if these ascensions happen at the end of the Trib-period, then there is no time remaining within the Trib-period for the fulfillment of these seven bowl events. This timing scenario would then preclude that these bowl events must find fulfillment sometime after the Trib-period.

This would mean that the wrath of God does not find completion within the Trib-period, but gets completed sometime after. This also forces the fulfillment of the bowl judgments into either the seventy-five day post-tribulation interval period of Daniel 12:12 or the Millennium of Rev. 20:4. Without going into a study about the details of these two post-tribulation periods, the fact is that it would make no sense for the wrath of God to be poured out in the bowl judgments during these two time frames.

5. THE TIMING RESTRICTIONS: The biblical text in Revelation 11:3 states that the ministry of the two witnesses is precisely 1260 days. This means logically that any end time scenario that would have the beginning and ending of their ministry less than 1260 days or more than 1260 days would seem to be in danger of contradicting the biblical text of this verse.

"And I will give power to my two witnesses, and they will prophesy one thousand two hundred and sixty (*1260*) days, clothed in sackcloth." (Rev. 11:3; *emphasis added*)

In order for the Antichrist's 1260-day period of rule over the world to synchronize with the same 1260 days that the Two Witnesses prophesy, the following must hold true. Let me explain.

It is commonly taught that the Antichrist performs the Abomination of Desolation, which is alluded to in Matthew 24:15, at the midpoint of the Trib-period. After this epic prophetic event, the Antichrist reigns as the world's leader for forty-two months, which is precisely 1260 days.

"And he, (*the Antichrist*), was given a mouth speaking great things and blasphemies, and he was given authority to continue for forty-two months." (Rev. 13:5; *emphasis added*)

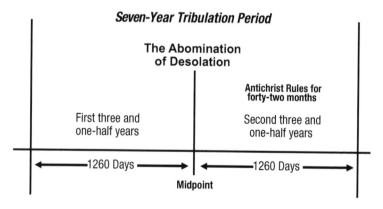

Seven-Year Tribulation Period

The Abomination of Desolation

Antichrist Rules for forty-two months

First three and one-half years | Second three and one-half years

◄——————1260 Days——————► ◄——————1260 Days——————►

Midpoint

The Antichrist rules in the second half of the Trib-period for 1260 days after which on day 1261, he is cast into the Lake of Fire as per Rev. 19:20. Therefore, if he is going to kill the Two Witnesses after they prophesy for 1260 days, he must do this prior to day 1261.

If the Two Witnesses prophesy in the second half of the Trib-period, this means that at the exact moment that the Antichrist begins his 1260 days, the Two Witnesses must also begin theirs. In this scenario the Two Witnesses can't come onto the scene a week or two after the Abomination of Desolation, otherwise it would be impossible for the Antichrist, dwelling in the Lake of Fire, to kill these two prophets in Jerusalem.

But there is a serious complication! Actually the Two Witnesses are on the earth for 1263.5 days, because after 1260 days, they get killed and lie dead in the streets of Jerusalem for *three-and-a-half days*.

> "When they, (*the Two Witnesses*), finish their (*1260 days of*) testimony, the beast, (*Antichrist*), that ascends out of the bottomless pit will make war against them, overcome them, and kill them. And their dead bodies *will lie* in the street of the great city (*of Jerusalem*), which spiritually is called Sodom and Egypt, where also our Lord was crucified. Then *those* from the peoples, tribes, tongues, and nations will see their dead bodies *three-and-a-half days*, and not allow their dead bodies to be put into graves." (Rev. 11:7-9; *emphasis added*)

During these additional *three-and-a-half days*, people around the world will see their dead bodies and give gifts to each other. This implies that the world watches the Two dead Witnesses after the Antichrist is cast into the Lake of Fire.

By way of review, the Two Witnesses get killed after prophesying for 1260 days and then they lie dead in Jerusalem for an additional *three-and-a-half days.* Then they resurrect and ascend to heaven and then the Seventh Trumpet sounds quickly thereafter. The sounding of the Seventh Trumpet segues into the unleashing of the Seven Bowl Judgments. These are the last seven plagues and Rev. 15:1 says, *"for in them the wrath of God is complete."*

The problem with the teaching that the Two Witnesses prophesy during the second half of the Trib-period, is that there aren't enough days within the Seven-Year Tribulation Period for the following events to happen:

1. The Two Witnesses to lie dead in the streets for *three-and-a-half days* (Rev. 11:7-9),

2. The Two Witnesses to resurrect and ascend to heaven after those *three-and-a-half* days (Rev. 11:11-12),

3. The earthquake to occur in the same hour that the Two Witnesses ascent to heaven that kills seven thousand people and destroys one-tenth of Jerusalem (Rev. 11:13),

4. The Seventh Trumpet to sound after all the above has happened (Rev. 11:14-19),

5. The completion of the wrath of God that happens through the Seven Bowl Judgments after the Seventh Trumpet sounds. (Rev. 15:1 and 16:1-21).

In the best-case scenario, for this second half of the Trib-period theory to work, the Antichrist must kill the Two Witnesses *three-and-a-half days* before he gets cast into the Lake of Fire. This seems virtually impossible considering the calendar of events above. It seems that those who subscribe to the timing of the Two Witnesses in the second half of the Trib-period, need to be very specific on their timetables, or they might end up with an incapacitated Antichrist who dwells in the Lake of Fire and is unable to kill the Two Witnesses.

6. CHAOTIC GLOBAL CONDITIONS: It was pointed out earlier in this chapter that when the Two Witnesses are killed, those people they tormented are rejoicing and passing out gifts to one another. If these two are killed at the very end of the Trib-period, then this rejoicing will be extremely short-lived because at that time the wrath of God is being poured out on them.

The Seven Seal Judgments

This Chapter presents the details and the timing of the Seven Seal Judgments.

The Seven Seals

Revelation 6:1-17 details the first Six Seals and Rev. 8:1-6 informs of the Seventh and last Seal. These Seven Seals find fulfillment in succession. The First Seal precedes the Second Seal, which precedes the Third Seal and so on and so forth.   All of the Seven Seals are opened after the Rapture, but before the Trumpet Judgments.

Most traditional Bible commentaries teach that the Seven Seals find fulfillment in the first three and one-half years of the Trib-period. They teach that the First Seal, which introduces the Antichrist on a white horse, is when the False Covenant of Daniel 9:27 gets confirmed and that act begins the seven years of tribulation.

In the *NEXT Prophecies* book, I present the basic logic behind this teaching in the chapter entitled, "*The Traditional View of the Seal Judgments of Revelation 6.*" In a comparative chapter called, "*The Alternative View of the Seal Judgments of Revelation 6,*" I point out the several potential flaws in this traditional timing theory. The chapter on the alternative view presents some new challenging ideas into this subject matter.

The Post-Rapture / Pre-Trumpet Timing of the Seven Seals

The Post-Rapture, but Pre-Trumpet timing of the Seven Seals is easily understood through the following details.

1. *Post-Rapture* - The Seal Judgments are opened in the aftermath of the events described in Revelation 4 and 5. These events climax with the opening of the heavenly scroll in Revelation 5. It was explained in the prior chapter entitled, *"The 144,002 Witnesses – Part One: the 144,000 Witnesses,"* that the Rapture event is fulfilled in Revelation 4:1. Thus, Rev. 4 and 5 detail events that take place in heaven after the Rapture, which makes the opening of the scroll that contains the Seven Seals a "Post-Rapture" event.

2. *Pre-Trumpet* - Rev. 8:1-6 points out that the opening of the Seventh Seal begins the Seven Trumpet Judgments. Thus, it is obvious that the Seven Seals precede the sounding of these trumpets, which makes them "Pre-Trumpet."

With these two prophetic understandings in place we know for certain that the Seven Seals are opened Post-Rapture, but how soon afterward? After the Rapture there is a gap of unspecified time that precedes the Tribulation. Is it possible that some of the Seals are opened in this gap, or is it conclusive that they patiently await their openings and fulfillments until the Trib-period? I invite you to read the *NEXT Prophecies* book to explore these timing topics more thoroughly.

Whatever that true timing of the Seven Seals turns out to be, all can agree that they are globally impacting predictions. They are summarized below.

First Seal: The White Horseman of the Apocalypse

"Now I saw when the Lamb opened one of the seals; and I heard one of the four living creatures saying with a voice like thunder, "Come and see." And I looked, and behold, a white horse. He who sat on it had a bow; and a crown was given to him, and he went out conquering and to conquer." (Rev. 6:1-2)

The First Seal involves the coming of the White Horseman of the Apocalypse. It is commonly taught that this represents the emergence of the Antichrist upon the world stage. Rev. 6:2 says that he goes forth *"conquering and to conquer."* The Greek word *nikaoô* is repeated in this verse. In addition to "conquering and to conquer," the word can be translated to *prevail, overcome, overpower* or *be victorious.*[31]

Ultimately, these conquering efforts lead the Antichrist to political prominence, military power and religious dominance. The Antichrist will *prevail* politically, *overcome* militarily and *overpower* religiously. He will become victorious in these three important arenas. He is wearing a Stefanos crown, which is a wreath or crown of victory. It is the type of crown that was awarded to a victor in the ancient athletic games, like the Greek Olympics.[32] Thus, he is victorious when he goes forth *conquering and to conquer.*

He prevails politically in Daniel 9:26-27 as the future prince, (political leader), that is called upon to confirm the all-important false covenant between Israel and another party. Modern-day comparisons of a political leader possessing similar respect would be US Presidents Jimmy Carter and Bill Clinton, who were called upon to confirm covenants between Israel and Egypt, (Carter), and Israel and Jordan, (Clinton).

As a powerful political leader, he achieves military power. In Daniel 11:40, he is waging and winning major wars. Once he achieves both political and military power, he uses them to springboard into religious dominance.

2 Thess. 2:4 foretells that in his capacity as a supreme religious figure, he will oppose and exalt himself above all that is called God or that is worshiped. Moreover, he will show himself off as god in the Temple of God.

Rev. 13:15 predicts that the False Prophet will be commissioned to build an image of the Antichrist and give *power* and breath to it.

These attributes will enable the image to speak, which in turn will be a contributing reason why many people will worship the Antichrist. Those who refuse will be beheaded as per this verse and Rev. 20:4. Many more details about the Antichrist will be provided in several of the upcoming chapters within this book.

Second Seal: The Fiery Red Horseman of the Apocalypse

> "When He opened the second seal, I heard the second living creature saying, "Come and see." Another horse, fiery red, went out. And it was granted to the one who sat on it to take peace from the earth, and that *people* should kill one another; and there was given to him a great sword." (Revelation 6:3-4)

The Fiery Red Horseman is given *a great sword*, which is a biblical typological representation of great wars. Perhaps on the scale of world wars. With this sword, the Red Horseman is permitted *to take peace from the earth.* This will likely prompt the world cries for "Peace and Safety" that are forthcoming as per 1 Thess. 5:3.

Third Seal: The Black Horseman of the Apocalypse

> "When He opened the third seal, I heard the third living creature say, "Come and see." So I looked, and behold, a black horse, and he who sat on it had a pair of scales in his hand. And I heard a voice in the midst of the four living creatures saying, "A quart of wheat for a denarius, and three quarts of barley for a denarius; and do not harm the oil and the wine."" (Revelation 6:5-6)

The introduction of the Black Horseman signifies that the darkest of times have fallen upon the earth. When world wars happen, severe suffering results. Famines occur as plagues and pestilences spread uncontrollably throughout the various warzones created by the Red Horseman. This creates a humanitarian crisis as refugees' surface and become stranded in the affected areas. The fact that the prior horseman wielded a great sword, implies that the global consequences of the second seal wars were catastrophic.

The third seal imposes the enormous burden upon the international community to resolve the disastrous dilemma before it burgeons out of control. It encourages the expeditious formation of a global government to deal with the escalating emergencies, like world starvation and disease control.

Presently, The Office for the Coordination of Humanitarian Affairs, (OCHA), and The Central Emergency Response Fund, (CERF), are among the United Nations agencies in place to deal with international emergencies. Perhaps they will be the organizations called upon to bring relief to the refugees. However, it appears more likely that the Pale Horsemen of the Apocalypse from the Fourth Seal will fulfill that future role.

Whatever international agency takes responsibility for administering aid to the afflicted, the Black Horseman instructs them to ration the world's food supplies. The price tag for the necessary food staples to survive becomes fixed at two days' wages. A denarius was the equivalent of a day's wage when this prophecy was written. One denarius will put a quart of wheat inside a family's gallon container and another denarius will fill the remainder of their vessel with three quarts of barley.

The third seal paints a grave picture for the poor, but it's not as distressing for the rich. The horseman concludes his instructions with the command, "*do not harm the oil and the wine.*" This alludes to the luxury items that only the rich will be able to afford. In other words, in the process of rationing the food, do not harm the economic engine that drives the financial recovery, which sustains the existence of the global government.

Fourth Seal: The Pale Horsemen of the Apocalypse

"When He opened the fourth seal, I heard the
voice of the fourth living creature saying, "Come
and see." So I looked, and behold, a pale horse.
And the name of him who sat on it was Death,
and Hades followed with him. And power was
given to them over a fourth of the earth, to kill
with sword, with hunger, with death, and by the
beasts of the earth." (Revelation 6:7-8)

As the seals progress in their chronological order, things go
from bad to worse as the world welcomes in the Pale Horsemen
of the Apocalypse. I say horsemen, rather than horseman, because
unlike its three predecessors the Pale horse has two riders. This
sinister tag team rides side saddle in their natural order, Death
followed by Hades. Death deals with the material departure of a
being from its body and Hades is concerned with the immaterial
aspect of a person after death, which is their soul. Presently, when
someone dies their soul is delivered to its destination, which is
either Heaven if they're saved or Hades if they're not.

Whoever, or whatever their manifestations represent, this
diabolical duo seemingly possess power and authority over a
quarter of the world's population to kill people via multiple
means. Unlike the second horseman who only had a great sword
in his sheath, Death and Hades have a lethal arsenal that enables
them *to kill with sword, with hunger, with death, and by the beasts
of the earth.*

In the prior chapter entitled, *"The False Covenant that Starts
the Seven-Year Tribulation Period,"* I mentioned the possibility
that Death and Hades might have control over one-fourth of the
world's surviving population at the time. The traditional teaching
is that Death and Hades kill a fourth of mankind, but that's not
necessarily what's being said here.

Let's unpack this possibility further. *Authority was given to them over a fourth of the earth...*

At a time when the world is experiencing strong satanic deception of 2 Thess. 2:9-10, and is recovering from devastating wars, severe famines and enormous economic scarcities, Death and Hades ride onto the scene. It appears that these two riders come to the rescue and harness global control over one-fourth of the world's surviving population. John Walvoord estimates this number of survivors at around 1 billion people.

If Death and Hades are called to restore order amidst the global chaos, then a global reach of 1 billion people would seem adequate to enable them to execute their campaign successfully. It is likely that some of the other 3 billion, (three-fourths of the earth), people are suffering on some levels from the consequences of the wars and famines. Perhaps Death and Hades commands their global network of about 1 billion to remedy the dire conditions occurring throughout the world.

However, for the benefit of receiving assistance from the global network of Death and Hades, the needy must follow their dictates. Those who dissent are put to death by either, *"the sword and with famine and with pestilence and by the wild beasts of the earth."*

It may mean that Death and Hades kill a fourth of the earth's population, which is what the traditional view teaches, but more than likely it implies that a quarter of the world's population are faithful followers of Death and Hades. These are devotees so committed to their cause that they are willing to kill their opposition. The fact that Hades takes a lead role in this massive operation infers that this involves a global religious crusade. This future scenario appears to be reminiscent of the historical inquisition periods when the Catholic Church was martyring the so-called Protestant heretics centuries ago.

The potential connections between Death and Hades as the Harlot of Revelation 17 and the Catholic Church of the end times were made in *the NEXT Prophecies* book. More on these connections will be presented later on in this book.

Fifth Seal: The Martyrs of the Apocalypse

"When He opened the fifth seal, I saw under the altar the souls of those who had been slain for the word of God and for the testimony which they held. And they cried with a loud voice, saying, "How long, O Lord, holy and true, until You judge and avenge our blood on those who dwell on the earth?" Then a white robe was given to each of them; and it was said to them that they should rest a little while longer, until both *the number of* their fellow servants and their brethren, who would be killed as they *were,* was completed."" (Revelation 6:9-11)

Among those being killed by Death and Hades are Post-Rapture believers. They are being martyred for professing the word of God and living out their Christian testimonies. True Christian believers may not be the only group Death and Hades are killing, but they are at least one of them.

This means that Death and Hades must be perpetrating a spiritual message that runs contrary to the gospel of Jesus Christ. The Fifth Seal Saints will hold fast, even to the point of death, to the biblical narrative, which is that Jesus Christ is the way, the truth and the life and the only means of salvation as per John 14:6.

This message of the Fifth Seal Saints must be antithetical to the teachings of Death and Hades. As such, the quarter of the world's population that adheres to the religious view presented by Death and Hades, is called upon in some fashion to martyr these Christian dissenters. The slaying of an untold number of Christians implies that the killing campaign of Death and Hades, is not religiously tolerant! Apparently, Death and Hades will not be propagating an ecumenical message, like *"all roads lead to heaven."*

Since the Fifth Seal Saints are being martyred after the Rapture, we can peer into the gap and Trib-period to see what entities are predicted to kill believers in the future. We find that there are two killing crusades of believers after the Rapture.

The Two Killing Crusades that Martyr Christians After the Rapture

Unlike the indiscriminate deaths that will inevitably result from the war(s) of the Second Seal, there exist two religious systems that discriminately martyr true Christian believers after the Rapture. These two are the Harlot and the Antichrist.

Per Revelation 17:6, the Harlot is *"drunk with the blood of the saints and with the blood of the martyrs of Jesus."* Per Revelation 13:15-17 and 20:4, the Antichrist in cahoots with the False Prophet will kill believers for refusing to receive the "Mark of the Beast."

Unless Death and Hades represents a third campaign of Christian martyrdom after the Rapture, which is not likely, then it must find association with either the Harlot or the Antichrist. It can't be related to the Antichrist for two reasons.

1. The Antichrist is the White Horseman and Death and Hades are the Pale Horsemen of the Apocalypse. These two horses carry distinctly different riders who operate independent of each other. The Antichrist is given a crown and instructed to go out conquering and to conquer. Death and Hades are given authority over a quarter of the earth's population to kill believers.

2. The Antichrist's killing crusade doesn't start until the middle of the Trib-period, but Death and Hades and the Harlot world religion begin their targeted murders beforehand.

Therefore, based upon the minor premises above, the major premise is that Death and Hades seemingly finds association with the Harlot world religion. Or, more boldly and directly stated; DEATH AND HADES are associated with "MYSTERY, BABYLON THE GREAT, THE MOTHER OF HARLOTS AND OF THE ABOMINATIONS OF THE EARTH."

Sixth Seal: The Wrath of the Lamb

> "I looked when He opened the sixth seal, and behold, there was a great earthquake; and the sun became black as sackcloth of hair, and the moon became like blood. And the stars of heaven fell to the earth, as a fig tree drops its late figs when it is shaken by a mighty wind. Then the sky receded as a scroll when it is rolled up, and every mountain and island was moved out of its place. And the kings of the earth, the great men, the rich men, the commanders, the mighty men, every slave and every free man, hid themselves in the caves and in the rocks of the mountains, and said to the mountains and rocks, "Fall on us and hide us from the face of Him who sits on the throne and from the wrath of the Lamb! For the great day of His wrath has come, and who is able to stand?"" (Rev. 6:12-17)

With the opening of the sixth seal judgment it becomes clear that wrath of God has arrived. A great earthquake and cosmic disturbances cause worldwide panic within all of mankind. They will seek places to hide upon the earth because of the widespread devastation.

The traditional view of the Seal Judgments teaches that the wrath of God begins with the opening of the first seal judgment and continues throughout the executions of the trumpet and bowl judgments. However, technically, there is no other specific mention in Revelation 6 about God's wrath coming upon the earth until the sixth seal judgment.

Whether or not the Fifth Seal Saints are actually martyred during the period of God's wrath could be debated, but regardless, by the time the sixth seal is opened, God's wrath has definitively come upon the earth.

In addition to its reference in the sixth seal judgment, God's wrath is alluded to in the trumpet and bowl judgments in the book of Revelation. Below are the following verses dealing with the connection between God's wrath and these judgments.

The sounding of the seventh trumpet, which segues into the outpouring of the seven-bowl judgments, makes it clear that God's wrath is being executed upon the earth.

> "Then *the seventh angel sounded* (His trumpet): .... The nations were angry, and *Your wrath has come*, And the time of the dead, that they should be judged, And that You should reward Your servants the prophets and the saints, And those who fear Your name, small and great, And should destroy those who destroy the earth." (Revelation 11:15a and 18; emphasis added)

At the conclusion of the seven-bowl judgments the wrath of God is complete.

> "Then I saw another sign in heaven, great and marvelous: seven angels having the seven last plagues, for in them the wrath of God is complete." (Revelation 15:1)

The additional related verses to God's wrath in its association to the bowl judgments are, Revelation 15:7, 16:1, and 19.

Seventh Seal: Prelude to the Seven Trumpets

"When He opened the seventh seal, there was silence in heaven for about half an hour. And I saw the seven angels who stand before God, and to them were given seven trumpets. Then another angel, having a golden censer, came and stood at the altar. He was given much incense, that he should offer it with the prayers of all the saints upon the golden altar which was before the throne. And the smoke of the incense, with the prayers of the saints, ascended before God from the angel's hand. Then the angel took the censer, filled it with fire from the altar, and threw it to the earth. And there were noises, thunderings, lightnings, and an earthquake. So the seven angels who had the seven trumpets prepared themselves to sound." (Rev. 8:1-6)

These verses take the readers into a powerful coming heavenly scene. So incredible are these happenings that all those who witness this stand in a moment of silence, which lasts for thirty minutes. Several things take place during this time span of silence. These events are:

- The Seven Angels, who are destined to sound off the Seven Trumpet Judgments, are given their instruments,

- Afterward, an angel proceeds to the altar with a golden censer that is filled with the prayers of the saints,

- Upon arriving at the altar, this angel is provided with *"much incense, that he should offer it with the prayers of all the saints upon the golden altar which was before the throne,"*

- The angel then empties out the prayers from within the censer, and along with the pleasing aroma of the smoke of the incense, they ascend before God,

- Upon emptying the golden censer, the angel fills it up with fire from the altar and throws it down to the earth,

- Concluding the thirty minutes of silence there are noises caused by *"thunderings, lightnings, and an earthquake,"* which result from the angel thrusting the fire filled censer to the earth.

Some questions that arise about the prayers of the saints are:

1. Which saints are being alluded to? Does this include prayers of all saints, including the Raptured believers, or is it a reference to those who become saints after the Rapture? For instance, the Fifth Seal Saints of Rev. 6:9-11 and the Tribulation saints of Rev. 7:9-17.

2. How many prayers are inside of the golden censer? If these prayers are from the saints throughout time, there could be trillions, or if they are from the left behind saints, they could number in the millions or billions.

3. What is the nature of these prayers? If they are only the prayers from the left behind saints, then they could have an emphasis on vindication for being unjustly persecuted and martyred.

Dr. Arnold Fruchtenbaum says the following about Rev. 8:1-6:

> *"In verses 1-2, the seventh seal is opened, and the seventh seal contains the second series of judgments, called the Trumpet Judgments. Verses 3-5 describe events in Heaven and earth just preceding the Trumpet Judgments. The act of adding incense to*

> *the prayers of the saints indicates that the Trumpet*
> *Judgments will answer the prayers of the saints,*
> *prayers already voiced in the fifth Seal Judgment. As*
> *a warning to the earth that the Trumpet Judgements*
> *are about to start, it is made to tremble with*
> *convulsions of nature. Then, in verse six, the seven*
> *angels prepare to sound the seven trumpets."*[33]

It's my personal opinion that, prior to the opening of the Seventh Seal, the Raptured saints who are in heaven will have already received an audience with God and a response from God to their specific prayers. Thus, I agree with Fruchtenbaum, that these specific prayers of Rev. 8:3-4, are likely from those who become saints after the Rapture.

These would be the prayers from persecuted and martyred saints that are stored up in the golden censer for the purposes of being offered to God at the time of the opening of the Seventh Seal. More specifically, the answer to the main petition of the Fifth Seal Saints below.

> "When He opened the fifth seal, I saw under the altar the souls of those who had been slain for the word of God and for the testimony which they held. And they cried with a loud voice, saying, *"How long, O Lord, holy and true, until You judge and avenge our blood on those who dwell on the earth?""* (Rev. 6:9-10; emphasis added).

The response from the Lord to this petition is:

> "Then a white robe was given to each of them; and it was said to them that they should rest a little while longer, until both *the number of* their fellow servants and their brethren, who would be killed as they *were,* was completed." (Rev. 6:11)

The Lord's reply is to rest patiently until after the three Post Rapture periods of Christian martyrdom have concluded. These three periods involve the martyrdom of the Fifth Seal Saints, the Fellow Servants of the Fifth Seal Saints and the Brethren of the Fellow Servants of the Fifth Seal Saints. In the *Next Prophecies* book, I write about these three periods of persecution in much more detail.

The Seven Trumpet Judgments

This chapter will explore the details and timing of the Seven Trumpet Judgments of Revelation 8:7-13, 9:1-21 and 11:15-19. If you thought the Seven Seal Judgments were bad, get ready to be doubly troubled by the next set of seven judgments. The Seven Trumpet Judgments includes the participation of eight good angels in heaven, but also involves the devastating activities of six bad angels and well over two hundred million demons.

The Details of the Seven Trumpet Judgments

First Trumpet: Vegetation Struck

> "The first angel sounded: And hail and fire followed, mingled with blood, and they were thrown to the earth. And a third of the trees were burned up, and all green grass was burned up." (Rev. 8:7)

These verses are to be interpreted literally. A toxic cosmic concoction of hail and fire mingled with blood is thrown to the earth. As a result a third of the trees and all green grass gets consumed by fire. This may mean all grass throughout the world gets adversely affected, but more than likely alludes to the green grass in the close proximity to the burned trees.

This is a supernatural attack, that likely gets targeted at heavily forested territories that are filled with lush vegetation, rather than vastly arid desert regions or arctic areas that are not. The nature of all of the Seven Trumpet Judgments is that each one is harmful and globally impacting. Burning up all the cactus in the desert between Palm Springs, California and Phoenix, Arizona, but leaving the heavily treed forests of Sequoia National Park or the tropical rain forests of Africa fully intact, may not make sense in this scenario.

Similarly, the burning of trees is probably likened to a major forest fire, whereby the flames from one tree sets ablaze a nearby tree and so on. It is not likely that one out of every three trees scattered throughout the earth gets targeted, and that nearby trees don't. This defies the nature of a forest fire and this judgment appears to be targeted geographically, rather than randomly.

The reason that identifying the potential locations of the trees and grass is important is so that the people living in heavily forested areas are made aware of the potential devastation coming to their area. We are told in the Fifth Trumpet Judgment, that people possessing the "Seal of God," will not be harmed, but we are not told that these believers are kept from harm's way in the preceding four Trumpet Judgments.

Second Trumpet: The Seas Struck

> "Then the second angel sounded: And something like a great mountain burning with fire was thrown into the sea, and a third of the sea became blood. And a third of the living creatures in the sea died, and a third of the ships were destroyed." (Rev. 8:8-9)

This imagery pictures a great volcanic mountain collapsing into some sea, or perhaps a flaming gigantic asteroid falling from the sky, which causes a third of the sea to become blood. This appears to be a specific sea in the singular, rather than multiple seas in plurality. Something resembling a solo massive burning mountain topples into a specific sea and in the process a third of the living creatures in that sea are killed and a third of the ships docked or traveling upon that sea are destroyed.

Presumably, it is a major sea or an ocean that supports a large fishing industry and is lined with robust commercial shipping ports, rather than a minor body of water housing a few fish and harboring a couple of row boats. We are not given the specific location, but the fact that the devastation is caused by "something like a great mountain," enables us to postulate that this sea is large in size and possibly targeted to inflict maximum damage on commercial shipments.

Is it either the Pacific, Atlantic, Indian, Southern or Arctic Oceans? We are not told. So, we caution people alive at that time when one-third of the trees are burned, to beware of all major seas and oceans because one of them is going to be adversely affected by the Second Trumpet Judgment.

Third Trumpet: The Waters Struck

> "Then the third angel sounded: And a great star fell from heaven, burning like a torch, and it fell on a third of the rivers and on the springs of water. The name of the star is Wormwood. A third of the waters became wormwood, and many men died from the water, because it was made bitter." (Rev. 8:10-11)

In this third judgment we learn that contaminated drinking water will cause the deaths of many men. The great star falling from heaven could be a star or large comet that people watch burn through the skies that strikes a third of the rivers.

This judgment is terribly frightening and its fulfillment is hard to fathom. How can a singular object fall on "a third of the rivers and on the springs of water?" It seems in this scenario that the rivers and springs must be centrally located rather than scattered throughout the world. Perhaps the object strikes a major waterway that affects the flow of the waters into the numerous tributaries that feed into it and flow out from it.

Another more plausible explanation is that the star called "Wormwood" may be a fallen angel with the ability to turn these affected rivers and streams into bitter waters. In the Bible the word star is often used as a typology for an angel and wormwood means a state or source of bitterness or grief. This alternative puts less emphasis on a geographical landing spot, which would restrict the affected waters to a central location, and presents the greater possibility that a third of the waters that become bitter are spread throughout various parts of the globe.

If this is the case, then Wormwood as a fallen angel, in relationship to being used to fulfill a trumpet judgment, represents the first of the six fallen angels used to execute some of these trumpet judgments. Below is a quote about this option from Dr. Arnold Fruchtenbaum.

> *"The third trumpet destroys one-third of the sweet water. Whenever the word star is used symbolically, it is a common symbol of an angel, and this is the case here. The angel's name is Wormwood, showing the angel to be a fallen one. This fallen angel causes one-third of the sweet water to turn bitter, which in turn causes the death of many. Fallen angels will be used on several occasions to render judgment on the earth, and this is one such occasion."[34]*

Fourth Trumpet: The Heavens Struck

"Then the fourth angel sounded: And a third of the sun was struck, a third of the moon, and a third of the stars, so that a third of them were darkened. A third of the day did not shine, and likewise the night." (Rev. 8:12)

The first three Trumpet Judgments affected the land and waters on parts of the earth, but this judgment affects the light shining upon all the earth. The sun, moon and a third of the stars are struck strategically so as to filter out light for a third of the day.

Does this mean daylight only extends for two-thirds of its usual time, or does it mean that daylight is filtered to only emit two-thirds of what is normal? Also, how will these conditions affect the ocean tides and frozen glacier formations? Studies have shown that shifting solar conditions can have a dramatic effect on the melting of glaciers, which in turn can lead to severe global flooding and other related catastrophes.

The Trumpet Interlude: The Flying Angel Announces the Three Woes

> "And I looked, and I heard an angel flying through the midst of heaven, saying with a loud voice, "Woe, woe, woe to the inhabitants of the earth, because of the remaining blasts of the trumpet of the three angels who are about to sound!"" (Rev. 8:13)

After the lights are dimmed down on earth from the Fourth Trumpet Judgment, the loudspeakers go on in heaven as an angel announces loudly *"Woe, woe, woe to the inhabitants of the earth, because of the remaining blasts of the trumpet of the three angels who are about to sound!"* Three is the number of perfection or completion in the Bible and thus, the echoing of *"woe"* three times emphasizes the complete severity of the *Fifth, Sixth* and *Seventh* Trumpet Judgments.

If you have been keeping a headcount of the angels, thus far, there have been four good trumpet angels and one bad angel called, *Wormwood.* Now enters the fifth good angel, who we'll call the "Announcing Angel." This angel only receives a cameo role, but his announcement enables us to know the timing of the Trumpet Judgments, which is explored at the end of this chapter.

From this point forward world events become extremely woeful, especially for unbelievers. They will be tormented so severely for five months that they will reach a point whereby they prefer death over the continued distress. This anguish is followed by many of their deaths, which causes many of those who survive to hate and blaspheme God.

Fifth Trumpet: The Locusts from the Bottomless Pit (Woe #1)

> "Then the fifth angel sounded: And I saw a star fallen from heaven to the earth. To him was given the key to the bottomless pit. And he opened the bottomless pit, and smoke arose out of the pit like the smoke of a great furnace. So the sun and the air were darkened because of the smoke of the pit. Then out of the smoke locusts came upon the earth. And to them was given power, as the scorpions of the earth have power. They were commanded not to harm the grass of the earth, or any green thing, or any tree, but only those men who do not have the seal of God on their foreheads. And they were not given authority to kill them, but to torment them for five months. Their torment was like the torment of a scorpion when it strikes a man. In those days men will seek death and will not find it; they will desire to die, and death will flee from them." (Rev. 9:1-6)

Before presenting the remaining details in Rev. 9:7-12, let's unpack these above six verses first. They introduce the sixth good angel, which is the fifth trumpet angel, as well as the second bad angel, who will be identified momentarily. Also, introduced are an untold number of locusts who likely represent demons, rather than insects. Most importantly, these verses introduce the first Woe Judgment.

Notice that the angel falls from heaven. It sounds like he was booted out of his heavenly abode. Then this angelic exile is given the keys to the bottomless pit. Observe that the locust occupants of this hot smoke-filled pit seem to have no problem with causing harm to humanity and, as the following verses will point out, they appear to be well equipped to handle this tormenting task. Below are a few other observations about the Fifth Trumpet Judgment.

OBSERVATION #1

- There is a contrast between the occurrences of the good angel of the First Trumpet Judgment that results in a third of the trees and all the green grass getting burned up and this bad angel, who instructs his demon locust *"not to harm the grass of the earth, or any green thing, or any tree."* Why is this?

I suspect that it is because Satan has instructed this bad angel named Apollyon to preserve what's left of the grass and trees because the devil has plans for planet earth when his seed the Antichrist achieves his full power and authority at the midpoint of the Trib-period. The Antichrist will set himself up as god, establish a global cashless society and seek to be worshipped by all of mankind. The absence of horticulture, agriculture and farming would be counterproductive to this end.

OBSERVATION #2

- Only those men who do not have the "Seal of God" on their foreheads are tormented as per (Rev. 9:4). This implies a couple things:

    1. These invaders have the ability to recognize who has the seal of God,

    2. They also have the ability to identify those who don't,

    3. That those being tormented are all unbelievers.

OBSERVATION #3

- That there is a way to avoid this tormenting period and it's called, the "Seal of God." This implies that:

1. All readers who do not currently have the Seal of God need to obtain it before the Fifth Trumpet Sounds!

2. Better yet; if the Rapture is still a pending prophetic event, those unsaved readers can receive Jesus Christ now as their Lord and Savior and avoid, not only the Fifth Trumpet Judgment, but all of the Seal, Trumpet and Bowl Judgments!

If you want to know what the "Seal of God" is, where to find it and how to obtain it, then read the chapter in this book entitled, "The Seal of God."

Fifth Trumpet: The Identity of the Locusts and description of their King Apollyon

> "The shape of the locusts was like horses prepared for battle. On their heads were crowns of something like gold, and their faces were like the faces of men. They had hair like women's hair, and their teeth were like lions' teeth. And they had breastplates like breastplates of iron, and the sound of their wings was like the sound of chariots with many horses running into battle. They had tails like scorpions, and there were stings in their tails. Their power was to hurt men five months. And they had as king over them the angel of the bottomless pit, whose name in Hebrew is Abaddon, but in Greek he has the name Apollyon." (Rev. 9:7-11)

These five verses provide us with more details into the identity and purpose of the locust invaders. These details enumerated below set them apart figuratively as demons, rather than literally as insects:

1. They originate from the bottomless pit, (v3) – This is not where locusts come from. Locusts go through egg, nymph and adult stages -- lacking the pupa stage. This means that actual locusts are birthed on the earth, whereas these demon locusts come from the bottomless pit.

2. They have power like scorpions, (v3), to strike men, (v5, v10) – Locusts don't even bite people, let alone sting or strike them like a scorpion.

3. They follow instructions not to "*harm the grass of the earth, or any green thing, or any tree*," (v4) – since locusts feed upon foliage and stems of plants such as herbs and grasses, it's not reasonable to assume they will ignore these fine locust delicacies.

4. These locusts of the Fifth Trumpet Judgment in no way resemble real locusts: (v7-9) –

   a. They are shaped like horses prepared for battle,
   b. On their heads were crowns of something like gold,
   c. Their faces were like the faces of men,
   d. They had hair like women's hair,
   e. Their teeth were like lions' teeth,
   f. They had breastplates like breastplates of iron,
   g. The sound of their wings was like the sound of chariots.

5. They are ruled by a fallen angel named "Apollyon," (v11) – Demons have fallen angel friends, but not locusts.

Speaking of the star fallen from heaven to the earth, whom was given the key to the bottomless pit, he is called Apollyon, which means "Destroyer." Thus, clearly this star represents the second bad angel used to execute the fulfillment of the Trumpet Judgments.

Are the Locusts A.I. Drones or Robots?

There is a relatively new theory being floated in prophetic circles that the locusts of the Fifth Trumpet Judgment may be drones or robots programmed with Artificial Intelligence (A.I.). I write about the potential problems with this teaching in the Chapter entitled, "*Technologies in the Tribulation Period.*"

OBSERVATION #4

- Observe that no information is provided in these verses about the future destination of Apollyon, nor his untold number of demons, after they are discharged from their Fifth Trumpet duties. What happens to all of these bad demons and their evil king at the end of the five-month period?

OBSERVATION #5

- These bad demons, along with their evil king Apollyon, seemingly lurch around on the earth for the remainder of the Trib-period, which will likely last about another 4 to 5 years. This means that they will likely rendezvous with the one-third of the fallen angels that lose the war in heaven between Satan and Michael in Revelation 12. This has the makings for a troublesome angelic reunion for all of mankind alive from that point forward. The details of this war in heaven will be discussed in *The LAST Prophecies – Volume 2* book.

The First Woe is Passed

"One woe is past. Behold, still two more woes are coming after these things." (Rev. 9:12)

The first of the three woe judgments concludes with the completion of the five-month demonic locust invasion. This solo verse above provides a clear break in the action between the passing of Woe #1 and the comings of Woe #2 and Woe #3. It serves as the segue that introduces Woe #2, which finds fulfillment through the Sixth Trumpet Judgment.

This verse uses the two Greek words *"meta tauta,"* which *means hereafter, afterward, after this,* or *after these things.* This reinforces the fact that after the first Five Trumpet Judgments the remaining two woes find fulfillment.

Sixth Trumpet: The Four Angels from the Euphrates

"Then the sixth angel sounded: And I heard a voice from the four horns of the golden altar which is before God, saying to the sixth angel who had the trumpet, "Release the four angels who are bound at the great river Euphrates." So the four angels, who had been prepared for the hour and day and month and year, were released to kill a third of mankind. Now the number of the army of the horsemen was two hundred million; I heard the number of them. And thus I saw the horses in the vision: those who sat on them had breastplates of fiery red, hyacinth blue, and sulfur yellow; and the heads of the horses were like the heads of lions; and out of their mouths came fire, smoke, and brimstone. By these three plagues a third of mankind was killed—by the fire and the smoke and the brimstone which came out of their mouths. For their power is in their mouth and in their tails; for their tails are like serpents, having heads; and with them they do harm. But the rest of mankind, who were not killed by these plagues, did not repent of the works of their hands, that they should not worship demons, and idols of gold, silver, brass, stone, and wood, which can neither see nor hear nor walk. And they did not repent of their murders or their sorceries or their sexual immorality or their thefts." (Rev. 9:13-21)

Woe #2 of the Sixth Trumpet Judgment involves five more angels and a 200-million-man army, which appears to be comprised of demons, rather than humans. One of the angels is good, but the other four are bad. This brings the tally of angels and demons that have thus far participated in the Trumpet Judgments to, seven good angels, six bad angels and well over 200 million demons.

Before the sounding of the Sixth Trumpet, four bad angels will be bound at the Euphrates River which courses through modern-day Syria and Iraq. They may already be bound there! Prior to their release, these angels prepare for a singular mission, which is not to spread good tidings of comfort and joy, but is to kill one-third of mankind! This could amount to well over a billion people at that time.

The number of human casualties will presumably be quite large because the size of the advancing army is 200 million strong. If only a small amount of people get killed, then this size of an army would be unnecessary. Also, if this army only targets only a select few within humanity, then this could not justifiably be classified as a Woe Judgment.

Who are these soldiers? Where do they come from? Are they killing people throughout the world, or only within the proximity of the Euphrates River? Are they killing believers or unbelievers, or both?

Who are these soldiers? Where do they come from?

Concerning the identity and origin of these soldiers, we are given clues in Rev. 9:17-19 from John's vision.

1. John saw horses with heads like lions and mouths that emitted fire, smoke and brimstone. These horses had tails like serpents having heads,

2. The apostle also saw horsemen riding these horses that were adorned with colorful breastplates of fiery red, hyacinth blue, and sulfur yellow.

Some believe that this alludes to the Chinese army for two primary reasons. *First*, the reference to the Euphrates River in Rev. 9:14 is also made in relationship to the "Kings of the East" in Rev. 16:12. They believe that the Kings of the East could allude to the Asian Kings of the Orient, which includes China.

Second, China once declared that it could field an army of 200 million men. Thus, the formula is: (Kings of the East + 200 million) = the Chinese Army.

Below are the three-fold problems with this theory:

1. The secondary reference to the Euphrates River in Rev. 16:12 alludes to the Sixth Bowl Judgment and not the Sixth Trumpet Judgment. There is no mention of the Kings of the East in correlation with the 200-million-man army of Rev. 9:14.

Connecting the Kings of the East with the 200 million army by mere association with the Euphrates would be like linking the Chicago Bears with the Chicago Cubs because they both play in Chicago. No, they are two distinct teams, that play two entirely different sports and they perform during separate seasons. Similarly, the Sixth Trumpet and the Sixth Bowl are two different judgments that occur at separate times.

2. The Chinese Army doesn't resemble the descriptions of these horses and horsemen. I like what Dr. Arnold Fruchtenbaum says along these lines.

"A person would be hard pressed to find just one Chinese person who looks like this, let alone two hundred million of them. The description given of

the army clearly rules out their being human and requires that they be demonic. Furthermore, the means by which the destruction of one-third of the world's population is accomplished (fire, smoke, brimstone), involves the supernatural rather than the natural."[35]

3. The Kings of the East may allude to leaders from Mesopotamia and not China. Scriptural references to the *"east"* usually alludes to Mesopotamia.[36]

Are they killing people throughout the world, or only within the proximity of the Euphrates River?

This is another valid question. What world populations are being affected by the Sixth Trumpet Judgment? Is this a global killing campaign, or does it only affect the peoples residing within the countries closest to the Euphrates River? If the latter is the case, then maybe those living at the time would want to be far removed from the Euphrates River. Keep in mind that any migration away from the Euphrates River areas, may involve navigation through the portions of the rivers and Sea that was previously turned to blood in the prior Trumpet Judgments.

Are they killing believers or unbelievers, or both?

Only unbelievers were being tormented for five months in Woe #1, but does that remain true for Woe #2? The clues in Rev. 9:20-21 seem to suggest that believers are also protected from the killings in Woe #2.

These two verses state that the two-thirds of mankind who were not killed by the plagues of smoke, fire and brimstone did not repent from their works, or their worship of demons and idols. *"And they did not repent of their murders or their sorceries or their sexual immorality or their thefts."*

This leads me to conclude that believers are spared from the Sixth Trumpet Judgment killings. Believers have repentant hearts, but these survivors above do not. However, just because believers might escape death at the hands of the 200 million demons, that doesn't mean they will not be distressed by the fire, smoke and brimstone. These types of plagues will undoubtedly create harsh living conditions in the affected territories.

Lastly, Joel 1:15-2:11 seems to give further details about the demonic invasions of Woe #1 and Woe #2. These verses describe the extremely harsh conditions that result from these invasions. There will be:

- Barns broken down, which results in withered grain (Joel 1:17),

- Restless cattle because there are no more pastures (Joel 1:18),

- The brooks are dry and the pastures burned by fire (Joel 1:20),

- People severely trembling, which could include believers (Joel 2:1),

- Atmospheric darkness and gloominess (Joel 2:2),

- Wildfires that turn places into desolate wastelands (Joel 2:3),

- People writhing in pain and pale in skin color (Joel 2:6),

- Well organized demonic armies that do not break their ranks, march in columns, run to and from within cities and break into houses like thieves to torment and kill people (Joel 2:7-9).

The Timing of the Seven Trumpet Judgments

The timing of the Seven Trumpet Judgments closely corresponds with that of the Two Witnesses. It was pointed out in the chapter entitled, "*The 144,002 Witnesses – Part Two: the 2 Witnesses*," that these two prophesy throughout the duration of the first half of the Trib-period. Therefore, the Trumpet Judgments also happen within this first half period.

> "And I will give *power* to my two witnesses, and they will prophesy, (*in the first*) one thousand two hundred and sixty days, (*of the Trib-period*), clothed in sackcloth." (Rev. 11:3; *emphasis added*)

Although the amount of days allotted for the Two Witnesses is numbered at 1260 days, the length of time that it takes for the Seven Trumpets to happen is unspecified. Therefore, it is possible that the Seven Trumpet Judgments could happen in less than 1260 days. Nonetheless, no matter how long the Seven Trumpet Judgments last, they closely correlate in time with the existence of the Two Witnesses.

The scriptural support for intertwining the timing of the prophesying of the Two Witnesses with the sounding of the Seven Trumpets, is provided in the *minor* and *MAJOR* premises below.

Minor Premise #1

The Two Witnesses get killed, resurrect and ascend to heaven after or about the same time as the fulfillment of the Second Woe Judgment, but before the start of the Third Woe Judgment. Rev. 11:7-13 informs that their deaths, resurrections and ascensions happen at the end of the 1260 days allotted to them. After their ascensions occur we are told that the second woe has passed and the third woe is coming quickly.

> "The second woe is past. Behold, the third woe is coming quickly." (Rev. 11:14)

Minor Premise #2

The second woe is the Sixth Trumpet Judgment and the third woe is the Seventh Trumpet Judgment. In Revelation 8:13 we are informed that after the first four Trumpet Judgments happen the remaining three Trumpet Judgments, due to their severity, are classified as the Three Woe Judgments.

> "And I looked, and I heard an angel flying through the midst of heaven, saying with a loud voice, "Woe, (#1) woe, (#2) woe, (#3) to the inhabitants of the earth, because of the remaining blasts of the, (*fifth, sixth and seventh*), trumpet of the three angels who are about to sound!"" (*Rev. 8:13; emphasis added*)

The breakdown is as follows:

Woe #1 = The Fifth Trumpet Judgment of Rev. 9:1-11.

Woe #2 = The Sixth Trumpet Judgment of Rev. 9:13-19.

Woe #3 = The Seventh Trumpet Judgment of Rev. 11:15-19, which segues into the outpouring of the Seven Bowl Judgments of Rev. 16.

Woe #1 is fulfilled over a period of five months as per Rev. 9:5, 10. After the events of Woe #1 take place we are told, "One woe is past. Behold, still two more woes are coming after these things." (Rev. 9:12).

Then follows Woe #2 that involves the killing of one-third of mankind by an army of two hundred million strong as per Rev. 9: 16. According to Rev. 11:14, which was quoted in *Minor Premise #1* above, the conclusion of these killings precedes or closely correlates in time with the ascension of the Two Witnesses of Rev. 11:12.

Minor Premise #3

Woe #3 happens after the ascension of the Two Witnesses, but Woe #1 happens prior to their deaths and it appears that Woe #2 does as well. Rev. 11:14 mandates that the conclusion of Woe #2 must conclude before or at the time of the ascension of the Two Witnesses.

The timeline below illustrates the likely timing and chronology of the Trumpet and Bowl Judgments.

MAJOR Premise #1

Seven-Year Tribulation Period

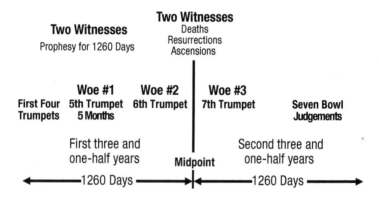

In order for Woe #1 to conclude before, and Woe #2 to conclude on or before, the Two Witnesses die, resurrect and ascend to heaven, the Fifth and Sixth Trumpet Judgments have to find fulfillment.

MAJOR Premise #2

In order for the Seventh Trumpet to sound quickly after the Two Witnesses ascend to heaven in Rev. 11:15, the first Six Trumpets had to have happened beforehand.

Conclusion

Based upon the *minor* and *MAJOR* premises above, the first Six Trumpet Judgments happen sometime within the 1260 days that the Two Witnesses are prophesying on the earth. These six judgments may not require a full 1260 days to be completed, but they can't happen after the Two Witnesses have ascended to heaven.

The Two Witnesses exist on earth in the first three and one-half years of the Trib-period. Therefore, we can safely conclude that at least the first Six Trumpet Judgments happen sometime within that same time span. In other words, these six judgments happen in the first half of the Trib-period. Then, the Seventh Trumpet Judgment kicks off the start of the second half of the Trib period.

The following names represent a small sampling of Bible prophecy teachers that believe the Trumpet Judgments happen in the first half of the Trib-period. Dr. Arnold Fruchtenbaum, Dr. Ron Rhodes, Tim LaHaye, Warren Wiersbe, Ed Hindson, Dr. David Reagan and Dr. Thomas Ice.

Ron Rhodes in his book entitled, *"The End Times In Chronological Order,"* on page 117 places the Trumpet Judgments in the first half of the Tribulation and on page 127, he places the death and resurrection of the two witnesses chronologically before the Antichrist breaks the covenant in Daniel 9:27 and the Abomination of Desolation spoken by Jesus in Matthew 24;15-22.

Tim LaHaye and Thomas Ice in their book entitled, *"Charting The End Times,"* on page 44 clearly place the seven trumpet judgments in the first half of the Tribulation Period.

Ed Hindson and Thomas Ice in their book called, *"Charting The Bible Chronologically"* place the Trumpet Judgments in the first half of the Tribulation Period before the Abomination of Desolation at the midpoint of the Tribulation Period in their "Book of Revelation Timeline" on page 118.

Do the Seven Trumpets Sound in the Second Half of the Tribulation Period?

There are some teachers today that believe the Trumpet Judgments happen in the second half of the Trib-period. The main argument from this camp is probably best voiced by Dr. Mark Hitchcock, who states the following.

> *"I place the trumpet judgments in the second half, really for one basic reason: the severity of them. Because Jesus says that the second half of the tribulation period, often called the great tribulation, will be unlike any other time that's ever been on the earth. Well, if you put the trumpets in the first half of the tribulation along with the seals you have half of the people dying in the first half of the tribulation, which would make that worse than the second half of the tribulation."*[37]

In reading Mark's statement above, you will see he gives two reasons for placing the Seven Trumpets in the second half of the Trib-period.

1. The severity of them

> *"I place the trumpet judgments in the second half, really for one basic reason: the severity of them. Because Jesus says that the second half of the tribulation period, often called the great tribulation, will be unlike any other time that's ever been on the earth."*

When it comes to the levels of severity between the Seal, Trumpet and Bowl Judgments, the Bowl Judgments appear to be of equal or greater harshness than the Trumpet Judgments. Unfortunately, we are not informed how many people die as a result of the Bowl Judgments, but in Rev. 15:1 we are told that God's wrath gets completed through the outpouring of these devastating judgments.

Perhaps the wrath that comes out through the Seven Bowl Judgments is sufficient enough to classify their fulfillment in the second half of the Trib-period as a time of Great Tribulation. Maybe we don't need to add the Trumpet Judgments to the Bowl Judgments to make this acknowledgement. The severity of the Seven Bowl Judgments is explained in the chapter entitled, "*The Seven Bowl Judgments,*" which will be included in "*The LAST Prophecies – Volume 2*" book.

2. The number of people dying

> *Well, if you put the trumpets in the first half of the tribulation along with the seals you have half of the people dying in the first half of the tribulation, which would make that worse than the second half of the tribulation.*"[38]

Thus, for the primary reason of how many people get killed between the Seal and Trumpet Judgments, he elects to leave the Seals in the first half of the Trib-period, but transport the Trumpet Judgments into the second half of the Great Tribulation.

The mathematical equation of determining that one-half of the world's population that Hitchcock alludes to during the Seal and Trumpet Judgments is simple and reflected in the example below.

It is commonly taught that the Fourth Seal kills one-fourth of mankind and the Fifth Trumpet subsequently kills another one-third of the world's population. Let's use the random example of 4 billion people to represent mankind going into the fulfillment of the Fourth Seal Judgment.

One-fourth would be 1 billion people. This would leave 3 billion people left after the killings occur from the Fourth Seal Judgment. Then one-third of the 3 billion survivors would also represent another 1 billion people killed from the Fifth Trumpet Judgment.

Thus you began with 4 billion people, but 2 billion get killed from the Fourth Seal and the Fifth Trumpet. These deceased could then represent the "*half of the people dying*" that Hitchcock alludes to.

One potential problem with Hitchcock's reasoning is that the Fourth Seal Judgment may not actually be killing one-fourth of mankind, which is what he believes as per the quote below.

"*In the fourth seal judgement one-fourth of the world will die (Revelation 6:8)...*" (Mark Hitchcock)[39]

Read the verse he alludes to below for clarification.

> "And I saw, and behold, a pale horse: and he that sat upon him, his name was Death; and Hades followed with him. And there was given unto them *authority over the fourth part of the earth*, to kill with sword, and with famine, and with death, and by the wild beasts of the earth." (Rev. 6:8, ASV; *emphasis added*)

It has commonly been taught that the pale horse ridden by Death and Hades is responsible for killing one-fourth of mankind. In an alternative interpretation, this may not be the case. A careful reading of the verse informs us that Death and Hades are only given authority over a fourth part of the earth. Some translations, like the New King James Version, use the word "power" instead of "authority."

Is this power and authority over a fourth part of the earth dealing with geographical landmass or world population? Most, me included, would answer world population.

So then, with this power and authority given to Death and Hades over such a large portion of the world's population, what do they decide to do with this enormous control? They opt to kill an unknown number of people through the multiple means described in Rev. 6:8. Among this nebulous number of victims are the Fifth Seal Saints of Rev. 6:9-11. They are martyred for voicing their religious descent against Death and Hades. We are told this in Rev. 6:9 that says they were, *"slain for the word of God and for the testimony which they held."*

In this alternative interpretation we don't know how many people actually get killed. It could be more or less than one-fourth of mankind. Now compare this Fourth Seal verse to the Fifth Trumpet verse below.

> "By these three *plagues* a third of mankind was killed—by the fire and the smoke and the brimstone which came out of their mouths." (Rev. 9:18, NKJV)

This verse clearly informs that a third of mankind gets killed, but the language in Rev. 6:8 above is less clear. Perhaps, Death and Hades kill a fourth of mankind, but maybe they only possess power over a fourth of the world's population. Maybe Death and Hades only kill a few million Fifth Seal Saints, rather than a full fourth of mankind? In the alternative interpretation, we don't know the actual number of those killed within mankind.

Therefore, if we put the emphasis on what defines "Great Tribulation" on the number of people who get killed from the Seal and Trumpet Judgments, then how can we be certain if that totals, *"half of the people dying,"* to quote Hitchcock.

The inseparability of the timing of the Two Witnesses and the Seven Trumpets

Mark Hitchcock also states below that the timing of the prophesying of the Two Witnesses occurs in the second half of the Trib-period in correlation with the timing of the Trumpet Judgments. He makes the point that the Two Witnesses and the Trumpet Judgments can't be separated in time.

> *"I put the trumpet judgments in the last half, and since the 2 witnesses (Rev 11) are placed within the trumpet judgments it makes sense that they're also in the second half. Also, the 7th trumpet sounds in Rev. 11:15 at the end of the tribulation right in the immediate context. Rev 11 is between the second and third woes (the 6th and 7th trumpets)."* (Mark Hitchcock quote is from an email to me from Mark on 5/19/19)

Although I disagree with placing the Two Witnesses and the Seven Trumpet Judgments into the Great Tribulation period, Hitchcock's quote above reinforces my minor and major premises made earlier in this chapter. These premises also recognized that Revelation 11, dealing with the timing of the Two Witnesses, *"is between the second and third woes (the 6th and 7th trumpets)."*

What is being distinguished by Hitchcock and me in correlation with Rev. 11:14, is that the first Six Trumpet Judgments happen prior to the deaths, resurrections and ascensions of the Two Witnesses in Rev. 11:7-13. Any attempts to disassociate the timing of the Two Witnesses from that of the Seven Trumpets appears to go against the Word of God as per Revelation 11:14. The Two Witnesses and the Seven Trumpets either operate together within the First or Second halves of the Trib-period, but they apparently can't be split apart.

Lastly, Hitchcock says, *"Also, the 7th trumpet sounds in Rev. 11:15 at the end of the tribulation right in the immediate context."* He states that the 7th trumpet sounds at the end of the Trib-period. The problems with this assessment were already explained in "REFUTATION #4: The Bowl Judgments" in the chapter entitled, *The 144,002 Witnesses – Part Two: the Two Witnesses,* but will be touched upon again below.

Below is a chronology of events that Mark Hitchcock believes will happen at the end of the Tribulation. [40]

- The bowl judgments are poured out in rapid succession (see Revelation 16).

- Commercial Babylon is destroyed (see Revelation 18).

- The Two Witnesses are killed by Antichrist and are resurrected by God three and a half days later (see Revelation 11: 7-12).

- Christ returns to the Mount of Olives and slays the armies gathered against Him throughout the land, from Megiddo to Petra (see Revelation 19:11-16; Isaiah 34:1-6; 63:1-6).

In Hitchcock's scenario the "*7th trumpet sounds in Rev. 11:15 at the end of the tribulation.*" This is likely why he suggests that "*The bowl judgments are poured out in rapid succession.*" They would have to be fulfilled rapidly because the 7th Trumpet, in his scenario, happens "*at the end of the tribulation.*" More specifically at the end of the 1260-day ministries of the Two Witnesses. In essence there is no time left for the Seven Bowl Judgments to be poured out in the Trib-period.

By way of review, the Seventh Trumpet is the prelude to the outpouring of the Seven Bowl Judgments. Read how important these last seven plagues are in the verse below.

> "Then I saw another sign in heaven, great and marvelous: seven angels having the seven last plagues, FOR IN THEM THE WRATH OF GOD IS COMPLETE." (Rev. 15:1; EMPHASIS ADDED)

How rapidly in succession can the Seven Bowl Judgements happen? These Bowl Judgments are summarized below as described in Revelation 16:

- Inflicting of loathsome sores (1st bowl),

- Sea turning to blood and killing all the sea creatures therein (2nd bowl),

- Rivers and Springs turning to blood (3rd bowl),

- Scorching of mankind with fires and great heat (4th bowl),

- Widespread of darkness and the gnawing of tongues from the pain of the sores (5th bowl),

- Drying of the Euphrates, enabling the world armies to gather for Armageddon (6th bowl),

- Great Earthquake that destroys end times Babylon (7th bowl).

Maybe these events will happen rapidly, but even still, in Hitchcock's scenario there is no time left in the Trib-period for these events to happen. The 1260 days end with the ascension into heaven of the Two Witnesses in Rev. 11:12 and then the Seventh Trumpet sounds in Rev. 11:15. This means that the last seven plagues that contain the completion of God's wrath don't happen until after the Trib-period has concluded. This also implies that they are not even part of the "Great Tribulation," that Jesus alluded to in Matthew 24:21.

Therefore, for the reasons presented above and in the chapter entitled, *The 144,002 Witnesses – Part Two: the Two Witnesses,* the arguments strongly favor that the first Six Trumpet Judgments happen in the first half of the Trib-period and the Seventh Trumpet sounds to start the second half of the Trib-period.

14

The Coming Jewish Temple

Up to this chapter the word "temple" has been used over eighty times in this manuscript. Over 90% of those usages have alluded to the coming Jewish Temple. This is because this future temple, which is often called "The Tribulation Temple," plays a central role in end times biblical prophecy. The Bible predicts it, the Jews are preparing to build it and so now it's time to write about it and evangelize through it.

This chapter will explore the following details concerning this Tribulation Temple:

1. The prophecies that acknowledge its future existence,
2. The timing of its building,
3. The functions performed within it,
4. Why it is unsanctioned,
5. The current preparations being made for its construction and operations,
6. How this coming Jewish Temple can be used to evangelize Jews.

1. The prophecies that acknowledge its future existence

A few of the primary direct and indirect verses that foretell of this future Tribulation Temple are quoted and explained below.

The Direct References to the Tribulation Temple

> *The First Temple Related Passage:* "Then I was given a reed like a measuring rod. And the angel

stood, saying, "Rise and measure the temple of
God, the altar, and those who worship there. But
leave out the court which is outside the temple,
and do not measure it, for it has been given to the
Gentiles."" (Rev. 11:1-2)

In these verses the apostle John undertakes the task of
measuring the coming "Temple of God." When John wrote this
verse around 95 AD there was no longer a "Temple of God" in
existence. The Second Jewish Temple had been destroyed by the
Romans about 25 years prior in 70 AD. Thus, this prophecy
introduces a future temple, which will be the Third Jewish Temple.

The timing of John's measuring takes place in the first half
of the Trib-period in correlation with the timing of the Two
Witnesses in Rev. 11:3-13. This means that this "Temple of God"
exists within the Trib-period, which is why some scholars opt to
call it, "The Tribulation Temple."

Notice that the Angel speaking to John instructs him not to
measure the outer court of the temple because it is given to the
Gentiles. This is a unique exception because the prior two Jewish
temples did not give their outer courts to the Gentiles. The fact
that the Tribulation Temple grants the outer court to the Gentiles
implies that the Jews will have to negotiate with whoever this
specific group of Gentiles are in order to even build their third
temple. Some suggest that these Gentiles are Israel's surrounding
Arab neighbors.

Presently Jordan, through the Waqf, has control over the
Temple Mount where the Jews want to build their third temple. The
Waqf is an Islamic trust which strictly limits non-Muslim visitation
on the Mount and bans prayer by non-Muslims. Presently, Jewish
prayer on the Temple Mount is completely forbidden. Jews may
enter only to visit the place, and only at limited times. Muslims are
free to pray on the Temple Mount however; Christians and Jews
may only visit the site as tourists.

Due to prayer restrictions upon Jews, stories have circulated about Jews purposely dropping coins onto the holy ground of the Temple Mount, while at the same time making pretend cell phone calls. They do this to disguise their true intentions, which are to bow down to the Lord in reverence when they stoop down to pick up the coins, and at the same time pray into the fake cell phone call. However, the day is rapidly approaching when they will no longer need to camouflage their prayers on the Temple Mount because they will control it.

If the Jews attempt to build this temple soon, while the Waqf is still in control, they would undoubtedly have to cut a deal with Jordan and the broader Arab world to accomplish this. Some Bible teachers believe that the false covenant of Daniel 9:27 is between the Arabs and the Jews. However, it was pointed out previously in this book that this theory is current event driven and lacks scriptural support.

My personal view is that the Gentiles referenced in Rev. 11:2 does not allude to the Islamic Arabs, but rather to the Harlot World Religion. I believe that Jordan will lose control of the Temple Mount when they are defeated by the IDF in Jeremiah 49:2 and Zephaniah 2:8-9 and that the Arabs will lose their voice in this matter when the IDF defeats them in Psalm 83, Zechariah 12:4-6 and elsewhere.

> "In that day, (*when Psalm 83 finds final fulfillment*),
> I will make the governors of Judah, (*the IDF*), like
> a firepan in the woodpile, and like a fiery torch in
> the sheaves; they shall devour all the surrounding,
> (*Arab*), peoples on the right hand and on the left,
> but Jerusalem shall be inhabited again in her own
> place—Jerusalem " (Zechariah 12:6; *emphasis
> added*)

After these above prophecies find fulfillment, the Muslims pride and joy, the "Dome of the Rock," that presently sits atop the sacred "Foundation Stone," which is where the Jews intend to build their coming temple, can be demolished by Israel. Then the Jews could move forward to build their third temple. However, in the process they likely meet with international resistance that forces them to give up the outer court to the Gentiles in Rev. 11:2. Upon releasing their exclusive rights to this important section of the temple compound, they can build their third temple.

> *The Second Temple Related Passage*: "Let no one deceive you by any means; for *that Day will not come unless the falling away comes first, and the man of sin is revealed, the son of perdition, who opposes and* exalts himself above all that is called God or that is worshiped, so that he sits as God in the Temple of God, showing himself that he is God." (2 Thessalonians 2:3-4)

These two verses also allude to the Temple of God. They inform that the man of sin, which is a reference to the Antichrist, will pompously sit in the future Jewish Temple and boast of himself as God. This event happens at the midpoint of the Trib-period and is yet another reason that the coming Temple is aptly called, the Tribulation Temple.

The Indirect References to the Tribulation Temple

> *The Third Temple Related Passage*: "Then he shall confirm a covenant with many for one week; But in the middle of the week He shall bring an end to sacrifice and offering. And on the wing of abominations shall be one who makes desolate, Even until the consummation, which is determined, Is poured out on the desolate." (Daniel 9:27)

This verse makes an indirect reference to the temple by alluding to the sacrifices and offerings that will take place in the Tribulation Temple. These religious activities will be terminated by the Antichrist "*in the middle of the week,*" which alludes to a week of years not days. This week refers to the Seven-Year Tribulation Period. This verse connects with 2 Thess. 2:3-4 quoted above. It evidences that the timing of when the Antichrist sits in the temple as God, occurs in the middle of the Trib-period.

> *The Fourth Temple Related Passage*: "Therefore when you see the 'abomination of desolation,' spoken of by Daniel the prophet, standing in the holy place" (whoever reads, let him understand), "then let those who are in Judea flee to the mountains." (Matthew 24:15-16)

Although Jesus doesn't replicate the terms, "the Temple of God," in these two verses, He does use the words, "the holy place," which is a reference to the temple. Since this act of the "Abomination of Desolation" didn't happen prior to the destruction of the Second Temple, this prophecy must refer to the coming Third Jewish Temple.

This quote from Jesus Christ rounds out the activities contained in 2 Thess. 2:3-4 and Daniel 9:27 above. The chain of events are as follows:

1. The Antichrist enters the Tribulation Temple at the midpoint of the Trib-period.

2. He stops the Jewish sacrifices and offerings taking place therein.

3. He goes into the holy place within the temple and performs a detestable act called the "Abomination of Desolation."

4. Then he "exalts himself above all that is called God or that is worshiped, so that he sits as God in the Temple of God, showing himself that he is God."

The Fifth Temple Related Passage: "Heaven is My throne, And earth is My footstool. Where is the house that you will build Me? And where is the place of My rest?" (Isaiah 66:1)

"*Where is the house that you will build Me*," is an indirect reference to the coming third temple. The fact that this question is asked by Isaiah the prophet eliminates the possibility that this alludes to the temple of his time. Isaiah knew the location of the First Temple was Jerusalem. This verse will be explained in its broader context later in this chapter to illustrate why the Tribulation Temple is unsanctioned by God.

2. The timing of its building and the functions performed within it

Although The Temple Institute and Temple Mount Faithful organizations in Jerusalem are chomping at the bit to have the third temple up and running, the current geopolitical circumstances do not permit this. However, after Israel prevails in the impending predominately Muslim wars of Psalm 83 and Ezekiel 38, the geopolitical picture will change dramatically.

Presently, Jerusalem is considered to be the third holiest city to Muslims behind Mecca and Medina in Saudi Arabia. Interestingly, the Bible references Jerusalem about a thousand times by approximately seventy different names, but the Islamic holy book called the Koran doesn't even mention this world renown city one time.

Inside of Islam's third holiest city are two major religious shrines, the Al Aqsa Mosque and the Dome of the Rock. Both of these are located upon the Temple Mount. In order for the Jews to build their third temple these shrines will likely have to be removed and Islam's stronghold on Jerusalem be released.

The odds of these things happening, apart from the fulfillment of the Psalm 83 and Ezekiel 38 wars, are extremely unlikely. The Psalm 83 war involves an inner circle of Muslim dominated nations that share common borders with Israel. These countries form into a confederacy that goes to war with Israel in an attempt to destroy the Jewish state and make Israel a forgotten name and place.

> "They have said, "Come, and let us cut them off from *being a nation, That the name of Israel may be remembered no more." (Psalm 83:4)*

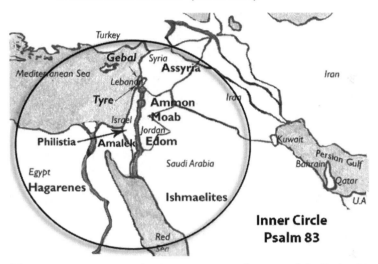

The image superimposes the ancient territorial names of the Psalm 83 Arab confederacy upon their modern-day equivalents.

The Arab confederacy that is displayed on the image is listed by their ancient names in Psalm 83:6-8. This grouping of countries came together in the Arab-Israeli war of 1948, but that was not a final fulfillment of the entire eighteen verses in the Psalm. Thus, Psalm 83:1-18 remains a prophecy in process that awaits its final fulfillment. However upon fulfillment, the IDF will win this prophetic war as per Psalm 83:9-18. In the aftermath of this war, Jordan's control of the Temple Mount will be removed and Islam's grip upon Jerusalem will become loosened.

Similarly, in the war of Ezekiel 38 Islam takes a big blow. This prophecy seems to follow on the heels of Psalm 83 and involves another predominately Muslim coalition that is led by Russia. Unlike Psalm 83, the Ezekiel 38 countries don't share common borders with Israel.

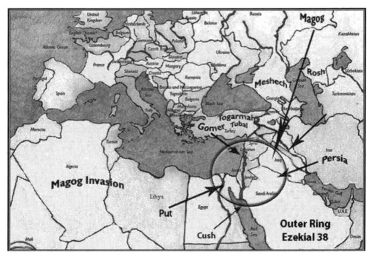

This image displays the Ezekiel 38 invaders alongside their modern-day equivalents.

This war is also won by Israel and in the aftermath Allah will have lost his Akbar in the greater part of the Middle East. Allahu Akbar means "god is most great." It alludes to Allah being the greatest god. Psalm 83 and Ezekiel 38 will disprove this boisterous Islamic claim, but more importantly, it will pave the way for the building of the Third Jewish Temple.

After the wars of Psalm 83 followed by Ezekiel 38, Israel will be:

- Victorious militarily (Obadiah 1:18, Ezek. 25:14, 37:10, Zechariah 12:6),

- Empowered politically (Daniel 12:7),

- Expanded territorially (Jer. 49:2, Zephaniah 2:8-9, Obadiah 1:19-20),

- Esteemed internationally (Ezek. 39:13),

- Temple ready religiously.

The supernatural defeat of the Magog invasion should get most Jews mindful of their God Jehovah and their belief in the need to build the Temple and reinstate the Mosaic Law to please Him. In the prior chapter entitled, "*The False Covenant that Starts the Seven-Year Tribulation Period,*" three clues were presented that suggest the rebuilding of the Temple is part of the true content of the false covenant. This implies that the Temple gets built, or at least becomes operational, promptly after the false covenant gets confirmed and the Trib-period starts.

In summary, the chain of events that likely lead to the actual building of the Tribulation Temple could be as follows:

1. The IDF wins the war of Psalm 83, which strips the Jordanian-based Waqf, from its control over the Temple Mount,

2. The Jews demolish the Dome of the Rock and the Al Aqsa Mosque to clear the Temple Mount site for construction of the Temple,

3. The other Muslim nations of the world, who were not part of Psalm 83, condemn the take down of these holy Islamic shrines and protest Israel's exclusive claims over the Temple Mount,

4. Some of these Muslim countries confederate to invade Israel in Ezekiel 38,

5. Jehovah supernaturally wins the war of Ezekiel 38,

6. The Jews turn more religious after witnessing Jehovah's victory in Ezekiel 38,

7. The Jews make strides to build their temple,

8. The Harlot world religion, which will be comprised mostly of Gentiles, with the support of the international community, disputes Israel's exclusive claims over Jerusalem and the Temple Mount. As a result, the Harlot's objections hinder the building of the temple, which causes the Jews to negotiate with these Gentiles to obtain permission to build their temple.

9. The False Covenant enables the Jews to build their Temple and gives the Gentiles the outer court along with access to travel through Jerusalem for forty-two months, which fulfills the prophecies in Rev. 11:1-3.

3. The functions performed within the Tribulation Temple

The Jews will repeat the same functions they performed in the prior two temples. They will fulfill the offerings and sacrificial requirements of the Mosaic Law. These sacrifices and offerings last up until the middle of the Trib-period, which is when the Antichrist enters into the Tribulation Temple and stops them.

> "Then he, (*the Antichrist*), shall confirm a covenant with many for one week; But in the middle of the week, (*upon entering the Tribulation Temple*), he shall bring an end to sacrifice and offering. And on the wing of abominations shall be one who makes desolate, Even until the consummation, which is determined, Is poured out on the desolate." (Daniel 9:27; *emphasis added*)

4. Why the Tribulation Temple is unsanctioned

The first two temples were sanctioned by God. In 1 Kings 6, Solomon was authorized to construct the First Temple, and in Ezra 1, King Cyrus of Persia sent the Jews back to Jerusalem to build the Second Temple. However, the Tribulation Temple does not appear to have God's stamp of approval upon it and neither do the sacrifices and offerings that will happen therein.

> ""Heaven *is My throne, And earth is My footstool. Where is the house that you will build Me? And where is the place of My rest? For all those things My hand has made, And all those things exist,*" Says the Lord. *"But on this one will I* look: On *him who is poor and of a contrite spirit, And who trembles at My word.*"" (Isaiah 66:1-2)

Through Isaiah God asks, *"Where is the house that you will build Me?"* This refers to an unbuilt Temple, but which one? It is not the First Solomonic Temple because it existed during Isaiah's time. Thus, its location was already known and there was no need to build it again. This Temple was destroyed by the Babylonians over a century after Isaiah's time around 586 BC.

> "He who kills a bull *is as if he slays a man*; He who sacrifices a lamb, *as if he breaks a dog's neck;* He who offers a grain offering, *as if he offers swine's blood; He who burns incense, as if he blesses an idol.* Just as they have chosen their own ways, (*of Temple worship*), And their soul delights in their (*sacrificial*) abominations,..." (Isaiah 66:3; *emphasis added*)

We can also rule out the Second Temple because in Isaiah 66:3, God is frowning upon the sacrifices of bulls and lambs, and He is displeased with the offerings of grain and incense. These types of sacrifices and offerings were required by Levitical Law to be performed in the First and Second Temples.

Therefore, the Temple in Isaiah 66:1 seems to be dealing with the Third Jewish Temple. This Temple will be built when God is most interested in *"him who is poor and of a contrite spirit, And who trembles at My (His) word,"* rather than animal sacrifices and grain offerings. In Isaiah 66:2, God is pleased with a poor and contrite spirit, but in Isaiah 66:3, He is indifferent to continuation of sacrifices and offerings.

In Isaiah 66:2 the priest who, *"kills a bull is as if he slays a man."* Slay is defined as the killing of a man or animal wantonly and in a violent way. The intentional or premeditated slaying of a man is called "First Degree Murder." Furthermore, Isaiah says that *"He who sacrifices a lamb, as if he breaks a dog's neck."* A dog is often called "Man's Best Friend," which presents another indictment against the priest who indulges in these sacrificial activities. These graphic bull and lamb examples explain how the Lord is displeased with the priestly sacrifices in the third temple.

God has always looked favorably upon a poor and contrite spirit, but why is He no longer pleased with the sacrifices and offerings that were obligatory acts performed within the two prior temples? The answer was already provided in the chapter entitled, *"Israel in the First Half of the Tribulation."*

That prior chapter pointed out that the Law and all of its sacrifices and offerings were established to be mankind's temporary tutor. The Law was intended to bring us to recognition through faith that Christ is the Lord and Savior. Christ fulfilled the Law and became the sacrificial "Lamb of God." His crucifixion was the ultimate atoning sacrifice that nullified the need for any further Temple sacrifices. The verse below and several other related verses were included in that previous chapter.

> "The next day John saw Jesus coming toward him, and said, "Behold! The Lamb of God who takes away the sin of the world!"" (John 1:29)

The continuation of sacrifices in the third temple amounts to abominations to God. They evidence a total disregard for the atoning sacrifice of Christ on the cross. Isaiah 66:3 acknowledges this by saying, *"their soul delights in their abominations."* Then Isaiah goes on to say:

> "So will I choose their delusions, And bring their fears on them; Because, when I called, no one answered, When I spoke they did not hear; But they did evil before My eyes, And chose *that in which I do not delight." (Isaiah 66:4)*

This above verse depicts the future religious leadership of Israel as being delusional. They are faulted for being unresponsive to God's call, deaf to God's word, doing evil in God's sight and performing sacrifices and offerings in which God no longer delights.

While the priests are performing the sacrifices and offerings inside the Temple, the Two Witnesses will be simultaneously speaking about the futility of these activities outside on the streets of Jerusalem. In large part, they represent God's call and words that fall upon the deaf ears of the religious leaders in Israel.

As a result of these offenses, God *"will choose their delusions."* Just like they choose to do abominations in which God does not delight, the Lord will choose their delusions in which they will not delight. The main delusion these religious leaders will face is the ultimate abhorrence in the unsanctioned Tribulation Temple and that is the, "Abomination of Desolation," spoken about by Daniel the prophet. This disgraceful act will be performed by the Antichrist.

The Temple sacrifices the priests will perform will be like "abominations" to God, so in turn they will get served with the "Abomination" of all abominations, which puts a complete stop to all future sacrifices and offerings in the Temple as per Daniel 9:27.

Then to top it off, while the Antichrist is still inside the Temple he, *"exalts himself above all that is called God or that is worshiped, so that he sits as God in the temple of God, showing himself that he is God."* (2 Thess. 2:4)

How's this scenario for a GRAND DELUSION to the religious leadership of Israel who will rebuff the Gospel preaching of the Two Witnesses and continue to reject Christ as the Messiah? In a blatant disregard for the atoning sacrifice of Christ, these Jewish priests will erroneously worship God by unnecessarily sacrificing animals. As a result, they will be submitted to the Antichrist, who will epitomize the ultimate form of false worship.

5. The current preparations being made for its construction and operations

In April of 2019, Moshe Feiglin, the head of the far-right quasi-libertarian Zehut party said that he wants to rebuild the Jewish Temple on the Temple Mount in Jerusalem immediately.

> *"I don't want to build a* (Third) *Temple in one or two years, I want to build it now."* [41]

The coming third temple is no longer a figment of Jewish imagination, but is about to become a reality. Some believe that this Temple could be constructed within a year or two, and that initially an altar could be established on location for Temple services and needs in the interim in a matter of just a few days.

A case in point is the Hanukkah dedication by the Sanhedrin in 2018. Concerning this important event, one news article reads;

> *"Sanhedrin Invites 70 Nations to Hanukkah Dedication of Altar for the Third Temple"* Israel Breaking News (11/29/18)

> *"The nascent Sanhedrin released a declaration to the 70 nations for Hanukkah to be read at a ceremony in Jerusalem on the last day of the holiday. The*

> *ceremony will include the consecration of a stone altar prepared for use in the Third Temple. The declaration is intended as an invitation to the nations to participate in the Temple and to receive its blessings. The altar is currently in the form of loose stone blocks ready to be transported to the Temple Mount and stored in a manner that will enable them to be transported and assembled at a moment's notice."[42]*

Additionally, the Temple Institute, the reestablished Sanhedrin and other Temple related organizations are preparing for all the required needs of an operational third temple. Architectural drawings exist and Levitical Priests are assigned and trained, including the required High Priest. Moreover, the Temple vessels and vestments are prepared, including the menorah, the table of showbread and the golden altar of incense.

Recently, I was even provided with some gold and silver coins that pictured images of the heads of US President Donald Trump and King Cyrus on one side and the coming Jewish Temple on the other. These coins are intended to generate revenues to be used toward the coming Temple.

This is an incredible reality that lines up perfectly with the biblical prophecies related to the Tribulation Temple. If you want to learn more about this Temple and stay apprised of its continued developments you can visit the following websites:

https://templeinstitute.org/ or http://templemountfaithful.org.

6. How this coming Jewish Temple can be used to evangelize Jews

While watching a Prophecy Watchers TV show that was hosted by Gary Stearman, I picked up some invaluable insights on how to evangelize to Jews by familiarizing them with the coming Temple. The show featured Pastor Billy Crone and can be viewed on YouTube under the show title of, *"Billy Crone: Trump, the Temple and the Antichrist."*

This chapter has provided information that can assist you in following a few sequential steps that can be used to evangelize a Jewish person. By asking the questions below and being able to follow up with interesting facts and answers, you just might lead a Jew or Jews to their Messiah, Jesus Christ.

QUESTION #1: Did you know that the Jews are preparing to build their third temple?

- Update the Jew(s) about the progression of activities being orchestrated to build their third temple. Inform them that this is not a figment of imagination, but is currently happening with real time application.

- Remind them that this is the third temple because the First Temple was destroyed by the Babylonians around 586 BC and the Second Temple was destroyed by the Romans in 70 AD. Interestingly, both temples were destroyed on the same day on the Hebrew calendar on the 9th of Av (Tisha b'Av).

- Inform them that these two Temples were considered architectural wonders of the ancient world.

- Most importantly, STARTLE them with the fact that the Temple priests are preparing to reinstate the practice of ANIMAL SACRIFICES. These animal killings won't be for sport, food or clothing needs, but for religious purposes, namely, for the atonement of sins. In fact, in celebration of Passover in 2018, hundreds of activists and supporters attended the annual exercise of the Passover sacrifice that was conducted for the first time next to the Southern Wall, at the foot of the Temple Mount. They actually slaughtered a real sacrificial lamb at the ceremony![43]

QUESTION #2: Did you know that the Bible predicted that this Third Temple would be built?

- Let them know that both the Old and New Testaments foretold that this third temple would be built and they are watching the fulfillment of Bible prophecy in the making. The scriptures were provided earlier in this chapter.

- Help them to realize how important this is as part of their historical religious heritage.

- Inform them that no other religious shrines or buildings are prophesied to be built in the future within the Bible, which makes the third temple unique and important.

After asking and answering the first two questions you should have the Jew(s) undivided attention, or at least piqued their interest to proceed with further questions and explanations. These two facts, that the Jews are going to build their Temple and the Bible predicted that they would, are real time and undeniable nuggets of information and should be exciting to Jews.

However, this information in and of itself is not necessarily going to get a Jew to receive Christ as their Messiah, but hopefully by now, the Jew is curious to know if the Bible foretells of any more information about their future.

QUESTION #3: Would you like to know more about what the Bible predicts about the future of Israel, the Temple and the Jewish people?

- Let them know that the Bible has much to say about these important topics.

- Share whatever you are capable of about these prophetic topics, but keep them focused upon the third temple. This is the topic that you used to captivate their attention.

QUESTION #4: Sadly, did you know that this Temple may have a very short lifespan?

- Alert them to the fact that, although the first two Temples each survived for over 400 years, this Temple is predicted to be violated in a short order of time by a charismatic world leader called the Antichrist.

- Let them know that their Hebrew prophet Daniel predicts that this world dictator will go into the Temple and permanently stop the sacrifices and offerings taking place inside.

By now a Jew should become disoriented. This is a disconnect. They could wonder, why and how does this happen? And, where is this a biblical prophecy? The Jew will likely applaud the fact that the temple is in Bible prophecy, but they should be stopped in their tracks to hear that the temple worship will be short-lived.

In love, let them know that's not all and then you level the boom by laying out the following predicted chronology of events.

- After stopping the Temple sacrifices, the Antichrist promptly attempts to exterminate the Jews. This is also predicted by a Hebrew prophet named Zechariah.

- It will be the worst genocidal attempt in Jewish history! Even worse than Hitler and the Nazis! The ancient prophecy declares that Two-thirds of the Jews will be killed at that time.

These statements should provoke the question about timing. HOW SOON will these terrible things take place? The honest answer, in light of the points already made about the Temple, is that these events could happen SOON, probably in the Jewish person's lifetime.

QUESTION #5: Did you know that over 2000 years ago that Jesus Christ warned about all of this in the Bible?

- Amazingly, in a discourse that He gave on the Mount of Olives, Jesus warned the people living in Judea at the time of the intrusion of the Temple by the Antichrist to flee immediately.

QUESTION #6: Would you like me to read from the Bible where Christ issued this warning?

- Read Matthew 24:15-22 to the person. Let them know that the "Abomination of Desolation" in these verses is what you were referring to when the Antichrist intrudes into the Temple and stops the priestly sacrifices and offerings. You can also read Daniel 9:27 to connect the dots of this prophecy.

THE NOT SO GOOD NEWS

Now it's time to present the better, but still not so good, news to the Jew.

- *The good news* is that the prophecy of Zechariah states that one-third of the Jews will survive the genocidal assault of the Antichrist.

The Jewish person might ask; "How is this good news?"

- The response from you to this question could be; "*I know, do the math... envision 3 Jews in a room, then realize that only one comes out alive... How do you like your chances that you are that sole one?*"

THE GREAT NEWS

Now it's time to give the Jew THE GREAT NEWS, which is that he or she can avoid this period of Great Tribulation, the Abomination of Desolation and the genocidal campaign of the Antichrist by receiving Christ right NOW!!!

(A smart Jew should be then grabbing his or her pen and saying, "WHERE DO I SIGN!")

NOTES TO REMEMBER WHILE WITNESSING TO THE JEW(S)

1. It's the real time strides toward building the predicted third temple that will likely hook them in on this journey to their salvation.

2. You are not making this stuff up!

3. God did not sugar coat the information within these prophecies and nor should you.

4. Explain the details and if they seek to receive Christ lead them in the prayer of salvation, which is presented in the appendix entitled, "The Sinner's Prayer of Salvation." If they don't want to receive Jesus Christ after the details are explained, LET GO and LET GOD do the rest!

15

The Harlot of Mystery Babylon in the Tribulation Period

After Jesus Christ catches His Bride of true believers up into heaven in the Rapture, Satan will use supernatural deception to elevate a type of female forgery in her place. In 2 Corinthians 11:2, the Christian believers are likened to chaste virgins, but in Revelation 17 the Bible alludes to this devilish imitation as:

> "The woman (*who*) was arrayed in purple and scarlet, and adorned with gold and precious stones and pearls, having in her hand (*was*) a golden cup full of abominations and the filthiness of her fornication, (*spiritual idolatry*). And on her forehead a name was written: MYSTERY, BABYLON THE GREAT, THE MOTHER OF HARLOTS AND OF THE ABOMINATIONS OF THE EARTH." (Rev. 17:4-5; *emphasis added*)

This Whore of Babylon is one of the first silk strands that Satan weaves into his clever web of deceit that is strategically designed to ensnare mankind in the end times. When he is no longer bound by the restraint of 2 Thess. 2:7, the Devil will immediately reveal his counterfeit crew, along with their scripts and props, and then proceed to thrust his well calculated layered campaign of spiritual deception upon an unsuspecting humanity. Satan's strategy involves the:

1. *Counterfeit Religion* of Ecclesiastical Babylon (Rev. 17),
2. *Counterfeit Gospel* of works (Rev. 13:15-17),
3. *Counterfeit Truth*, which is "The Lie" (2 Thess. 2:11),
4. *Counterfeit Trinity* of Revelation 16:13 who are:
   1. False Prophet as the unholy spirit in the flesh (Rev. 13:11-16),
   2. Antichrist as the false messiah, (Rev. 6:1-2, 2 Thess. 2:3-4),
   3. Satan as the false god (2 Thess. 2:9),
5. *Counterfeit Cashless Economy* of Commercial Babylon (Rev. 18).

It was duly noted above that when Satan is free to do so, he unleashes a *"well calculated layered campaign"* of supernatural deception. The Devil has prepared a double religious jeopardy for humankind. The first part involves the "Scarlet Harlot," who is the whore of Babylon, and the second segment involves the "Scarlet Beast," representing the Antichrist.

> "So he, (*the angel*), carried me, (*the apostle John*), away in the Spirit into the wilderness. And I saw a woman sitting on a *scarlet beast* which was full of names of blasphemy, having seven heads and ten horns. The *woman was arrayed in purple and scarlet.*" (Rev. 17:3-4a; emphasis added)

These two sinister characters are fittingly adorned in scarlet, as this brilliant red hue is the biblical color rendering for sin.

> ""Come now, and let us reason together," Says the Lord, "Though your sins are like scarlet, They shall be as white as snow; Though they are red like crimson, They shall be as wool."" (Isaiah 1:18)

Observe that the *Scarlet Harlot* sits on the *Scarlet Beast* in Rev. 17:3. This pictures the Harlot initially in the superior position while the Antichrist temporarily plays the supportive role. This is further evidenced in Rev. 17:7, which acknowledges the Antichrist "carries" the harlot during the time of her tenure.

> "But the angel said to me, "Why did you marvel? I will tell you the mystery of the woman and of the beast that carries her, which has the seven heads and the ten horns."" (Rev. 17:7)

This unholy alliance is short lived because ultimately, not too long later, the ten kings of Rev. 17:16-17 will desolate the harlot and submit their power and authority to the Antichrist. However, this chapter is about her and not him and it will present the details about, timing for, mystery behind, and identity of this mysterious woman of Revelation 17.

The Details of the Harlot

The particulars about the Harlot are tabulated and briefly explained below. The Harlot:

- *Rules over many nations*, which means that the Harlot has a global reach - (Rev. 17:15).

- *Is headquartered in a great city*, meaning that she represents a very real and specific organization, rather than an allegorical concept - (Rev. 17:18).

- The Harlot's *city is located upon 7 hills*, which further evidences the realness of the organization and also provides an important clue about the location of the Harlot's headquarters - (Rev. 17:9).

- *Panders to political leaders* and serves as *the religious opiate of the masses*, which means that she is a religion possessing both a church and state relationship - (Rev. 17:2).

> "with whom the kings, (*political leaders*), of the earth committed fornication, (*spiritual idolatry*), and the

inhabitants of the earth, (*the masses*), were made drunk, (*opiated*), with the wine of her fornication (*spiritual idolatry*)" - (Rev. 17:2; *emphasis added*).

- *Martyred believers in the past* and will martyr believers *in the future*, meaning that whatever religion the Harlot represents, it has a history of killing Christians and is predicted to repeat this behavior again - (Rev. 17:6).

- *Killed 2 or more holy apostles*, which narrows down the choices of the global religion and the great city where it's located - (Rev. 18:20).

- "Rejoice over her, O heaven, and you holy apostles, (*in the plural, meaning two or more*), and prophets, for God has avenged you, (*your deaths of martyrdom*), on her!" (Rev. 18:20; *emphasis added*)

- *Guilty of great crimes and sins*, meaning that whatever this religion is, it has a traceable sinful history - (Rev. 18:5).

- *Will be hated and desolated by the Ten Kings*, which means that the reign of the Harlot world religion has an expiration date - (Rev. 17:16).

- *Will be replaced by the Antichrist*, meaning that the Antichrist no longer serves in a subservient position to the Harlot, but gets promoted to his role as the charismatic world leader, which initiates part two of Satan's layered campaign over mankind - (Rev. 17:17).

The Timing of the Harlot

For the reasons about to be explained, it appears that the Harlot punches in on the timeclock promptly after the Rapture and then clocks out at the midpoint of the Trib-period. Determining the end point of the Harlot's reign involves deductive reasoning that is scripturally supported. Estimating the start point of the Harlot requires some speculation derived from logic.

The Start Point for the Harlot

It's logical to assume that after the Rapture, which is also when the restraint upon Satan gets removed, that the Devil will promptly unleash the first leg of his two-legged campaign upon mankind. Why would he wait? When these two epic predictions occur, it is doubtful that Satan will slap his forehead and ask his fallen angelic cohorts, "*Oh no, what should we do now?*"

Satan has likely long been preparing for the moment that he can showcase his supernatural capabilities to man, which is what happens when he is no longer restrained. The process is explained in 2 Thess. 2:7-12 and outlined below.

1. The restrainer, who prevents Satan from using his supernatural powers to deceive mankind, unlocks the handcuffs and permits Satan to display his hidden powers. (2 Thess. 2:7)

2. Satan promptly reveals his point man the Antichrist, who initially carries the Harlot Queen to her heights, but ultimately rules over the world after the Ten Kings dethrone her in Rev. 17:16. (2 Thess. 2:8)

3. In the process of moving the Antichrist into his ultimate post as the world's leader, Satan utilizes "all power, signs, and lying wonders." These paranormal means are outsourced in a deceptive manner in order to influence people who are perishing to believe in what the Bible calls, "The Lie." (2 Thess. 2:9-12)

In 2 Thess. 2:1-2 the believers in Thessalonica were concerned that the Rapture had happened and they were left behind. The apostle Paul dispelled their concerns in 2 Thess. 2:3-12. Many

Bible expositors, including me, teach that Paul's explanation in those verses correlated the timing of the Rapture with the removal of the restraint upon Satan.

Thus in theory, Satan props up the Harlot who sits on the Antichrist in Rev. 17:3 shortly after the Rapture occurs and the restraint upon him is removed. This implies that the Harlot emerges as the global religion in the Post-Rapture / Pre-Trib time gap period. Her dominion is during this time gap until the middle of the Trib-period, which is when the Ten Kings desolate her.

The End Point of the Harlot

> "And the ten horns, (*ten kings*), which you saw on the beast, these will hate the harlot, make her desolate and naked, eat her flesh and burn her with fire. For God has put it into their hearts to fulfill His purpose, to be of one mind, and to give their kingdom to the beast, (*Antichrist*), until the words of God are fulfilled." (Rev. 17:16-17; *emphasis added*)

These two verses explain that the ten kings unite to eliminate the Harlot in order to elevate the Antichrist. This is the point whereby stage one of mankind's double religious jeopardy ends and stage two begins.

> ""So they, (*mankind*), worshiped the dragon, (*Satan*), who gave authority to the beast, (*Antichrist*); and they worshiped the beast, saying, "Who is like the beast? Who is able to make war with him?" And he was given a mouth speaking great things and blasphemies, and he was given authority to continue for forty-two months."" (Rev. 13:4-5; *emphasis added*)

These above two verses tell us what happens after the Harlot gets deposed. World worship gets deflected from the Harlot to Satan and his representative, the Antichrist. This period spans forty-two months, which most Bible prophecy experts agree, is the last three and one-half years of the Trib-period.

The ten kings do away with the Harlot and then at that time give their authority to the Antichrist. With the backing of the ten kings on his resume, the Antichrist exercises this authority over the world throughout the second half of the Trib-period. Deductive reasoning enables us to conclude that the transfer of authority from the Harlot to the Antichrist happens in the middle of the Seven-Year Tribulation Period, which reserves the final three and one-half years for the rule of the Antichrist.

The Mystery of the Harlot

> "And on her forehead a name was written: MYSTERY, BABYLON THE GREAT, THE MOTHER OF HARLOTS AND OF THE ABOMINATIONS OF THE EARTH. I saw the woman, drunk with the blood of the saints and with the blood of the martyrs of Jesus. And when I saw her, I marveled with great amazement." (Rev. 17:5-6)

In his vision of this mysterious woman, the apostle John sees a title tattooed on her forehead. This heading informs us that this MOTHER OF HARLOTS, represents a biblical mystery. The reality that this is dealing with a true biblical mystery is proven by the following two important factors:

1. The word mystery is separated from the identity of BABYLON THE GREAT, by a comma in Revelation 17:5, MYSTERY, BABYLON THE GREAT,... Some translations like, the RSV, NIV and the NET go so far as to use a colon to distinctly separate the words of "Mystery" from "Babylon."

2. The angel translating the vision to John clearly states that, "BABYLON THE GREAT, THE MOTHER OF HARLOTS," is indeed a "mystery."

> "But the angel said to me, "Why did you marvel? I will tell you the mystery of the woman and of the beast that carries her, which has the seven heads and the ten horns. (Rev. 17:7)

A biblical mystery in the New Testament is something that was hidden in the Old Testament, but becomes revealed in the New Testament. The revealing can come from different sources. For instance, Christ reveals to the apostle John the mystery of the "Seven Stars and Seven Golden Lampstands."

> "The mystery of the seven stars which you saw in My right hand, and the seven golden lampstands: The seven stars are the angels of the seven churches, and the seven lampstands which you saw are the seven churches." (Rev. 1:20)

In the case of the mystery related to the timing that believers receive their resurrected bodies, the apostle Paul discloses this.

> "Behold, I tell you a mystery: We shall not all sleep, but we shall all be changed in a moment, in the twinkling of an eye, at the last trumpet. For the trumpet will sound, and the dead will be raised incorruptible, and we shall be changed." (1 Corinthians 15:51-52)

In the case of the mystery behind the MOTHER OF HARLOTS, the translating angel informs John of the important details about the Harlot. What the angel reveals is explained in the following three verses:

1. "Here is the mind which has wisdom: The seven heads are seven mountains, (hills in some translations), on which the woman sits." (Rev. 17:9; emphasis added)

2. "Then he said to me, "The waters which you saw, where the harlot sits, are peoples, multitudes, nations, and tongues." (Rev. 17:15)

3. "And the woman whom you saw is that great city which reigns over the kings of the earth." (Rev. 17:18)

In Revelation 17:18, John discovers that the Harlot is headquartered in a great city. In Revelation 17:9, he learns the geographical location of the great city is upon seven hills. Revelation 17:15 explains that the Harlot has a global reach, that it becomes a religion that is embraced worldwide by multitudes of people in various nations that have diverse languages.

When John received the revelation, Rome was the city that was known as, "The City on Seven Hills." The Romans even minted a coin at the time that featured the "Goddess Roma" sitting on these infamous seven hills.

Further evidencing that the great city is Rome, I will paraphrase what the angel said, "*the woman* (with the tattooed forehead) *whom you saw* (in your vision John)" *is that great city* (of Rome) *which* (currently) *reigns over the kings of the earth*" . . .

From John's perspective that clearly represented the city of Rome. John lived during the reign of the Roman Empire.

Thus, the mystery explained in Rev. 17:7 quoted above also involves, "*the beast that carries her, which has the seven heads and the ten horns.*" In this context, *the beast that carries her* likely alludes to the political support that the Antichrist provides for the Harlot within their unholy church and state alliance.

The seven heads and the ten horns are attributes associated with the beast. The seven heads appear to represent the historical Gentile empires of Egypt, Assyria, Babylon, Persia, Greece, Rome (past) and Rome (revived). Whereas seven heads are interpreted chronologically, the ten horns represent a group of ten kings contemporarily that will exist at the same time as the Harlot and Antichrist.

The Identity of the Harlot

Satan has had ample time to paganize a specific religion in preparation of becoming the dominant global religion of the Harlot. This has to be a religion that remains mostly intact after the Rapture. Moreover it needs to be fully functioning, internationally based and well established so that the Antichrist can align himself with it when he comes upon the world scene.

In addition to being left behind, functional, international and well established, the candidate religion for becoming the Harlot must be:

1. Headquartered within a great city,
2. Sitting atop seven mountains or hills,
3. Stained with the shed blood of martyred believers in the past,
4. Responsible for the killing of two or more of the holy apostles,
5. Reigning over the kings of the earth during the apostle John's time,
6. Guilty of historical crimes and sins.

There exists only one active religion that meets all of these requirements in full and it's the Roman Catholic Church. It is headquartered in Rome, which is *the city that reigned over the kings of the earth* during John's time.

Rome is sometimes referred to as the eternal city that *sits on seven hills.* Presently these hills still exist under the names of Aventine, Caelian, Capitoline, Esquiline, Palatine, Quirinal, and Viminal.

During the historical periods of the Catholic Inquisitions many Christian believers were killed as heretics, which fulfills the Rev. 17:6 requirement of the shed *blood of the saints* in the past. Below is a quote related to this from the American Theologian Albert Barnes who lived between December 1, 1798 – December 24, 1870.

> *"The meaning here* (Revelation 17:6) *is, that the persecuting power referred to had shed the blood of the saints; and that, in its fury, it had, as it were, drunk the blood of the slain, and had become, by drinking that blood, intoxicated and infuriated. No one need say how applicable this has been to the papacy* (Roman Catholicism) *... Let the blood shed in the valleys of Piedmont; the blood shed in the Low Countries by the Duke of Alva; the blood shed on Bartholomew's day; and the blood shed in the Inquisition, testify."*[44]

Two or more of the *holy apostles* were killed either in Rome or by the orders delivered from Rome matching up with Rev. 18:20. History tells us that the Apostle Paul was beheaded in Rome and the Apostle Peter was crucified under the Roman Emperor Nero. In addition, there is historical evidence that the Apostle Andrew was crucified by the order of a Roman governor and the Apostle James, the brother of the Apostle John was killed by a client king of Rome.

Both Pagan and Papal Rome have long lists of historical crimes and sins. Some are listed below.

> "Pagan Rome ended and Papal Rome began with the CROSS! Imperial Rome became PAPAL Rome on October 28, 312 A.D., when Constantine exchanged the eagle for the cross: And not only so, but he (Constantine) also caused the sign of the salutary trophy

to be impressed on the very shields of his soldiers; and commanded that his embattled forces should be preceded in their march, not by golden eagles, as heretofore, but only by the standard of the cross. (Eusebius, Life of Constantine, p. 545)."[45]

"For her sins are piled as high as heaven and God has remembered her crimes." (Rev. 18:5 HCSB)

Pagan Rome

- Put to death God's Son the Savior Jesus Christ.

- Martyred Christians for over 3 centuries.

- Killed 1.1 million people around 70 AD. These were mostly Jews according to Jewish historian Josephus.

- Destroyed the Second Jewish Temple and the city of Jerusalem in 70 AD.

- Destroyed Jerusalem again in 135 AD.

- Killed hundreds of thousands of more Jews around 132-135 AD.

Papal Rome

- Expelled all Jews from Spain in 1492 AD.

- Expelled all Jews from Portugal in 1497 AD.

- Killed tens of thousands of Jews in the Crusades.

- Killed Hundreds of thousands of Protestants for hundreds of years during the inquisitions. (*There are numerous sources that say the amount of people killed worldwide by Rome runs into the millions).*

• Responsible for as many as 100,000 victims of sexual abuse in the United States alone. (according to an article in the National Catholic Reporter). *What about worldwide?*

In my book entitled *The Next Prophecies* I go into enormous details about the prophetic connections between the Harlot of Revelation 17 and the Catholic Church of the future. In that book I explain the following:

1. Why the other popular candidate cities of Jerusalem, New York, Mecca and rebuilt Babylon Iraq, are not likely the great city of the Harlot.

2. How the judgment of Ecclesiastical Babylon in Revelation 17 is different than the judgment of Commercial Babylon in Revelation 18.

3. That the Harlot is the other signatory with Israel of the False Covenant of Isaiah 28:15-18 and Daniel 9:27.

4. Why the Harlot of Revelation 17 probably represents the horsemen of Death and Hades in the Fourth Seal Judgment of Rev. 6:7-8.

5. How the Harlot is responsible for the deaths of the Fifth Seal Saints of Rev. 6:9-11.

6. Why the Catholic Church represents the Gentiles that are given control of the outer court of the Tribulation Temple and access to trod over Jerusalem for three and one-half years in Rev. 11:1-2.

7. How the letter to the Church of Thyatira in Rev. 2:18-29 has a prophetic application to the Catholic Church.

8. That the Catholic Church is "amillennial," and as such does not believe in a Pre-Tribulation Rapture. Thus, the Catholic clergy won't be surprised if they are left behind, but will still hold to the thinking that the Catholic Church is the one true church.

9. That the Catholic Church gets left behind and ends up in the Great Tribulation period.

10. Why the Marian apparitions are demonic and will likely continue to happen after the Rapture.

11. How Mary worship within the Catholic Church is likened in the Bible to the prophetess Jezebel in the letter to Thyatira in Rev. 2:20.

The comparisons below between Jezebel and the Catholic version of Mary are copied from the *Next Prophecies* book. They are related to these damning verses below.

> "Nevertheless I have a few things against you, (*the Catholic Church*), because you allow that woman Jezebel, (*the demonic Mary imposter*), who calls herself a prophetess, to teach and seduce My servants to commit sexual immorality, (*spiritual idolatry*), and eat things sacrificed to idols. And I gave her time to repent of her sexual immorality, and she did not repent, (*Mary worship in the Catholic Church will continue*). Indeed I will cast her into a sickbed, and those who commit adultery with her into great tribulation, (*the second half of the Trib-period*), unless they repent of their deeds. I will kill her children with death, (*Catholics will die during the Great Tribulation period*), and all the churches shall know that I am He who searches the minds and hearts. And I will give to each one of you according to your works." (Rev. 2:20-23; *emphasis added*)

Jezebel's Traits	End Time Harlot's Traits
A queen 1 Kings 16:29-31	*A queen* Revelation 18:7
Encourages idolatry 1 Kings 21:25-26	*Encourages idolatry* Rev. 2:20; 17:4
Described as a harlot 2 Kings 9:22	*Described as a harlot* Rev. 17:1, 5; 19:2
She uses witchcraft 2 Kings 9:22	*Uses witchcraft* Isaiah 47:9, 12; Rev.18:23
Seductress; Outward beauty 2 Kings 9:30	*Seductress; Outward beauty* Rev. 17:4
Sheds the saints blood 2 Kings 9:7	*Sheds the saints blood* Rev. 17:6; 19:2
Massacres God's prophets 1 Kings 18:4	*Massacres God's prophets* Rev. 18:24
She is destroyed 2 Kings 9:33-37	*She is destroyed* Rev. 17:16; 18:8

For more well researched information on the Harlot World Religion, I highly recommend the following books that are available on Amazon Kindle.

- *Queen of All: The Marian apparitions' plan to unite all religions under the Roman Catholic Church,* by authors Jim Telow, Roger Oakland and Brad Myers

- *Messages from Heaven: A Biblical Examination Of The Queen Of Heaven's Messages In The End Times,* by Jim Tetlow

16

The Kings in the Tribulation Period

Presently, there are 195 countries in the world. This total comprises 193 countries that are member states of the United Nations and 2 countries that are non-member observer states: the Holy See (Vatican) and the State of Palestine. This number of nations excludes Taiwan because it is represented by the People's Republic of China.[46]

Most all of these countries have a government and a political leader or a royal ruler. The Bible often refers to these national heads of state as kings. This chapter will explore the kings that exist during the Trib-period. These are the Donald Trump's, Vladimir Putin's and Benjamin Netanyahu's of the last of the last days. Their governing decisions will heavily influence the direction that the world takes at this most critical point in human history.

These leaders will be reacting to cataclysmic cosmic, economic, geographic and geo-political repercussions resulting from the unprecedented divine judgments of God and the deceiving supernatural signs and wonders coming from Satan.

Excluding the Scarlet Harlot Queen and the Scarlet Beast King, who is also called the "little horn" in Daniel 7:8, the list of additional powerful end times political potentates includes:

- The Kings of the Earth (Rev. 6:15, 16:14, 17:2, 18:3, 9 Rev. 19:19),

- The Ten Kings (Daniel 7:24, Rev. 17:12-13), who are also called:

- Ten Horns (Daniel 7:7, 20, 24 Rev. 12:3, 13:1, 17:3, 7, 12, 16),

- Ten Toes (Daniel 2:40-41),

- The Kings of the East (Rev. 16:12),

- The King of the South (Daniel 11:40),

- The King of the North (Daniel 11:40).

Some Bible commentaries fail to differentiate between all of the above kings, especially when it comes to the Ten Kings in relationship to the Kings of the Earth. The explanations below will evidence the clear distinctions, and in some instances, the commonalities between these various groupings of kings. For instance, the Kings of the East are a subset of rulers that emerge out from the Kings of the Earth, but the Ten Kings likely do not. The Ten Kings receive their kingdoms and authority in one hour with the Antichrist as per Rev. 17:12.

The Kings of the Earth

The largest contingency of kings in the end times are the Kings of the Earth. Although there are approximately 195 world leaders presently, that number will likely drop as a result of the fulfillment of the following prophetic events:

- Isaiah 17, which predicts the destruction of Damascus, could eliminate Syria's President,

- Jeremiah 49:1-6 and Zephaniah 2:8-9, which involves the toppling of Jordan and the annexing of territory by Israel, could remove the King of Jordan,

- Psalm 83, the climactic concluding Arab-Israeli war prophecy, could be problematic for the continued existence of Lebanon's leader,

- Ezekiel 38, which involves the massive invasion of Israel from a northern coalition, could eliminate several rulers from the defeated invading countries of Russia, Turkey, Iran, Libya and several of the other coalition nations,

- Revelation 6:3-4, which is when major wars happen, could be a time when Pakistan and India and / or North Korea and South Korea experience the use of nuclear weapons. These wars could remove national leaders also.

Therefore, however many countries and their kings survive into the Trib-period, the passages below tell their future stories as the infamous Kings of the Earth.

Revelation 6:15-17 – The Kings of the Earth will go into hiding when the Wrath of the Lamb comes. They will seek refuge in the caves and in the rocks of the mountains.

Revelation 16:12-16 – During the outpouring of the Sixth Bowl Judgment many of the Kings of the Earth will be approached by Satan, the Antichrist and False Prophet in the form of demonic spirit beings that look somewhat like frogs. This false trinity will perform signs in an attempt to influence the Kings of the Earth to gather for battle in the place called Armageddon for the climactic battle between the Antichrist and Jesus Christ.

Revelation 17:2 and 18:3 – The Kings of the Earth fully support the idolatry of the Harlot World Religion.

Revelation 18:9 – The Kings of the Earth weep and lament when they see commercial Babylon destroyed in one hour by the Lord.

Revelation 19:19 – The Antichrist assembles with the Kings of the Earth to make war against Jesus Christ at Armageddon.

The Kings of the East

The Kings of the East are alluded to one time in the connecting verses below:

> "Then the sixth angel poured out his bowl on the great river Euphrates, and its water was dried up, so that the way of the kings from the east might be prepared. And I saw three unclean spirits like frogs *coming* out of the mouth of the dragon, out of the mouth of the beast, and out of the mouth of the false prophet. For they are spirits of demons, performing signs, *which* go out to the kings of the earth and of the whole world, to gather them to the battle of that great day of God Almighty." (Rev. 16:12-14)

The Kings of the East appear to be among the first grouping of kings, from within the Kings of the Earth, to make their way to Armageddon for the final battle between the Antichrist and his armies against Jesus Christ in, "*that great day of God Almighty.*" When the Sixth Bowl Judgment occurs, "the great river Euphrates" dries up, which prepares the way for their travel westward to Armageddon.

It's interesting to note that God uses a Bowl Judgment to enable His enemies an unobstructed pathway to partake in a battle against His Son Jesus Christ. This Euphrates scenario beckons a few questions.

1. Is it a miracle? Could it be rightly called "THE MIRACLE AT THE EUPHRATES?"

2. Is it just a damning up of the river and not a miracle?

3. How much of the 1740-mile-long Euphrates dries up? Is it all of it or just a wide enough stretch to facilitate the deployment of the Kings of the East?

Before addressing the potential miracle, it is important to note that the water levels of the Tigris and Euphrates rivers have been declining. Dams built upriver in Turkey, Syria and Iran since the 1970s have reduced the flow of water that reaches Iraq by as much as half and the situation is about to get worse. One related headline came out on July 2, 2018 from the Independent that read:

"Catastrophic drought threatens Iraq as major dams in surrounding countries cut off water to its great rivers..."

THE MIRACLE AT THE EUPHRATES

In light of the facts that this event happens as the result of a Bowl Judgment at a time when the supernatural is the natural and the paranormal is the new normal, and simultaneously the false trinity, clothed in the form of frog-like demonic bodies, is performing signs in Rev. 16:14, I'm inclined to call this, "THE MIRACLE AT THE EUPHRATES," and that this supernatural event dries up the entire 1740 miles.

Remember by this time most, if not all, the world's rivers and streams have either been polluted or turned to blood by the Third Trumpet and Third Bowl Judgments. If the Euphrates is a bloody waterway then drying it up entirely would be a blessing.

If this is a true miracle, then what must the Kings of the East be thinking has happened to facilitate their ease of deployment for this climactic end times war? They will probably attribute THE MIRACLE AT THE EUPHRATES to the signs being performed by the false trinity per Rev. 16:14. The drying up of the Euphrates along with whatever other signs are being performed, will likely convince the Kings of the East that they will be victorious in the final battle.

Who are these kings and why is God making their mobilization across the Middle East easier? The primary choices for the identity of the Kings of the East are that they are either from Asia or Mesopotamia.

One of the advocates for these kings coming from Mesopotamia is Dr. Arnold Fruchtenbaum, who writes,

> *"The consistency of usage requires identifying the kings of the east as referring to Mesopotamian kings rather than China."* ...For now it is sufficient to point out that the east in Scripture is always Mesopotamia and never China."[47]

A brief history lesson on Mesopotamia is presented in the quote below from *"The Ancient History Encyclopedia."*

> *"Mesopotamia (from the Greek, meaning 'between two rivers') was an ancient region located in the eastern Mediterranean bounded in the northeast by the Zagros Mountains and in the southeast by the Arabian Plateau, corresponding to today's Iraq, mostly, but also parts of modern-day Iran, Syria and Turkey. The 'two rivers' of the name referred to the Tigris and the Euphrates rivers and the land was known as 'Al-Jazirah' (the island) by the Arabs referencing what Egyptologist J.H. Breasted would later call the Fertile Crescent, where Mesopotamian civilization began."*[48]

One foreseeable problem with the Kings of the East originating from Mesopotamia is that their march toward Armageddon begins directionally from east of the Euphrates, then crosses over the dried-up Euphrates riverbed and ultimately ends up approximately 600 miles to the west in Armageddon. From the list of modern-day countries in the encyclopedia quote above, only a portion of these nations are to the east of the Euphrates and among those, namely Iran and Eastern Iraq, there may not be many soldiers for the Kings of the East to muster.

Iran will have likely been hard hit by the disaster, potentially nuclear, in Elam of Jeremiah 49:34-39. This catastrophe appears to be followed promptly thereafter by the Ezekiel 38 war involving the defeat of Persian troops. A map of modern-day Iran consists of ancient Elam that hugs the Persian Gulf and Persia, which encompasses the land to the east of Elam.

According to the power index of GFP (www.globalfirepower. com), Iraq is currently ranked no. #53 among world armies, and the Iraqi army could also be adversely affected when the Psalm 83 war prophecy finds final fulfillment. They appear to be identified in Psalm 83:8 as a member of the Arab confederacy under the banner of ancient Assyria. When the Psalm was penned about 3000 years ago, Assyria mostly encompassed modern-day Northern Syria and Northern Iraq.

Dr. Mark Hitchcock believes that the Kings of the East represent the Far East, such as China and Korea. In his book entitled, "Middle East Burning," he writes,

> "The simplest and most suitable explanation for understanding "the kings from the east" (Revelation 16:12) is to take the passage literally. The kings of the East are kings from the East or "of the sun rising" – that is, they are monarchs who originate from the Far East. All that we know about these nations, then, is that they come from the east of the Euphrates River to gather at Armageddon for the final great conflict of the ages. The kings of the East probably include the nations of the Far East, such as China and Korea."[49]

Dr. David Reagan, Dr. Chuck Missler, I and several other Bible teachers also believe that the Kings of the East come from Asia.[50]

Thus, it is likely that the military force coming from the Far East is numerous and formidable. China alone has an estimated 2.7 million military personnel[51] and is ranked no.#3 among world armies.[52]

If the Kings of the East are advancing from Asia with potentially millions of military personnel and many armored fighting vehicles to come war against Jesus Christ, then why is God making their deployment across the Middle East easier by drying up the Euphrates River? Why not flood the Euphrates to impede their travels and make mobilization more difficult, which would serve to discourage and tire out the advancing troops?

Is the Lord using the "Rope-a-Dope" fighting technique to trick His enemies? This is a boxing tactic of pretending to be trapped against the ropes, goading an opponent to throw tiring ineffective punches.

The answer seems to be found in Joel 3. Joel provides some details about this final battle between Jesus Christ and the Antichrist.

> "I will also gather all nations, And bring them down to the Valley of Jehoshaphat; And I will enter into judgment with them there..." (Joel 3:2a)

> "Proclaim this among the nations: "Prepare for war! Wake up the mighty men, Let all the men of war draw near, Let them come up. Beat your plowshares into swords And your pruning hooks into spears; Let the weak say, 'I *am* strong.' " Assemble and come, all you nations, And gather together all around. Cause Your mighty ones to go down there, O Lord. "Let the nations be wakened, and come up to the Valley of Jehoshaphat; For there I will sit to judge all the surrounding nations."" (Joel 3:9-12)

"Multitudes, multitudes in the valley of decision! For the day of the Lord *is* near in the valley of decision." (Joel 3:14)

The Lord wants to make this the final battle. All adversarial nations are to gather, the mighty will be wide awake, the farmers will bring swords, the fisherman will have spears, the weak will believe they are strong. If I may be so bold to suggest; it's like the Lord is saying,

> "*Come one, come all. Let the unbelieving multitudes assemble in the valley of decision. Bring your A-game. Hit Me with your best shots. Let there be no excuses. Do you blasphemers of God and murderers of the saints want a piece of Me, come and get it. I will show you Who is the KING OF KINGS and LORD OF LORDS once and for all!*"

Isaiah says that Jesus Christ wins this great battle single-handedly.

> "I (*Jesus Christ the Messiah*) have trodden the winepress alone, And from the peoples no one *was* with Me. For I have trodden them in My anger, And trampled them in My fury; Their blood is sprinkled upon My garments, And I have stained all My robes. For the day of vengeance *is* in My heart, And the year of My redeemed has come. I looked, but *there was* no one to help, And I wondered That *there was* no one to uphold; Therefore My own arm brought salvation for Me; And My own fury, it sustained Me." (Isaiah 63:3-5; *emphasis added*)

With all of this in mind, my advice to a Chinese soldier living in the Trib-period is:

> "*Don't cross a dried-up Euphrates River and end up in Armageddon with the rest of the troops, because you won't survive! Instead, accept Christ as your Savior, and though it could cost you your life to do this, your rewards are great in heaven.*"

The Ten Kings, Ten Horns and Ten Toes

The Ten Kings, also referred to as the Ten Horns in Daniel 7:24 and Rev. 17:12, play a major role in the Trib-period. It is likely that these Ten Kings are also referred to as the Ten Toes in Daniel 2:41-42. Their story is summarized in the verse below.

> "The ten horns *are* ten kings *Who* shall arise from this kingdom. And another shall rise after them; He shall be different from the first *ones,* And shall subdue three kings." (Daniel 7:24)

The Ten Kings arise from the revived Roman Empire along with the Antichrist who becomes the eleventh king. Three of the Ten Kings eventually get subdued by the Antichrist, which then leaves a total of eight kings remaining as noted in Rev. 17:11.

Revelation 17: 12-14 – The Ten Kings are all appointed to their respective kingdoms in one hour in a political alliance with the Antichrist. They all agree to transfer their power and authority to the Antichrist. Ultimately, these kings, excluding the three that get subdued, go with the Antichrist to Armageddon to fight Jesus Christ. They lose!

> "These (*kings*) will make war with the Lamb, (*of God*) and the Lamb (*Jesus Christ*) will overcome them, for He is Lord of lords and King of kings; and those *who are* with Him *are* called, chosen, and faithful." (Rev. 17:14; *emphasis added*)

Revelation 17:16-17 – Before three kings get subdued by the Antichrist and the surviving seven kings are later overcome by Jesus Christ, the Ten Kings will *"hate the harlot, make her desolate and naked, eat her flesh and burn her with fire."*

> "And the ten horns, *(ten kings)*, which you saw on the beast, these will hate the harlot, make her desolate, *(remove all her priests from their pulpits)*, and naked, *(strip her of all wealth)* eat her flesh *(eradicate her religious practices)*, and burn her with fire, *(burn all of her religious teachings)*. For God has put it into their hearts to fulfill His purpose, to be of one mind, and to give their kingdom to the beast, until the words of God are fulfilled." (Rev. 17:16-17; *emphasis added*)

The four graphic details in these two verses of; *"make her desolate, naked, eat her flesh and burn her with fire,"* involve much more than wrapping yellow crime scene tape around the Vatican, slapping a few padlocks on Catholic cathedral doors and hanging up a sign that says, "CLOSED FOR BUSINESS!" NO; the Ten Kings remove every last vestige of this pagan religions existence because the shift of all global religious worship, commercial wealth and political power is now going to the Antichrist.

The Ten Kings are of one mind to eliminate the Harlot and to give their kingdom to the Antichrist. From his book, *There's a New World Coming*, Hal Lindsey states the following about this transitional event.

> "The question that logically comes to mind is, "When the Antichrist destroys this Harlot in the middle of the Tribulation, does he destroy some geographical location from which she rules? I personally don't think so, since that would mean destroying his own kingdom, for it is in the Antichrist's kingdom that the Harlot

has dominated. For example, if someone today wanted to break the power of the Roman Catholic Church, he wouldn't have to blow up Vatican City or the city of Rome. Assassinations of the Pope and the cardinals and bishops of the church, plus a destruction of some of the major seminaries and church buildings, and a confiscation of church property and wealth would finish the organization. I believe something like this will happen when the Antichrist destroys the false ecclesiastical system that seeks to smother him. He will purge its leaders and confiscate all its wealth. Then he will establish himself as the religious leader of the world and consolidate all worship in himself."[53]

The desolation of the Harlot occurs at the midpoint of the Trib-period, which leaves the second three and one-half years of the Trib-period available for the Antichrist to do all of his dastardly deeds.

Daniel 7:25 says that the Antichrist will speak "pompous words" against God, will "persecute" believers and "intend to change times and law" "*for a time and times and half a time,*" which amounts to three and one-half years. Rev. 13:5 informs that the Antichrist will be given a "great mouth to blaspheme" God and "authority" as the world's leader "*for forty-two months,*" which spans the entire second half of the Trib-period.

Revelation 17:13 says that the Ten Kings "*are of one mind, and they will give their power and authority to the beast.*" Rev. 17:17 says that they are "*of one mind, and to give their kingdom to the beast.*"

So, the progression of events are:

FIRST, at some future eventful one-hour the Ten Kings are appointed to their kingdoms and given exclusive authority over them. This is apparently not the result of a normal political election, which involves a campaign process that costs money and takes time, but happens by some sweeping executive order of the Antichrist.

SECOND, to oblige the Antichrist for receiving their swift appointments to their respective kingdoms, they all agree to pledge their allegiance and obedience to his rule. They become subservient to the Antichrist, but at a time when he, the Scarlet Beast, is still supporting the Scarlet Harlot's religious existence.

THIRD, at some point, which probably occurs shortly after their appointments, the Ten Kings come to hate the Harlot and then proceed to eradicate her pagan religious system. Rev. 17:17 says that God has put it into their hearts for His purposes to give their kingdom to the Antichrist. This enables the Antichrist to move into his full position of authority as the world leader.

FOURTH, accomplishing a victory over the Harlot, the kingdom that they convey to the Antichrist likely includes the wealth of their individual kingdoms and that of the Harlot, which they can obtain as the spoils of their victory over her. In receipt of the wealth of the Harlot and the Ten Kings, the Antichrist can proceed now to rule the world and establish His international cashless economy in Rev. 13:16-17. In this commercial system no one will be able to buy or sell unless they take the "Mark of the Beast."

Who are the Ten Kings and Where are their Kingdoms?

This is the fifty-million-dollar question. Some believe they are:

- Ten rulers from the Arab populations listed in Psalm 83:6-8. This is not likely because the Pre-Tribulation fulfillment of Psalm 83 occurs prior to the emergence of the Ten Kings in the Trib-period.

Also, after Psalm 83 these countries are war-torn and in the cases of Jordan, and parts of Lebanon, Syria and Egypt, annexed into a future Greater Israel. It is unlikely that the Antichrist will give authority over a kingdom to a king or politician from a conquered Arab state. Additionally, these Arabs are mostly Islamic and the Antichrist will be pushing his own non-Islamic brand of false religion through the ten kingdoms. (The expansion of Israel is explained in my book entitled, *The Now Prophecies*.)

- Ten leaders from amongst the Ezekiel invaders in Ezekiel 38:1-6. This is advocated primarily by Joel Richardson, who believes in an Islamic Antichrist and an Islamic Harlot. This possibility is likewise not likely because these invaders appear to be conquered prior to the Trib-period.

The similar logic above about Psalm 83 can be applied here. Would the Antichrist select a ruler from a defeated country? Additionally, most of these invading countries are Islamic as well. Moreover, there are only nine, not ten, populations listed in Ezekiel 38:1-6. (I write about the Pre-Tribulation timing of Ezekiel 38 in my book entitled, *The Next Prophecies*.)

On a related side note, Joel Richardson and I debated the topic of the identity of Mystery Babylon. Joel advocated for an Islamic Harlot based out of Mecca and I argued the case that the Catholic Church headquartered in Rome was the likely candidate for this mysterious woman of Revelation 17. The event turned out to be an important three-hour discussion between Christian brothers, rather than an aggressive debate between adversaries possessing opposing views. This debate is highly instructional and available at my bookstore at *www.prophecydepot.com*. It is entitled, "*The Identity of Mystery Babylon: Mecca or Rome.*"

- Ten politicians that are selected from the world at large. At the time the world at large will be reeling from wars and divine judgments and recovering from resultant famines, scarcities and pestilences. As such, sorting through the assortment of world politicians, that are not already among the Kings of the Earth, could be a daunting proposition, but it is a possibility. However, the next option, which appears to be the most logical one, should rule out all these other three afore listed scenarios.

- Ten European politicians that come from the revived Roman Empire. This view is best presented by Dr. Arnold Fruchtenbaum in his book entitled, *The Footsteps of the Messiah, A Study of the Sequence of Prophetic Events.* I have already quoted from Fruchtenbaum's book several times and I highly recommend it to everyone that is serious about the study of Bible prophecy. It's available through Amazon or by scrolling through the bookstore at *www.ariel.org.*

Fruchtenbaum points out that when it comes to understanding the identity of the Ten Kings that the dream of Nebuchadnezzar in Daniel 2 needs to be compared to Daniel's dream with visions in his head described in Daniel 7.

Nebuchadnezzar's dream, which is detailed in Daniel 2:31-33, had a head of fine gold, a chest and arms of silver, a belly and thighs of bronze, and two legs of iron with feet having ten toes that were partly of iron and partly of clay. This dream represented the four dominant Gentile Empires and their futures. These empires are Babylon (gold), Medo-Persia (silver), Greece (bronze) and Rome (iron mixed with clay). Daniel's dream recorded in Daniel 7 also alluded to these four empires.

As a result of comparing the details between these two chapters, Fruchtenbaum provides the following outline of the fourth Gentile Empire, which is the Roman Empire.

The Fourth Empire

a. The United Stage – The Roman Empire
b. The Two Division Stage – The East-West Balance of Power

    c. The One World Government Stage

    d. The Ten Division Stage – The Ten Kingdoms

    e. The Antichrist Stage.[54]

How this outline translates is that the *United Stage* was the historic Roman Empire. The *Two Division Stage*, which is represented by the two legs of the image, followed around 364 AD when the Roman Empire split between the East and West. The Western Roman Empire remained headquartered in Rome, but the Eastern leg moved to Constantinople. Fruchtenbaum says:

> "*In the original division of the east-west axis, these two cities controlled the balance of power. Since then the centers of the balance of power have shifted, but it has remained an east-west division... The eastern division of power remained in Constantinople until 1453, when it collapsed in the Turkish invasion. When Constantinople fell, the political rulers fled northward into Russia and infiltrated the government there. The rulers called themselves Czars, which is Russian for "Caesar." Eventually, the eastern balance of power was centered in the Soviet Union and included the Communist block of nations.... The western division of power remained in Rome.*"[55]

It's interesting to note that *Czar* is Russian for *Caesar* and *Kaiser* is German for *Caesar*. Russia is part of the eastern leg of the divided Roman Empire and Germany belongs to the western leg of the empire.

The evolvement from the *Two Division Stage* into the *One World Government Stage* is predicted in the verse below.

> "Thus he said: 'The fourth beast, *(of the Roman Empire)*, shall be A fourth kingdom on earth, Which shall be different from all other kingdoms,

And shall devour the whole earth, Trample it and break it in pieces.'" *(Daniel 7:23; emphasis added)*

The, *"And shall devour the whole earth,"* detail references a future attribute of the Roman Empire. After the Roman Empire splits between the east and the west, it revives itself in some capacity to devour the whole earth. Then, as per the verse below, it morphs from the *One World Government Stage* into the *Ten Division Stage.*

> "The ten horns are ten kings Who shall arise from this kingdom. And another shall rise after them; He shall be different from the first ones, And shall subdue three kings." (Daniel 7:24)

In Daniel's vision he saw the Roman Empire in the form of a fourth beast that had ten horns on its head in Daniel 7:20. These turn out to be the ten kings that emerge out from the world government. Then, the next verse in succession identifies the final stage of the revived Roman Empire as the Antichrist Stage.

> "He, *(the Antichrist)*, shall speak *pompous* words against the Most High, Shall persecute the saints of the Most High, And shall intend to change times and law. Then *the saints* shall be given into his hand For a time and times and half a time." (Daniel 7:25; *emphasis added*)

Fruchtenbaum summarizes the Ten Division Stage as follows:

> *"It has become common today to refer to the ten kingdoms as being in Europe only, especially the European Union. But the text does not allow for this kind of interpretation. At the very best, the European Union might become one of the ten, but it could hardly become all of them...More consistent with Daniel's prophecy is the recommendation of*

*the Club of Rome that the world be divided into ten
administrative districts to avoid a world economic
collapse."*[56]

The Club of Rome was founded in 1968 and after evaluating
200,000 equations they issued a report in 1974. The gist of the
report distinguished that ten world regions could be formed to
hedge against the potential of a future global economic crisis.[57]

Daniel 7:24 predicted that the Antichrist will subdue three of
the ten kings. This appears to happen after the Harlot's desolation
in Rev. 17:16, which makes it clear that all ten of the kings
participate in her overthrow. They are all on board at that time
and they transfer their kingdoms to the Antichrist. However, three
kings develop a change of heart for some reason.

Why do three kings rebel after the fact? I suggest that they
all jump on the bandwagon in support of the Antichrist political
and economic agendas, which includes the global cashless society
of Rev. 13:17. They all agree with the Antichrist that the Harlot
World Religion will ultimately become an obstacle to their
collective success. As such, they eliminate this Whore of Babylon
at the request of the Antichrist.

Then, possessing enormous power under his belt, the Antichrist
proceeds to enter into the Third Jewish Temple and, *"exalts himself
above all that is called God or that is worshiped, so that he sits as God
in the temple of God,"* and shows himself off that he is God, as
predicted in 2 Thessalonians 2:4.

In my thinking, this over the top act becomes unacceptable to the
political aspirations of the three kings. Everything was acceptable to
them up to that unexpected point. Upon witnessing his bold behavior,
they will likely reason, we just eliminated one global religion in favor
of a comprehensive political and commercial solution, the last thing
we need now at this critical juncture of time is another alternative
world religion run by a charismatic religious fanatic.

I could be wrong, but I have yet to uncover a more logical explanation that causes three kings to rebel and ultimately be subdued.

Summarizing the Ten Kings

In my estimation, the Antichrist rezones the world into ten regions and then appoints ten qualified politicians from within his administration to implement his political and economic policies within these provinces. These are the Ten Kings. The Antichrist expects these ten kings in his court to be yes men and for a while they all are.

One of the first orders of business that the Antichrist commands of his team, is the elimination of the Harlot religious system and the confiscation of all her wealth. The second order of business is to establish a global cashless economic system within the ten newly created districts. Up to this point, the Ten Kings are all in agreement with the wishes of the Antichrist.

After these things are fulfilled, the Antichrist promotes himself as the world's supreme religious leader and that's the point where he alienates three of the ten kings. These could have been former Catholics who the Antichrist had convinced that Catholicism was a problematic religion that had turned pagan. But, when they witness the Antichrist declare that he's God, they decide, probably collective decide, that he MUST BE STOPPED!

The King of the South and The King of the North

As we conclude this chapter on the end times kings, the final two to mention are both referenced the same verse below.

> "At the time of the end the king of the South shall attack him; (*the Antichrist*), and the king of the North shall come against him like a whirlwind, with chariots, horsemen, and with many ships;

and he shall enter the countries, overwhelm,
(*subdue*), them, and pass through." (Daniel
11:40; *emphasis added*)

These two kings are subdued by the Antichrist. They could
be two of the three rebellious kings, or they could be two entirely
different kings. Whoever they are, they have a problem with the
Antichrist's attempt to take over their respective countries.

The King of the South and the King of the North are each
spoken of eight times in Daniel 11. Most agree that the first seven
references to these kings identify the King of the North as Syria
and the King of the South as Egypt. There are historical events that
appear to make this a correct assessment. However, this may not
be the same case of national identity in Daniel 11:40.

After the impending destruction of Damascus in Isaiah 17:1
and the desolation of other major Syrian cities in Isaiah 17:9, Syria
may not even exist at the time. Also, the prophecy predicts that the
King of the North will come against the Antichrist like a "*whirlwind,
with chariots, horsemen, and with many ships.*" It is doubtful that
after the projected prophetic fulfillments of Isaiah 17, that Syria
will even have a navy, let alone "*many ships.*" Presently the navy is
the smallest component within Syria's entire armed forces.

The King of the South is not likely Egypt because, in Daniel
11:40 this king attacks the Antichrist, but in the two verses below
it's the Antichrist that does the attacking of Egypt along with
Libya and Ethiopia.

"He, (*the Antichrist*), shall stretch out his hand
against the countries, and the land of Egypt shall
not escape. He shall have power over the treasures
of gold and silver, and over all the precious things
of Egypt; also the Libyans and Ethiopians shall
follow at his heels." (Daniel 11:42-43; *emphasis
added*)

17

Believers in the Tribulation Period

Although all Christian believers will be removed from the earth via the Rapture, there will be an innumerable multitude of replacements that exist afterward. These believers come to faith either within the Post-Rapture / Pre-Trib time-gap or in the Trib-period.

> "After these things I looked, and behold, a great multitude which no one could number, of all nations, tribes, peoples, and tongues, standing before the throne and before the Lamb, clothed with white robes, with palm branches in their hands." (Rev. 7:9)

The fact that this group stands *before the throne and before the Lamb* indicates that they are believers. The white robes represent their garments of salvation. These are believers from around the globe that come from, *all nations, tribes, peoples, and tongues.* The clue as to the timing of their existence is in the opening words, *After these things,* which are the two Greek words, *meta tauta.*

These believers come to their saving faith (*meta tauta*), after these things below:

1. The Church Age has run its course in Revelation 2 and 3.

2. The True Church is removed from earth and pictured in heaven in Revelation 4 and 5.

3. 144,000 Witnesses emerge as earthly evangelizers in Revelation 7:1-8.

This chapter will explore the following topics:

*   The method of salvation after the Rapture.

*   The relationship between the Holy Spirit and the Post-Rapture believer.

*   The two killing crusades that martyr Christians after the Rapture.

*   The three periods of Post Rapture Christian martyrdom.

The method of salvation after the Rapture

> "Nor is there salvation in any other, for there is no other name (*than Jesus Christ*) under heaven given among men by which we must be saved." (Acts 4:12; *emphasis added*)

> "Jesus said to him, "I am the way, the truth, and the life. No one comes to the Father except through Me." (John 14:6)

When it comes to a person's salvation after the Rapture, there is no biblical basis to deviate from the one and only scripturally supported way of salvation. No additional name, no new truth and no freshly paved pathway to heaven is provided in scripture apart from Jesus Christ. Thus, the same method for salvation for the Church Age believers applies to the Post-Rapture believer. The means of achieving this is provided in the appendix entitled, "The Sinner's Salvation Prayer."

The relationship between the Holy Spirit and the Post-Rapture believer

A Church Age believer is blessed to receive the indwelling of the Holy Spirit. Does this process carry over to the Post-Rapture believer? Some teach that the role of the Holy Spirit changes when Jesus Christ comes and catches up His Bride the Church up into heaven.

The thinking, in part, is that the Holy Spirit is the restrainer of Satan in 2 Thess. 2:6-7 and when the Church gets raptured, the Holy Spirit reverts back to His former role as depicted in the Old Testament. These advocates refer to a verse in the Psalms that pointed out that the Holy Spirit could be taken from someone.

"Do not cast me away from Your presence, And do not take Your Holy Spirit from me." (Psalm 51:11)

The Holy Spirit does not appear to remove Himself from the earth when the Rapture occurs, however at or around the same time, He backs off from hindering Satan any further. In other words He presently is multi-tasking and performing the following functions:

1.   Indwelling believers (John 14:17),
2.   Helping believers (John 14:16, 26, 15:26, 16:7),
3.   Speaking to believers (Rev. 2:7, 11, 17, 29 Rev. 3:6, 13, 22),
4.   Teaching believers (John 14:26),
5.   Testifying about Jesus Christ (John 15:26),
6.   Convicting the world of sin, righteousness and judgment (John 16:18),
7.   Restraining Satan and lawlessness (2 Thess. 2:6-7).

When the Rapture happens, all that we are told is that the Holy Spirit stops doing #7, which is the restraining of Satan and lawlessness. However, we are not informed if He stops performing the functions of #1 through #6 above. In fact, there are two references in the book of Revelation that imply the Holy Spirit remains active on earth after the Rapture.

> "Then I heard a voice from heaven saying to me, "Write: 'Blessed are the dead who die in the Lord from now on.'" "Yes," says the Spirit, "that they may rest from their labors, and their works follow them."" (Rev. 14:13)

In this verse the Holy Spirit is fulfilling functions #2, #3, and #4. He is *helping, speaking* and *teaching* Post-Rapture believers by preparing them for the reality of martyrdom and informing them that they are blessed, will have rest from their labors and that their service to God will be rewarded.

> "And the Spirit and the bride say, "Come!" And let him who hears say, "Come!" And let him who thirsts come. Whoever desires, let him take the water of life freely." (Rev. 22:17)

In this verse the Holy Spirit is fulfilling functions #2, #3, #4, #5 and #6. He is *helping* by *speaking* the invitation to *"Come"* and *"take the water of life freely,"* which according to John 4:10-15 and 7:37-39, *testifies of Jesus Christ.* This also *teaches* the manner of salvation and how to evangelize… *"And let him who hears say, "Come!"* In other words, the Spirit and bride say come, but also him who hears should echo the same evangelical invitation to *"Come!"* Lastly, the reference to *"him who thirsts"* is a function of *convicting* that individual *of sin, judgment and righteousness.*

However, in the two verses above we are not specifically told if the Holy Spirit is still fulfilling function #1 of the continued indwelling of believers. The three reasons that I believe that He indwells Post-Rapture believers are below.

1. All believers appear to be benefactors of the NEW COVENANT.

> "Behold, the days are coming, says the Lord, when I will make a new covenant with the house of Israel and with the house of Judah— not according to the covenant that I made with their fathers in the day that I took them by the hand to lead them out of the land of Egypt, My covenant which they broke, though I was a husband to them, says the Lord. But this is the covenant that I will make with the house of Israel after those days, says the Lord: I will put My law in their minds, and write it on their hearts; and I will be their God, and they shall be My people." (Jeremiah 31:31-33)

The New Covenant is a promise to get God's divine law into the minds of believers by writing it on their hearts. This is not laser technology, rather it involves the indwelling of the Holy Spirit, Who, living inside the believer indelibly etches God's law upon their hearts. This is a miraculous process and not a technological undertaking. The verse below explains how the sacrificial blood of Jesus Christ relates to the New Covenant.

> "Likewise He also took the cup after supper, saying, "This cup is the new covenant in My blood, which is shed for you."" (Luke 22:20)

At the last supper, which is celebrated as the Holy Communion that commemorates the sacrifice of Jesus Christ for the atonement of all sins, Jesus declares that His blood was shed on behalf of the New Covenant. When covenants were made historically, blood was shed as a sacrifice to validate the covenant. Without the shedding of blood a covenant lacked the appropriate confirmation.

The covenantal process typically involved the slaughter of animals and the division of their body parts, in such a way as to create a pathway for the covenanting parties to pass through. The respective parties would walk together through the bloody mess and the implication afterward was; *"If either of us breaks this covenant in the future, may we become likened to the gory scenario we just created and walked through."*

This acknowledgement was intended to bind the parties into the specific performances of their promises to one another. A biblical example of this process is the Abrahamic Covenant written about in Genesis 15.

The following verses demonstrate the important role of the Holy Spirit in relationship to the implementation of the New Covenant.

> "And I will pray the Father, and He will give you another Helper, that He may abide with you forever—The (*Holy*) Spirit of truth, whom the world cannot receive, because it neither sees Him nor knows Him; but you know Him, for He dwells with you and will be in you." (John 14:16-17; *emphasis added*)

> "But the Helper, the Holy Spirit, whom the Father will send in My name, He will teach, (*write upon your heart*), you all things, (*God's divine law*) and bring to your remembrance (*and get into your mind*) all things that I said to you." (John 14:26; *emphasis added*)

In these three John 14 verses above, Jesus points out that He will ask God the Father to send the Holy Spirit to believers to help them. The process is not for the world at large which, *cannot receive, because it neither sees Him nor knows Him,* but for believers only. The Holy Spirit is to indwell and abide with the believer forever. From the vantage point of being with and within the believer, the Holy Spirit, *first* teaches all things relative to God and *second*, brings that information to remembrance.

In other words, the Holy Spirit performs the functions of the New Covenant. The blood of Jesus was the confirmation of the New Covenant, but the Holy Spirit takes responsibility for the Jeremiah 31:33 commitment, which said; *"I will put My law in their minds, and write it on their hearts."*

When Jesus made these Holy Spirit pledges above, it was prior to the commencement of the Church, which happened months later in the Acts 2 Pentecost account. This might imply that these Holy Spirit activities are for all believers whether they accepted Christ just prior to Pentecost, during the Church Age, or after the Rapture.

2. The Holy Spirit is promised to abide with and indwell a believer FOREVER.

John 14:16-17 was quoted above. These verses speak about the intimacy and permanency of the relationship between the Holy Spirit and a believer. Perhaps this only applies to a Church Age believer, but these verses don't seem to make that specification. Thus, the abiding and indwelling of believers likely occurs after the Rapture.

3. Since the method of salvation is the same after the Rapture, why wouldn't the indwelling of the Holy Spirit also remain the same after the Rapture?

It would seem to make most sense that the salvation of someone and the ensuing incorporating of that person into the New Covenant would still involve:

a. Accepting Christ as the Savior,
b. Receiving the indwelling of the Holy Spirit as a Helper,
c. Getting God's law into their minds by writing it upon their hearts.

Unless there is clear biblical evidence that excludes Post-Rapture believers as benefactors of the New Covenant, or that specifically acknowledges the termination of the Holy Spirit's indwelling ministry, then I for one will continue to teach and encourage all believers that the Holy Spirit will usher them into the New Covenant through the miraculous process of dwelling within them.

The two killing crusades that martyr Christians after the Rapture

Receiving Jesus Christ as one's Lord and Savior after the Rapture will be an amazing and courageous achievement. This is because it will likely end in a martyr's death. After the Rapture there are at least two religious systems that discriminately persecute and kill true Christians.

These two are the Harlot and the Antichrist. Per Revelation 17:6, the Harlot is *"drunk with the blood of the saints and with the blood of the martyrs of Jesus."* Per Revelation 13:15-17 and 20:4, the Antichrist will kill believers for refusing to receive the "Mark of the Beast."

Another problem facing the person that puts off their salvation until after the Rapture is that receiving Christ will not necessarily be a popular choice. This is because Satan will be misleading the masses through supernatural deception into thinking there is an alternative truth and reality that refutes the biblical narrative. Through powerful signs and lying wonders, the Devil will be promoting what the 2 Thess.2:9-11 calls, "The Lie."

Someone who accepts Christ after the Rapture won't flip a coin to make this decision. It will involve counting the cost of following Christ and seeing through overpowering influential deception.

In addition to the martyrdom verses above, an additional passage of scripture describes Christian martyrdom. It is discoverable in the verses below.

> "When He opened the fourth seal, I heard the voice of the fourth living creature saying, "Come and see." So I looked, and behold, a pale horse. And the name of him who sat on it was Death, and Hades followed with him. And power was given to them over a fourth of the earth, to kill with sword, with hunger, with death, and by the beasts of the earth. When He opened the fifth seal, I saw under the altar the souls of those who had been slain for the word of God and for the testimony which they held." (Rev. 6:7-9)

These verses imply that the pale horsemen of the Apocalypse, named Death and Hades, are responsible for the slain souls of the Fifth Seal Saints. Death and Hades could represent a third independent source that martyrs Post Rapture believers, but more than likely these tandem riders are an embodiment of either the Harlot or the Antichrist.

Death and Hades do not likely represent the Antichrist for two reasons.

1. The Antichrist is the White Horseman and Death and Hades are the Pale Horsemen of the Apocalypse. These two horses carry distinctly different riders who operate independent of each other. The Antichrist is given a crown and instructed to go out conquering and to conquer. Death and Hades are given authority over a quarter of the earth's population to kill believers.

2. The Antichrist's killing crusade doesn't start until the middle of the Trib-period, but Death and Hades and the Harlot world religion begin their targeted murders beforehand.

Therefore, based upon these two reasons above, the logical conclusion is that Death and Hades seemingly find association with the Harlot world religion. Or, more boldly and directly stated; DEATH AND HADES are associated with "MYSTERY, BABYLON THE GREAT, THE MOTHER OF HARLOTS AND OF THE ABOMINATIONS OF THE EARTH."

If this is the case then whoever THE MOTHER OF HARLOTS represents could be the personification of the fourth horsemen of Death and Hades. In this book generally, and in the *Next Prophecies* book specifically, I have pinned the tail of the donkey on the Roman Catholic Church as the world religion of the Harlot.

One might ask, "*Why would the self-acclaimed "One-True Christian Church" called, Roman Catholic Church, kill true Christian believers?*" My answer, provided in the form of a corresponding question is, "Why did this same religious institution kill scores of true believers during the inquisitions of the centuries past?" During those dark ages, it was about following the Catholic way or hitting the highway and being labeled as a heretic. This paragraph leads to the pertinent point of the prophetic verse below.

> "I saw the woman (*Harlot*), drunk with the blood of the saints, (*during the past Catholic inquisitions*), and with the blood of the martyrs of Jesus, (*in future Catholic inquisitions*). And when I saw her, I marveled with great amazement." (Rev. 17:6; *emphasis added*)

Below are a couple of quotes that deal with the past and future aspects of this verse. The next two quotes also connects the Roman Catholic Church with the harlot religion.

> "*The meaning here* (Revelation 17:6) *is, that the persecuting power referred to had shed the blood of the saints; and that, in its fury, it had, as it were, drunk the blood of the slain, and had*

become, by drinking that blood, intoxicated and infuriated. No one need say how applicable this has been to the papacy (Roman Catholic Church) … Let the blood shed in the valleys of Piedmont; the blood shed in the Low Countries by the Duke of Alva; the blood shed on Bartholomew's day; and the blood shed in the Inquisition, testify."[58] (American Theologian Albert Barnes - December 1, 1798 – December 24, 1870)

"*When the true church is caught up* [raptured]… *the Roman Catholic "church" will see a great revival. For a time she has been stripped of the temporal power she once had, but it will be restored to her… And she was drunken with the blood of the Saints and with the blood of the martyrs of Jesus, so that John wondered with a great wonder. Such were her cruel, wicked, Satanic deeds in the past…It could never be true of the literal Babylon. Nor does it mean, as Romish expositors of this book claim, pagan Rome, for if it meant the persecutions under the Roman Emperors, John would not have wondered with a great wonder. And the last page of her* (Roman Catholic Church) *cruel, horrible, persecutions is not yet written. When she comes to power again, she will do the same thing.*" (Arno C. Gaebelein) [59]

Let me add a caveat about the Catholic Church. Although the religious institution gets left behind and apparently functions as the Harlot World Religion, that doesn't mean that every Catholic gets left behind also. A Catholic that has been born again and received Jesus Christ as their Lord and Savior, prior to the Rapture, will be Raptured! They will be caught up into the clouds in the twinkling of an eye along with everyone else who has made this same conversion.

The three periods of Post Rapture Christian martyrdom

Thus, there are at least two Christian killing crusades after the Rapture, first is that of the Harlot and second by the Antichrist. These campaigns take place over the three primary Post-Rapture time-periods. They are:

1. The Post-Rapture / Pre-Tribulation gap period,
2. The first half of the Trib-period,
3. The second half of the Trib-period, also referred to as the "Great Tribulation."

These time frames of martyrdom can be determined in part by interpreting the Lord's response to the pleadings of the Fifth Seal Saints. First we will look at the pleadings and second we will explore the response.

The Pleadings of the Fifth Seal Saints

> "When He opened the fifth seal, I saw under the altar the souls of those who had been slain for the word of God and for the testimony which they held. And they cried with a loud voice, saying, "How long, O Lord, holy and true, until You judge and avenge our blood on those who dwell on the earth?" (Rev. 6:9-10)

The traditional view of the seal judgments teaches that these saints of the fifth seal are martyred during the Tribulation period. Below is the quote from Dr. John Walvoord that is repeated from a prior chapter concerning the identity of the saints of the fifth seal.

> *"These are obviously martyrs, mentioned in more detail in Revelation 7. This makes it clear that souls will be saved in the Great Tribulation, but many of them will be martyred."*

The problem I have with this interpretation is found in the telling question that these martyred saints ask: *"How long, O Lord, holy and true, until You judge and avenge our blood on those who dwell on the earth?"*

If these saints of the fifth seal are martyred in the "Great Tribulation," shouldn't they know how much longer until the Lord judges and avenges their blood that was shed by the earth dwellers? Wouldn't they have witnessed the confirmation of the Daniel 9:27 seven-year covenant that starts the Tribulation period? Wouldn't they be able to accurately identify their existence within the seven-year timeline?

The pleadings are voiced because the killing spree perpetrated by Death and Hades is so deadly that these saints cry out with a loud voice for an answer as to how much longer it will continue. These saints have already been slain for the word of God and for their testimonies, but they are obviously concerned for their loved ones who are still alive and grappling with the onslaught of Death and Hades.

The fact that they don't know how much longer these killings will continue, strongly suggests that they have been martyred during the Post-Rapture / Pre-Tribulation gap period. This period has no specific time attributed to it in the Scriptures.

The timing of the slaying of the Fifth Seal Saints can be logically deduced by realizing that if the Seven-Year Tribulation Period had already started, they would be able to calendar the days remaining until the Second Coming of Christ. The problem is that they don't know how much longer until Christ's return and that's why they ask this timing related question?

I mean, these men and women were slain for the word of God. The fact that the Trib-period lasts for seven years is repeated numerous times in several different ways in the Scriptures. They must know that the Trib-period is coming and how long it lasts, but apparently they just don't know "how long" until it starts.

It's important to recognize that when the saints of the fifth seal make their decision to accept Christ as their Savior, they will do this knowing full well that it could cost them their lives. Before they are martyred, these saints convert to Christianity at a time in the future when the prophetic awareness is at an all-time high. They will have likely witnessed the fulfillment of some or all of the *NOW Prophecies* which were listed in the prior chapter entitled, *"Recapping the NOW and NEXT Prophecies."*

The Lord's Response to the Fifth Seal Saints

Back to the pertinent question asked by the Fifth Seal Saints, *"How long, O Lord, holy and true, until You judge and avenge our blood on those who dwell on the earth?"* The Lord's response to their question is interesting. He sums up the metric of time by identifying their Christian condition. Christ says that He will return when the full number of believers who are martyred for their faith is complete. Christ identifies the three phases of Christian martyrdom for them.

> "Then a white robe was given to each of them; (*Group 1*) and it was said to them that they should rest a little while longer, until both the number of *"their fellow servants"* (*Group 2*) and *"their brethren,"* (*Group 3*) who would be killed as they were, was completed." (Rev. 6:11; emphasis added)

The three phases of Christian martyrdom after the Rapture, apparently breakdown in the manner described below.

1. *The Post-Rapture / Pre-Tribulation gap period:* (*Group 1*) - This phase is when the *Fifth Seal Saints* are slain. They are likely among those killed by the Harlot, who is "the woman" in Revelation 17:6, who is "drunk with the blood of the saints and with the blood of the martyrs of Jesus."

2. *The first half of the Trib-period:* (*Group 2*) - The second phase involves the *"fellow servants"* of the *Fifth Seal Saints*. They are seemingly killed during the first half of the Trib-period by the same executioner as the *Fifth Seal Saints*. The Harlot is drunk with their blood also. The fact that they are martyred by the same hands appropriately classifies them as *fellow servants* with the *Fifth Seal Saints*.

3. *The second half of the Trib-period:* (*Group 3*) - The final phase of martyrdom involves the *"brethren"* of the *fellow servants* who previously died in the second phase. By the time the *brethren* are martyred, the Harlot will have been desolated by the ten kings in Rev. 17:16. This means the *brethren* are killed by a different source. The *brethren* are beheaded by the Antichrist for refusing to worship him by taking his "Mark of the Beast." The fact that they die during the Trib-period adequately categorizes them with the *fellow servants*, who also died in the Trib-period, as *their brethren*.

The martyrdom that takes place during the killings of groups one and two of the Fifth Seal Saints, martyred during the gap, and their fellow servants, killed in the first half of the Trib-period, will be via the methods below.

> *"And power was given to them,* (Death and Hades as the Harlot world religion), *over a fourth of the earth, to kill with sword, with hunger, with death, and by the beasts of the earth."* (Rev. 17:8; emphasis added).

Those martyred in group 3 by the Antichrist will be beheaded for rejecting his "mark of the beast."

> "And I saw thrones, and they sat on them, and judgment was committed to them. Then I saw

the souls of those who had been beheaded for their witness to Jesus and for the word of God, who had not worshiped the beast or his image, and had not received his mark on their foreheads or on their hands. And they lived and reigned with Christ for a thousand years." (Rev. 20:4)

3 Periods of Post-Rapture Christian Martyrdom

False Covenant Confirmed		Ten Kings Desolate Harlot	
Harlot kills *5th Seal Saints*	**Harlot kills** *Fellow Servants* of 5th Seal Saints	**Antichrist Beheads** *Brethren* of Fellow Servants	
Post-Rapture Pre-Trib Time-Gap *"How Long oh Lord?"*	First three and one-half years 1260 Days	Midpoint	Second three and one-half years 1260 Days

18

Technologies in the Tribulation Period

"When they, (*the Two Witnesses*), finish their testimony, the beast, (*the Antichrist*) that ascends out of the bottomless pit will make war against them, overcome them, and kill them. And their dead bodies *will lie* in the street of the great city, (*of Jerusalem*), which spiritually is called Sodom and Egypt, where also our Lord, (*Jesus Christ*), was crucified. Then *those* from the peoples, tribes, tongues, and nations will see their dead bodies three-and-a-half days, and not allow their dead bodies to be put into graves." (Revelation 11:7-9; *emphasis added*)

This prophecy was written by John the Apostle about 2000 years ago at a time when it was utterly impossible for a worldwide audience to see two dead bodies lying in the streets of Jerusalem.

"Then those who dwell in the cities of Israel will go out and set on fire and burn the weapons, (*of the Magog invaders*), both the shields and bucklers, the bows and arrows, the javelins and spears; and they will make fires with them for seven years. They will not take wood from the field nor cut down *any* from the forests, (*for alternative fuel or energy purposes*), because they will make fires with the weapons; and they will

> plunder those who plundered them, and pillage
> those who pillaged them," says the Lord God."
> (Ezekiel 39:9-10; *emphasis added*)

This prophecy was written by Ezekiel the Prophet over 2500 years ago at a time when there weren't enough bows, arrows, javelins and spears in the world, let alone in the arsenals of the Magog invaders, to make bonfires throughout Israel for one year, let alone seven years.

These are just two among several prophecies that required the future creation of a technology to facilitate their final fulfillment. When the biblical prophecies were penned upon their parchments centuries ago, the authors did the best they could, within the limitations of the vernaculars of their time, to provide us with the details of their predictions.

The vocabularies of the ancient Hebrew prophets didn't include terms like Computers, Navigation Satellites, Drones or A.I., (artificial intelligence). These incredible individuals were given the daunting task of explaining the globally impacting events of the end times.

Some of us today would have likely declined to respond to such a calling. If I was given the responsibility 2000 years ago to explain the origin and identity of the Antichrist, or Gog of Magog, I would have probably ☞ pointed my index finger to the east and said: "*Oh yeah, those guys, they are up to no good and they went that-a-way.*"

This chapter will attempt to identify in the present a few of the technologies that were predicted in the past.

WWW. (World Wide Web) and Flying Machines

> "But you, Daniel, shut up the words, and seal the
> book until the time of the end; many shall run to
> and fro, and knowledge shall increase." (Daniel
> 11:4)

Daniel was informed of a future time when transportation methods would be improved and knowledge would be increased. As time passed:

1. Pens became keyboards,
2. Ancient parchments became computers,
3. Tribal talk became Social Networks,
4. Horse and buggies became cars,
5. Covered wagons became buses and trains,
6. Chariots became tanks, and stealth fighter jets,
7. Sailing ships became nuclear submarines,
8. Canoes became cruise liners,
9. Flying machines became commercial airliners.

Daniel 11:4 has multiple applications for the end times and since these applications are being fulfilled now, this is another indicator that these are the last days.

First, the Internet opened up the information age and knowledge in general has increased dramatically. Almost any topic someone wants to research is available over the Internet in just seconds.

Second, trips to far away locations that would take months-worth of travel can be made now in a day's time. One week in the summer of 2018, I spoke in America and the next week I taught in Australia. Thus, people are now traveling to and fro and to faraway places that were once considered unchartered territories.

Third, the vision that Daniel was told to seal up pertained to end times events that he wouldn't necessarily understand, nor be affected by. They were prophecies concerning a future final generation. Since these prophecies are starting to be revealed, this implies that they have become unsealed, which is further evidence that this is the "*time of the end.*"

Satellite Technologies

In 1957, "Sputnik 1" was sent into orbit, which gave the former Soviet Union the distinction of launching the first human made object into space. Shortly afterwards, on January 31, 1958 NASA launched America's first satellite into space called, "Explorer 1."

Since Sputnik 1, about 8,100 satellites from more than 40 countries have been launched. According to a 2018 estimate, some 4,900 remain in orbit, of those about 1,900 were operational; while the rest have lived out their useful lives and become space debris.[60]

There are several different types of satellites, but for the purposes of this chapter we will only explore, Communication and Drone Satellites.

Communication Satellites are satellites placed in orbit around the earth in order to relay television, radio, and telephone signals. These devices are primarily used for television, telephone, radio, internet, and military applications. Through these satellites the fulfillment of the following prophecies becomes possible.

> "Then *those* from the peoples, tribes, tongues, and nations will see their dead bodies three-and-a-half days, and not allow their dead bodies to be put into graves." (Rev. 11:9)

This prophecy opened up this chapter. Rumor has it in times past that Bible skeptics would quote this verse to argue against the inerrancy of scripture. They would ask, *"How can someone living far outside of Jerusalem "see" two dead bodies lying on the streets of that city?"*

Well, the answer is *"Communication Satellites."* These days one is not required to be an eyewitness of an event to see it. They will be able to watch it secondhand, live or prerecorded on TV, or over the Internet via a personal computer or a smart phone.

The same holds true for the prophecies below.

> "The kings of the earth who committed fornication and lived luxuriously with her will weep and lament for her, when they see the smoke of her burning, standing at a distance, (*secondhand*), for fear of her torment, saying, 'Alas, alas, that great city Babylon, that mighty city! For in one hour your judgment has come.'" (Rev. 18:9-10; *emphasis added*)

This prophecy finds fulfillment at the end of the Trib-period. It is not likely that every king upon the earth will be assembled on location at end times Babylon to watch its one-hour destruction firsthand. In fact, we are told just the opposite that, "*they see the smoke of her burning, standing at a distance.*"

> "'For in one hour such great riches came to nothing.' Every shipmaster, all who travel by ship, sailors, and as many as trade on the sea, stood at a distance and cried out when they saw the smoke of her burning, saying, 'What *is* like this great city?'" (Rev. 18:17-18)

The one-hour destruction of commercial Babylon is also seen secondhand by every "*shipmaster*," "*sailor and as many as trade on the sea.*" This grouping also, "*stood at a distance and cried out when they saw the smoke of her burning,*" when they watched it through Communications Satellite technologies.

Some teach that this verse requires that the city of commercial Babylon must be near a deep-water seaport to in order for them to see the burning smoke. Although this city could be near such a port, due to the video technologies that exist today, it is not necessarily a mandatory requirement for the fulfillment of this prophecy.

Drone Satellites are involved in both aviation arenas and in space technologies. A drone refers to an unpiloted aircraft or spacecraft. Another term for it is an "unmanned aerial vehicle," or UAV. Technically speaking, spaceborne drones could include cargo spacecraft, satellites and machines that leave Earth, although they aren't usually referred to as such.[61]

Some Bible prophecy teachers, like Pastor Billy Crone, are making an interesting connection between drone technologies and A.I. (*Artificial Intelligence*) developments. A.I. is a field of computer science that deals with machine intelligence, which is the information-based intellect demonstrated by machines, in contrast to the natural intelligence displayed by humans.

Some of the most advanced uses of A.I. is found in the field of Robotics, which is the branch of technology that deals with the design, construction, operation, and application of robots. Billy Crone is at the forefront of explaining the potential prophetic connections between drones, A.I. and Robots.

When Billy Crone and I taught together in Vancouver, Canada in October of 2018 at the Prophecy Source conference (https://www.prophecysource.com/), Billy informed me that he was on the cusp of discovering multiple prophecies involving these technologies. His studies are still in the early stages and I encourage you to visit his website to stay apprised of his discoveries in this area. Billy Crone's website is: (https://www.getalifemedia.com/).

Within the developing area of study of Drones, A.I. and Robotics in relationship to Bible prophecy, there are some that suggest the locusts of the Fifth Trumpet Judgment may actually be drones or robots that are fitted with A.I. Although, I do believe that A.I. made drones and / or robots will likely play a role of some sort in Bible prophecies, I don't think they are part of the Fifth Trumpet Judgment. Below are some of my reasons for dismissing this possibility.

Are the Locusts of the Fifth Trumpet Judgment A.I. Robots?

One of the prophetic details that some believe identifies drones in the Fifth Trumpet Judgment is found in the verse below.

"And they, (*the locusts*) had breastplates like breastplates of iron, and the sound of their wings *was* like the sound of chariots with many horses running into battle." (Rev. 9:9; *emphasis added*)

These advocates who believe the locusts are drones suggest that the, "*breastplates like breastplates of iron, and the sound of their wings was like the sound of chariots with many horses running into battle,*" implies that these are likely A.I. robots or drones.

If this was the only detail about these locusts, then their idea could have credibility. However, there are many other details scattered through Rev. 9:1-11, that I believe mitigate against this possibility. I point out in the chapter called, "*The Seven Trumpet Judgments*" that they are probably demons.

Some of the problems with this teaching are listed below.

- The majority of breastplates for human soldiers have been made of bronze or iron for centuries. Thus, this is not a new or unique detail that can only now be attributed to A.I. robots.

- The Locusts originate from the smoke that comes out of the bottomless pit, rather than a Robot manufacturing factory somewhere. (Rev. 9:2-3)

- The commander of these locusts is the fallen angel named Apollyon rather than an A.I. programming specialist. (Rev. 9:11)

- The Locusts only torment men for five months, which poses the question: "Will an A.I. robot know the limits between killing and tormenting someone?" One tormented person that dies at the hands of an A.I. robot seemingly nullifies this entire theory. The pertinent verse is below.

  "In those days men will seek death and will not find it; they will desire to die, and death will flee from them." (Rev. 9:6)

It is difficult to think that a robot or drone would know its limitations to be in compliance with this prophetic detail.

- Will a robot be able to determine who has the seal of God? The locusts receive specific instructions in the verse below.

  "They were commanded not to harm the grass of the earth, or any green thing, or any tree, but only those men who *do not have the seal of God* on their foreheads." (Rev. 9:4; *emphasis added*)

It would seem that determining who has the seal of God would require spiritual rather than technological discernment. Such selectivity is something that apparently Apollyon possesses as the commander of the tormenting locusts. If the locusts are demons, which is what I and some others believe, then the locust would also perhaps have the ability to decipher who to torment.

The Global Cashless Society of the Antichrist

"He causes all, both small and great, rich and poor, free and slave, to receive a mark on their right hand or on their foreheads, and that no one may buy or sell except one who has the mark or the name of the beast, (*the Antichrist*) or the number of his name." (Rev. 13:16-17; *emphasis added*)

It is commonly taught that the fulfillment of this prophecy requires a technology. It doesn't have to, but it likely does. Technically, the Antichrist could establish a system of commerce that requires a consumer to tattoo an identification mark on their right hand or on their foreheads in order to receive an approval to buy and sell. However, this would be a global economic nightmare that is easily avoided by using technologies that presently exist.

The use of current and developing technologies could have numerous advantages to this crazed world leader, who ultimately covets the spiritual worship of all mankind. He could:

1. Centralize all commerce,
2. Monitor the flow of all goods and services globally,
3. Reduce the traditional crimes of thievery and bank robbery,
4. Track the whereabouts of every marked individual,
5. Consolidate and control all the personal records of every marked individual.

These are just a few advantages of using technologies to establish a global cashless society. The commercial system of the Antichrist is also well detailed in Revelation 18. The clues found within these details also support the probability that the Antichrist employs technologies for his cashless society:

- The merchants worldwide must be able to grow rich from the abundance of the system (Rev. 18:3),

- The system must be able to oversee a vast internationally integrated shipping industry that is capable of transporting commercial goods to global markets. (Rev. 18:17-19),

- The system must be centralized in one location in order for it to be capable of being destroyed in one hour (Rev. 18:10),

- The system must facilitate the ability for consumers to promptly purchase goods that are manufactured abroad. Some of the commercial goods described in the verses below appear to be coming from different exporting countries.

> "Merchandise of gold and silver, precious stones and pearls, fine linen and purple, silk and scarlet, every kind of citron wood, every kind of object of ivory, every kind of object of most precious wood, bronze, iron, and marble; and cinnamon and incense, fragrant oil and frankincense, wine and oil, fine flour and wheat, cattle and sheep, horses and chariots, and bodies and souls of men." (Rev. 18:12-13)

Presently, the world markets are gradually moving away from cash and credit card transactions in favor of the Blockchain technology, which utilizes digital currencies. Digital currency is the blanket term used to describe all electronic money, that includes both virtual currency and cryptocurrency. Digital currencies can only be owned and spent using electronic wallets or designated connected networks.

Digital currency exhibits properties similar to physical currencies, but can allow for instantaneous transactions and borderless transfer-of-ownership. This type of financial exchange medium would enable the Antichrist to promptly accomplish the five commercial advantages identified above.

Promptly, is the key word here. This is because the Antichrist has only a short forty-two-month period to work within in order to put his cashless society in place. He will need to implement it in the NOW when he is able!

> "And he, (*the Antichrist*), was given a mouth speaking great things and blasphemies, and he was given authority to continue for forty-two months." (Rev. 13:5; *emphasis added*)

The chronology of events begins with:

1. The Ten Kings desolating the Harlot world religion and stripping this system of its wealth (Rev. 17:16),

2. The Ten Kings turn over all of the Harlot's and their wealth to the Antichrist promptly thereafter (Rev. 17:17),

3. Upon receiving this enormous wealth the Antichrist instructs the False Prophet to centralize all commercial activity under one cash free economic system (Rev. 13:15),

4. Upon centralizing his system he forces mankind to utilize his cashless system in order to buy or sell any and all goods and services (Rev. 13:16).

The Antichrist can't be omnipresent like God, Who searches the hearts and minds of people as per Jeremiah 17:10, but this devilish last days world leader will be able to track the whereabouts of every individual marked into this global computerized economic system.

Israel Converts Modern-Day Weapons into Energy for Seven Years

This chapter closes out with one of its opening passages dealing with the burning of enemy weapons for seven-years by the Israelis. Ezekiel 39:9-10 predicts the following:

*   Israelis will set fire and burn the weapons of the defeated Magog invaders for seven years.

    "Then those who dwell in the cities of Israel will
    go out and set on fire and burn the weapons, both
    the shields and bucklers, the bows and arrows,
    the javelins and spears; and they will make fires
    with them for seven years." (Ezekiel 39:9)

- This process will eliminate the need for Israelis to chop and gather wood from the fields and forests.

  "They will not take wood from the field nor cut down any from the forests." (Ezekiel 39:10a)

- The Israelis will make fires with these enemy weapons instead.

  "Because they will make fires with the weapons." (Ezekiel 39:10b)

- They will plunder and pillage these enemies in retaliation for invading Israel.

  ""They will plunder those who plundered them, and pillage those who pillaged them," says the Lord God." (Ezekiel 39:10c)

First, let's explore the last bullet point. The Magog coalition invades Israel to plunder and pillage the Jewish state. This backfires and Israel ends up doing the plundering and pillaging. This evidences that God's foreign policy toward the Gentiles, which was established over 4000 years ago is still effectually intact even at this future time.

At that time, God promised Abraham that the Gentiles who cursed him would be cursed in retaliation.

"I will bless those who bless you, And I will curse him who curses you; And in you all the families of the earth shall be blessed." (Genesis 12:3)

This "*Curse For Curse In Kind*" policy has been displayed throughout Israel's history in some of the examples below.

Exodus 14 - The Red Sea Crossing: This epic event pertained to the Hebrew exodus out of Egypt in pursuit of the Promised Land.

Pharaoh of Egypt and his army attempted to kill the Hebrews at the Red Sea, but the sea miraculously parted so that the Hebrews could cross over to the other side on dry ground.

While the Red Sea remained separated, Pharaoh led his army into the midst of these divided waters to their doom. The waters converged upon them so that all Egyptians who entered were killed. So, the *Curse For Curse In Kind* aspect was employed in that, Pharaoh and his armies tried to curse the Jews at the Red Sea, but instead, the Red Sea cursed them.

Another example occurred nearly a millennia later during the time of Queen Esther. The historical account concerned the plan of then Persian Prime Minister Haman to kill the Jews living in Persia and hang Esther's adopted father Mordechai. Haman's plan failed, as the Jews fought back and survived, but instead of Mordechai getting hung in the gallows, Haman did.

> "So they hanged Haman on the gallows that he had prepared for Mordecai. Then the king's wrath subsided." (Esther 7:10)

Thus, the *Curse For Curse In Kind* aspect manifested in the reversal of Haman being hung in the same gallows that he had prepared to hang Mordechai. These are only two examples, among several others, that demonstrated how God's Gentile foreign policy applies on both national (Egypt) and personal (Haman) levels.

In the Ezekiel 38 and 39 prophecy this *Curse For Curse In Kind* policy shows itself again, in that Israel plunders and pillages the invaders, rather than vice versa. The other interesting note is found in correlating what happened to Joseph, when his brothers intended to harm him, with how the Ezekiel invaders intend to harm Israel.

> "But as for you, (*Joseph's brothers*), you meant evil against me, (*Joseph*); but God meant it for good, in

> order to bring it about as it is this day, to save many
> people alive." (Genesis 50:20; *emphasis added*)

This could perhaps be comparably paraphrased to apply in the Ezekiel 38 case as follows:

> "But as for you, (*Ezekiel 38 invaders*), you meant
> evil against me, (*Israel*); but God meant it for
> good, in order to bring it about as it is this day,
> to save many people alive."

Remember that God puts the hooks in the jaw of the Ezekiel invaders to bring them against Israel. They invade Israel with evil intentions, but God, who according to Romans 8:28 knows how to convert bad things into good, blesses Israel in the end analysis.

> "I will turn you around, put hooks into your jaws,
> and lead you out, with all your army, horses,
> and horsemen, all splendidly clothed, a great
> company with bucklers and shields, all of them
> handling swords." (Ezekiel 38:4)

> "And we know that all things work together for
> good to those who love God, to those who are the
> called according to *His* purpose." (Romans 8:28)

- Israelis will set fire and burn the weapons of the defeated Magog invaders for seven years.

Now let's explore the first bullet point above. This detail prompts a couple of questions.

1. Why? Why will Israel burn these weapons? Why don't they incorporate them into their own arsenals? These are likely state of the art weapons that Israel could use militarily.

2. What is the nature of these weapons? Are they primitive, *"shields and bucklers, the bows and arrows, the javelins and spears"* as Ezekiel 39:9 reads, or was the prophet attempting to describe in the vocabulary of his time, the advanced ABC (Atomic, Biological and Chemical) weapons that currently exist within the Ezekiel invaders arsenals?

Why will Israel burn these weapons? Ezekiel 39:10 explains that the Israelis burn these weapons to make fires with them. They elect this method because it enables the Jews to let the trees in the fields and forest continue to grow. This verse states that, *"They will not take wood from the field nor cut down any from the forests."*

What kind of fires are they going to use these weapons for over the course of seven years? Are these going to be big bonfires, or are they going to be used for household and civilian purposes like cooking, heating and public utilities? Cooking and heating were customary domestic uses of fire prior to the invention of gas and electricity. If the latter is the case, then the use of these weapons for fires could be for fuel and energy purposes, rather than to build campfires and roast marshmallows.

If this means that Israel converts the enemies' weapons into fuel and energy resources, they must have a technology in place to accomplish this. Perhaps the prophet was attempting to inform us that when Ezekiel 38 happens, the enemies will have advanced weapons and Israel will possess the technological wherewithal to convert them into sources of fuel for domestic usages.

Even still, why will Israel burn these weapons for domestic consumption, rather than utilize them militarily? The likely reason is because they don't need them, or at least not all of them, for military uses. The answer is not because Israel won't know how to use them militarily. Presently, Israel possesses the ability to purchase American fighter jets and then modify them to better fit their fighting needs. Below is a related headline from the Jerusalem Post that was published on May 11, 2016.

*'ISRAEL ONLY COUNTRY ALLOWED BY US
TO MODIFY NEW STEALTH FIGHTER JETS'*

The possible reason that Israel won't necessarily need all of these weapons for military means, is because they will be dwelling securely having deployed their IDF to win a war over their Arab enemies, which would fulfill the Psalm 83 prophecy. This victory would enable them to become the safe dwelling Israel described in the verse below.

> "You (*Magog invaders*) will say, 'I will go up against a land (*Israel*), of unwalled villages; I will go to a peaceful people (*Israelis*), who dwell safely, all of them dwelling without walls, and having neither bars nor gates'"—(Ezekiel 38:11; *emphasis added*)

The verse describes geopolitical conditions within Israel before the Ezekiel coalition invades the Jewish state, not after. This suggest that the Jews felt relatively safe in advance of the Ezekiel invasion, and therefore after witnessing God supernaturally defeat the Magog invaders, as described in Ezekiel 38:18-39:6, they felt doubly secure.

Then, adding fuel to the fire, after the fulfillments of Psalm 83 and Ezekiel 38, Israel enters into the False Covenant of Daniel 9:27, which makes the Jews in Israel even feel more safe and secure. So that by the time the Antichrist barges into their Third Temple and commits the "*abomination of desolation*" that Jesus speaks about in Matthew 24:15, the IDF is powerless to prevent this. Perhaps at that time, they may regret having burned, rather than kept, the Magog invaders weapons?

Why do they burn the weapons for seven years? Is this because that's when all the weapons have been burned, or is it because something happens to halt the further weapons burning process? The answer may be that the cessation results when the Antichrist performs the "abomination of desolation."

This is the pivotal prophetic event that Jesus Christ warns about in Matthew 24. This abominable act happens at the midpoint of the Trib-period.

> "Therefore when you see the 'abomination of desolation,' spoken of by Daniel the prophet, standing in the holy place" (whoever reads, let him understand), "then let those who are in Judea flee to the mountains. Let him who is on the housetop not go down to take anything out of his house. And let him who is in the field not go back to get his clothes.'" (Matthew 24:15-18)

Jesus warns the Jews to flee immediately and not continue to burn weapons. This is because He realizes that the Antichrist will begin his Jewish genocidal campaign at that time. There may be more weapons left to burn, but no time left to do so.

Thus, the Jews could burn weapons for three and one-half years prior to the Trib-period and continue to do so for the first three and one-half years within the Trib-period, but not at all during the second half of the Trib-period. This is one of the reasons prophecy experts like Dr. Ron Rhodes, Dr. Arnold Fruchtenbaum, Dr. David Reagan, I and others believe that Ezekiel 38 find fulfillment prior to the Trib-period.

Israel Burns Weapons for Seven Years

	False Covenant Confirmed	**The Abomination of Desolation**	
Israel burns weapons for 3.5 years in peace	**Israel burns weapons for 3.5 years in pseudo peace**	**Jews flee, stop burning weapons, & Antichrist attempts Jewish genocide**
Church Age and Post-Rapture / Pre-Trib Time-Gap	First three and one-half years of Trib-Period	*Midpoint*	Second three and one-half years of Trib-Period

So in conclusion of this last section, it appears as though Ezekiel was foretelling of a time whereby the Jews would possess the technological capability of converting highly advanced weapons into fuel and energy related sources.

19

How to Obtain the Seal of God

The Seal of God was introduced in the chapter entitled, The Seven Trumpet Judgments. It is alluded to in the verses below that deal with the Fifth Trumpet Judgment. This judgment is the first of the three devastating "Woe Judgments" in the book of Revelation.

Fifth Trumpet: The Locusts from the Bottomless Pit (Woe #1)

> "Then out of the smoke locusts came upon the earth. And to them was given power, as the scorpions of the earth have power. They were commanded not to harm the grass of the earth, or any green thing, or any tree, but only those men who do not have *the seal of God* on their foreheads. And they were not given authority to kill them, but to torment them for five months. Their torment was like the torment of a scorpion when it strikes a man. In those days men will seek death and will not find it; they will desire to die, and death will flee from them." (Rev. 9:3-6; *emphasis added*)

In that prior chapter the following observations were made about the Seal of God:

1. Only those men who do not have the Seal of God on their foreheads are tormented as per (Rev. 9:4).

2. These demonic locust invaders have the ability to distinguish between who has, and who does not have, the Seal of God on their foreheads.

3.   The only way to avoid being tormented by these demonic invaders is to obtain the Seal of God.

This chapter will explain:

1.   The Seal of God is only given to believers,
2.   What the Seal of God is,
3.   The advantages of receiving the Seal of God,
4.   How to receive the Seal of God now!

The Seal of God is only for believers

The Greek word for seal that is used above in Revelation 9:4 is "sphragis." Strong's Hebrew and Greek Dictionaries defines (G4973), the word "sphragis," as either; *a signet; a fencing in, a protecting from misappropriation, a stamp impressed (as a mark of privacy, or genuineness), or literally a seal.*

The word "sphragis" is used a total of 16 times in the New Testament. It is used 11 times to describe the Seal Judgments of Rev. 6:1-17 and 8:1. In these instances the word identifies a stamp impressed upon a series of parchments that bind them into a scroll. This is expressed in the two verses below.

> "And I saw in the right *hand* of Him who sat on the throne a scroll written inside and on the back, sealed with seven seals. Then I saw a strong angel proclaiming with a loud voice, "Who is worthy to open the scroll and to loose its seals?" (Rev. 5:1-2)

The other five usages of the word are listed and explained below.

1.   *"And he (Abraham) received the sign of circumcision, a seal of the righteousness of the faith which he had"*… (Romans 4:11a)

This is the first use of the word in the New Testament. This use of this word for seal is directly related to a believer's faith in God. Abraham believed in God.

2.   *"Am I (Paul) not an apostle? Am I not free? Have I not seen Jesus Christ our Lord? Are you not my work in the Lord? If I am not an apostle to others, yet doubtless I am to you. For you are the seal of my apostleship in the Lord."* (1 Corinthians 9:1-2)

This usage by the apostle Paul informs that those who believe in God serve as a testament to his apostleship.

3.   *"Nevertheless the solid foundation of God stands, having this seal: "The Lord knows those who are His,"...* (2 Timothy 2:19a)

This usage of seal connects the Lord with those who believe in Him. The Lord knows who they are.

4.   *"Then I saw another angel ascending from the east, having the seal of the living God. And he cried with a loud voice to the four angels to whom it was granted to harm the earth and the sea, saying, "Do not harm the earth, the sea, or the trees till we have sealed the servants of our God on their foreheads.""* (Revelation 7:2-3)

These verses allude to the 144,000 Witnesses who are all believers in God. Revelation 7:3 says that these witnesses are sealed as servants of God.

5.   *"They were commanded not to harm the grass of the earth, or any green thing, or any tree, but only those men who do not have the seal of God on their foreheads."* (Rev. 9:4)

These, like the 144,000 witnesses, are sealed by God on their foreheads. Perhaps it is only the 144,000 that are being referred to here, but more than likely it applies to all believers alive at this future time.

In each of these five instances above only believers are alluded to. Therefore, it is safe to conclude that the Seal of God is only given to believers.

In addition to these verses above, there are more details about what happens when a believer becomes sealed by God. A close examination of the Greek word "sphragizo," which is a derivate of the Greek word "sphragis," enlightens us that the Holy Spirit plays an integral part in the sealing process.

Strong's Hebrew and Greek Dictionaries defines (G4972), the word "sphragizo" as follows; The word is from (G4973), "sphragis". It means, *to stamp (with a signet or private mark) for security or preservation (literally or figuratively); by implication to keep secret, to seal up.*

The verses below comprehensively explain the Seal of God process.

> "Now He, (*God the Father*), who establishes us, (*The Apostle Paul and disciples Silvanus and Timothy*),[62] with you, (*The believer*), in Christ, (*God the Son*), and has anointed us *is* God, who also has sealed, (*sphragizo*), us and given us the, (*Holy*), Spirit in our hearts as a guarantee." (2 Cor.1:21-22; *emphasis added*)

This passage unites the Trinity with the believer in a spiritual symbiotic union. The guarantee is the indwelling Holy Spirit within our hearts.

> "In Him, (*Jesus Christ*), you, (*The believer*), also *trusted,* after you heard the word of truth, the gospel of your salvation; in whom also, having believed, you were sealed, (*sphragizo*), with the

Holy Spirit of promise, who is the guarantee
of our inheritance until the redemption of the
purchased possession, to the praise of His glory."
(Ephesians 1:13-14; *emphasis added*)

These two Ephesians verses above emphasize the critical role
of the gospel message of salvation in the process. The sequence of
events are as follows:

1. A person hears the "word of truth," which is the gospel
    message of salvation,

2. They believe it,

3. Then they receive it; meaning they accept Jesus Christ as
    their Lord and Savior,

4. Having heard, believed and received, they put all of their
    trust "In Him," (*Jesus Christ*),

5. As a result of their decision to become a believer, they are
    sealed with the Holy Spirit,

6. The Holy Spirit serves as the spiritual guarantor of the
    believers eternal redemption.

    "And do not grieve the Holy Spirit of God, by
    whom you were sealed, (*sphragizo*), for the day
    of redemption." (Ephesians 4:30; *emphasis added*)

Finally, after a believer has undergone the six steps outlined
above from Ephesians 1:13-14, they are instructed to, "not grieve
the Holy Spirit." This is in large part because, in addition to sealing
the believer for the day of his or her redemption, the Holy Spirit
is transforming the believer into the likeness of Jesus Christ. This
undertaking is performed in accordance with Romans 8:28-29
through the method described in John 14:26.

"But the Helper, the Holy Spirit, whom the Father
will send in My name, (*To serve as the Seal of God*),
He will teach you, (*The believer*), all things, and
bring to your remembrance all things that I said
to you." (John 14:26; *emphasis added*)

"And we know that all things work together
for good to those who love God, (*The
believers*), to those who are the called according
to *His* purpose. For whom He foreknew, He also
predestined *to be* conformed to the image of His
Son, that He might be the firstborn among many
brethren." (Romans 8:28-29; *emphasis added*)

What the Seal of God is

The Seal of God is essentially God's stamp of divine approval
and spiritual protection   upon the believer. It is a form of
identification that separates the believers from the unbelievers. In
the book of Revelation it appears to be a tangible impression that
is placed upon the foreheads of the believers. If this is the case, that
would explain how the invading locusts of Revelation 9:4 could
identify their targets. By way of reminder, they are instructed to
torment "*only those men who do not have the seal of God on their
foreheads.*"

However, it could also be an intangible identifier that is only
visible to the Trinity, angelic hosts (good and fallen), demonic
realms and those that have a special spiritual discernment. An
example of this visibility into the invisible realm is found in the
biblical story of Elisha and his servant in the verses below.

"So he answered, "Do not fear, (*The invading
Syrians*) for those who *are* with us *are* more than
those who *are* with them." And Elisha prayed,
and said, "Lord, I pray, open his eyes that he may
see, (*What is invisible to the naked eye*)." Then

the Lord opened the eyes of the young man, and he saw, (*Into the invisible realm*). And behold, the mountain *was* full of horses and chariots of fire all around Elisha. So when *the Syrians* came down to him, Elisha prayed to the Lord, and said, "Strike this people, I pray, with blindness." And He struck them with blindness according to the word of Elisha." (2 Kings 6:16-18; *emphasis added*)

Another very likely probability, is that the Seal of God is the invisible indwelling of the Holy Spirit inside the believer. The 2 Cor. 1:21-22, Ephesians 1:13-14 and 4:30 verses provided above all explained the integral role of the Holy Spirit in the Seal of God process. This was a topic also explored in the prior chapter called, "Believers in the Tribulation Period." The biblical precedent for this possibility is found in the verses below.

"And I will pray the Father, and He will give you, (*Seal you with*), another Helper, that He may abide with you forever—The (*Holy*) Spirit of truth, whom the world cannot receive, because it neither sees Him nor knows Him; but you know Him, for He dwells with you and will be in you." (John 14:16-17; *emphasis added*)

The invisible indwelling of the Holy Spirit, whom the world cannot see, inside of the believer, epitomizes the true definition of faith as expressed in the passage below.

"Now faith is the substance of things hoped for, the evidence of, (*invisible*), things not seen. For by it the elders obtained a *good testimony. By faith we understand that the worlds were framed by the word of God, so that the, (visible), things which are seen were not made of things which are visible.*" (Hebrews 11:1-2; *emphasis added*)

If you are a believer presently, you possess the Seal of God via the indwelling of the Holy Spirit. Although you can't see Him, you can know Him, because "*He dwells with you and will be in you.*"

The Seal of God versus the Mark of the Beast

The Seal of God exists in stark contrast to the Mark of the Beast, which is a tangible identifier reserved for unbelievers in the Great Tribulation Period. The Greek word for this form of identification is "charagma."

Strong's Hebrew and Greek Dictionaries define it as *a scratch or etching, that is, stamp (as a badge of servitude), or a mark.* "Charagma" appears in Revelation. 13:16-17, 14:9,11, 15:2 16:2, 19:20, 20:4 and in each instance it alludes to the Mark of the Beast, which is described below.

> "He causes all, both small and great, rich and poor, free and slave, to receive a mark on their right hand or on their foreheads, and that no one may buy or sell except one who has the mark or the name of the beast, or the number of his name. Here is wisdom. Let him who has understanding calculate the number of the beast, for it is the number of a man: His number *is* 666." (Rev. 13:16-18)

The Mark of the Beast is subject matter for the follow up Volume 2 sequel book that is presently untitled. Those who receive this mark will be pledging their spiritual allegiance to the Antichrist and partaking in his cashless society. The verses below warn of the grave consequences to unbelievers for doing this.

> "Then a third angel followed them, saying with a loud voice, "If anyone worships the beast and his image, and receives *his* mark on his forehead or on his hand, he himself shall also drink of the

wine of the wrath of God, which is poured out full strength into the cup of His indignation. He shall be tormented with fire and brimstone in the presence of the holy angels and in the presence of the Lamb. And the smoke of their torment ascends forever and ever; and they have no rest day or night, who worship the beast and his image, and whoever receives the mark of his name."" (Rev. 14:9-11)

The Forehead in the Book of Revelation

It is interesting to note that the Seal of God, in Revelation 7:3 and 9:4 and the Mark of the Beast in Revelation 13:16 are located upon the foreheads of the subjects. In the case of the Mark of the Beast, this appears to be a tangible identifier. The forehead is alluded to in, Rev. 7:3, 9:4, 13:6, 14:1, 14:9, 17:5, 20:4, 22:4.

In Rev. 17:5 below it is dealing with the Harlot World Religion.

"And on her forehead a name *was* written: MYSTERY, BABYLON THE GREAT, THE MOTHER OF HARLOTS AND OF THE ABOMINATIONS OF THE EARTH."

In this instance, the tattooed forehead of the whore of Babylon is symbolic. "THE MOTHER OF HARLOTS," represents a global pagan religion, but the apostle John's eyes were opened in a vision to see this religious institution embodied as a woman. This instance, like all of the other above Revelation usages of forehead, connect it with the primary bodily location of spirituality. It seems to be the go between that links the mind, heart and soul of an individual. This is also the case in the verse below, but in a much more positive prophecy.

" And there shall be no more curse, but the throne of God and of the Lamb shall be in it, and His servants shall serve Him. They shall see His face, and His name *shall be* on their foreheads. There shall be no night there: They need no lamp nor light of the sun, for the Lord God gives them light. And they shall reign forever and ever." (Rev. 22:3-5)

In this verse, the name of Jesus Christ is imprinted, probably symbolically, upon the foreheads of His believers. What better physical location than a forehead to be close to one's mind and its thoughts? It appears that the forehead serves as the bodies billboard when it deals with spiritual matters.

The Forehead in the Hindu Religion

In the Hindu religion the devotees place a dot on their foreheads, which is called a "Bindi." This practice has a strong religious application. Below is a quote about this Hindu custom, which also connects the forehead as the representative body location of spirituality.

> *"Around 3000 BC, the rishi-muni (ancient seers of Hinduism) wrote the Vedas, in which they described the existence of areas of concentrated energy called the chakras. There are seven main chakras that run along the center of the body, and the sixth one (called the ajna chakra, the "brow chakra" or "third eye chakra") occurs exactly where the bindi is placed. In Sanskrit, ajna translates as "command" or "perceive," and is considered the eye of intuition and intellect. According to the Vedas, when something is seen in the mind's eye or in a dream, it is also seen by ajna. Thus, the bindi's purpose is to enhance the powers of this chakra, specifically by facilitating one's ability to access their inner wisdom or guru, allowing them to see the world and interpret things in a truthful, unbiased manner as well as forsake their ego and rid*

*their false labels. Hindu tradition holds that all people
have a third inner eye. The two physical eyes are used
for seeing the external world, while the third focuses
inward toward God. As such, the red dot signifies
piety as well as serving as a constant reminder to keep
God at the center of one's thoughts.*"[63]

Unfortunately for the Hindus, none of their gurus ever rose
from the grave to authenticate their spiritual teachings. Thus their
Bindi is at best ornamental and cultural and does not seal them for
their redemption!

In contrast, Jesus Christ rose from the grave, and in so doing,
validated everything He taught while He was alive on earth. His
resurrection is an integral part of the entire gospel of salvation
message.

"For I delivered to you first of all that which I also
received: that Christ died for our sins according
to the Scriptures, and that He was buried, and
that He rose again the third day according to the
Scriptures." (1 Cor. 15:3-4)

If Christ did not resurrect from the grave, then the most
popular Bible verse in Christianity is of no value.

"For God, (*The Heavenly Father*), so loved the
world that He gave His only begotten Son, (*Jesus
Christ*), that whoever believes in Him, (*Hopefully
this is you*), should not perish but have everlasting
life, (*Why? Because He is Risen*)." (John 3:16;
emphasis added)

The advantages of receiving the Seal of God

There are incredible benefits that come with receiving
the Seal of God. A few of them are listed below:

- An abundant life now (John 10:10),

- An everlasting life in the hereafter (John 3:16),

- An immortal body forever (1 Corinthians 15:50-54),

- A mansion in heaven (John 14:1-6),

- An escape from God's Wrath, if you receive Christ prior to the Trib-Period (Luke 21:36),

- A reprieve from the locust torment of the Fifth Trumpet Judgment, if you receive Christ prior to that time (Rev. 9:4),

- A choice seat in the First Resurrection (Rev. 20:4-6),

- A heavenly reward ceremony (2 Cor. 5:9-11),

- A face to face meeting with Jesus Christ (1 Cor. 13:12),

- A name in the Lamb's Book of Life (Rev. 21:27),

- A place in the eternal order where this is no more death, sorrow or crying (Rev. 21:4).

These are a small sampling of the advantages of becoming a believer.

How to receive the Seal of God now

If you are ready to make the wisest decision and take the biggest step that you can ever make in your lifetime, then receive Jesus Christ right now as your personal Lord and Savior. Remember that, "*the Lord knows those who are His,*"... (2 Timothy 2:19a). He also knows those who are not!

> "Therefore God also has highly exalted Him
> and given Him the name which is above every
> name, that at the name of Jesus every knee should
> bow, of those in heaven, and of those on earth,
> and of those under the earth, and *that every
> tongue should confess that Jesus Christ is Lord, to
> the glory of God the Father." (Philippians 2:9-11)*

These critically important verses apply to you one way or another. Presently, you are alive and among *"those on earth,"* but at some point you will be dead and numbered among *"those under the earth."* It's your call, either you voluntarily take a knee now, if you haven't already done so, and confess that Jesus Christ is Lord, or you involuntarily fall to your knees later as described in the process below.

The Great White Throne Judgment

> "Then I saw a great white throne and Him who
> sat on it, from whose face the earth and the
> heaven fled away. And there was found no place
> for them. And I saw the dead, small and great,
> standing before God, and books were opened. And
> another book was opened, which is *the Book* of Life.
> And the dead were judged according to their works,
> by the things which were written in the books. The
> sea gave up the dead who were in it, and Death
> and Hades delivered up the dead who were in
> them. And they were judged, each one according
> to his works. Then Death and Hades were cast
> into the lake of fire. This is the second death. And
> anyone not found written in the Book of Life was
> cast into the lake of fire." (Rev. 20:11-14)

The Great White Throne Judgment is the just trial for all unbelievers. They are all brought front and center from the dead, *"those under the earth,"* to stand before God. Then, they are all judged according to their works, which will all fall short before the righteousness that is required to dwell in the presence of God in heaven. This is why they all wind up in the Lake of Fire, which is an entirely different and extremely undesired zip code.

Below are a few important scriptures for unbelievers to study now, well in advance of this final White Throne Judgment. They set the standard for why this judgment is so terminal for those who don't have Jesus Christ representing them at this divine hearing.

> "My little children, these things I write to you, so that you may not sin. And if anyone sins, we have an Advocate with the Father, Jesus Christ the righteous. And He Himself is the propitiation for our sins, and not for ours only but also for the whole world." (1 John 2:1-2)

This encouraging verse points out that Jesus Christ will be anyone's Advocate, as long as they receive Him as their Savior. The next verse explains why that is important.

> "For He, (*God the Father*), made Him, (*God the Son*), who knew no sin *to be sin for us, that we might become the righteousness of God in Him.*" (2 Cor. 5:21; emphasis added)

Christ possesses the required righteousness of God. According to the prophet Isaiah we don't.

> "All we, (*This includes* you and me), like sheep have gone astray; We have turned, every one, to his own way; (*Oh yeah, I have been there and done that*), And the Lord has laid on Him, (*Jesus Christ the Messiah*), the iniquity of us all. (Isaiah 53:6; emphasis added)

Every unbelieving knee will drop and every unbelieving

tongue will confess that Jesus Christ is Lord at the time of the White Throne Judgment. This is because they won't have Jesus Christ, Who possesses the required Righteousness of God, as their Advocate. They will serve as their own defense attorney. They will present their case of the sheep that had gone astray and has turned to his or her own way. That won't cut the mustard, especially when God the Father sacrificed His only begotten Son, Jesus Christ on their behalf, and they rejected Him!

Former US President Abraham Lincoln said it best, "*He who represents himself has a fool for a client.*" Why would you make such a foolish decision at the most important trial of your eternal existence? DON'T DO IT! DON'T BE THAT FOOL!

If you want to avoid the Great White Throne Judgment and being cast into the Lake of Fire, then receive Jesus Christ as your personal Lord and Savior RIGHT NOW! Follow the steps outlined in the Appendix entitled, The Sinners Salvation Prayer. Listen to these invitational words below from Jesus Christ.

> "Behold, I *(Jesus)* stand at the door and knock. If anyone *(Including you)* hears My voice and opens the door, I will come in to him and dine *(Have a salvation relationship)* with him, and he with Me. To him who overcomes I will grant to sit with Me on My throne, as I also overcame and sat down with My Father on His throne." (Rev. 3:20-21; *emphasis added*)

Appendix 1
The Sinner's Salvation Prayer

"In an acceptable time I have heard you, And in the day of salvation I have helped you." Behold, now *is* the accepted time; behold, now *is* the day of salvation. (2 Corinthians 6:2)

"And you shall love the Lord your God with all your heart, with all your soul, with all your mind, and with all your strength. This is the first commandment."" (Mark 12:30)

The most important decision one can make in their entire lifetime is to receive Christ as their personal Lord and Savior. It is the sinner's passport to paradise! It's an all-inclusive package that provides a forgiven and changed life on earth now and a guaranteed future admission into heaven afterward.

Without God's forgiveness, the sinner cannot enter into heaven because earthly sin is not allowed to exist there. Otherwise, it would not be rightfully called "heaven." Jesus was sent into the world to provide a remedy for man's sin problem. The Bible teaches that we are all sinners and that the wages, (what we deserve), of sin is death, (spiritual separation from God forever). But God so loved us that He wanted to make a way so anyone could be forgiven and thus be allowed to enter heaven. God doesn't want anyone to perish, and has been patient with us so that we can turn from sin and find forgiveness, (by faith), in His son, Jesus.

"For God so loved the world that He gave His only begotten Son, [*Jesus Christ*] that whoever believes in Him should not perish but have everlasting life. (John 3:16, NKJV).

> And this is eternal life, that they may know You, the only true God, and Jesus Christ [*Begotten Son of God*] whom You have sent." (John 17:1-3, NKJV).

These passages point out that people are perishing to the great displeasure of God, who loves them immeasurably. He wishes that none would perish, but that everyone would inhabit eternity with Him and His only begotten Son, Jesus Christ. Quintessential to eternal life is the knowledge of these two concepts.

Sin Separates Us from the Love of God

The apostle John reminds us in 1 John 4:8, 16 that God is love, but man lives in a condition of sin, which separates him from God's love. Romans 8:5-8 explains how sin manifests into carnal behavior that creates enmity between God and man.

> "So then, those who are in the flesh cannot please God." (Romans 8:8, NKJV).

The book of Romans instructs that sin entered into the world through Adam, and spread throughout all mankind thereafter. Additionally, Romans informs that sin is the root cause of death, but through Jesus Christ eternal life can be obtained.

> "Therefore, just as through one man [*Adam*] sin entered the world, and death through sin, and thus death spread to all men, because all [*men*] sinned." (Romans 5:12; emphasis added).

> "All we like sheep have gone astray; We [*mankind*] have turned, every one, to his own way; And the

LORD has laid on Him [*Jesus Christ*] the iniquity of us all." (Isaiah 53:6; emphasis added).

"For the wages of sin *is* death, but the gift of God *is* eternal life in Christ Jesus our Lord." (Romans 6:23, NKJV).

If this makes sense to you, and you:

1. Have humbled yourself to recognize that you are a sinner, living under the curse of sin, which has separated from your Creator.

2. Believe that Jesus Christ took your punishment for sin so that you could be pardoned, as the only way to be saved

3. Want to repent and start letting God make changes in your life to be in a right relationship with God,

4. And, want to do it right now,

Then you have come to the right place spiritually. It is the place where millions before you, and many of your contemporaries alongside you, have arrived.

Fortunately, you have only one final step to take to complete your eternal journey. This is because salvation is a gift of God. Christ paid the full price for all sin, past, present, and future, when He sacrificed His life in Jerusalem about 2000 years ago. Your pardon for sin is available to you through faith in the finished work of Jesus Christ, which was completed upon His bloodstained cross. His blood was shed on our behalves. He paid sins wages of death on our account.

You must now take the final leap of faith to obtain your eternal salvation. It is your faith in Christ that is important to God.

"But without faith *it is* impossible to please [*God*] *Him*, for he who comes to God must believe that He is, and *that* He is a rewarder of those who diligently seek Him." (Hebrews 11:6, NKJV; emphasis added).

"In this you [*believer*] greatly rejoice, though now for a little while, if need be, you have been grieved by various trials, that *the genuineness of your faith, being much more precious than gold that perishes,* though it is tested by fire, may be found to praise, honor, and glory at the revelation of Jesus Christ, whom having not seen you love. Though now you do not see *Him,* yet believing, you rejoice with joy inexpressible and full of glory, receiving the end of your faith—the salvation of *your* souls." (1 Peter 1:6-9, NKJV).

Before the necessary step to salvation gets introduced it is important to realize and appreciate that salvation is a gift provided to us through God's grace. We didn't earn our salvation, but we must receive it. If you are one who has worked hard to earn everything you have achieved in life then you are to be commended. However, apart from living a sinless life, which is humanly impossible, there is nothing you as a sinner could have done to meet the righteous requirement to cohabitate in eternity with God. In the final analysis, when we see our Heavenly Father in His full glory, we will all be overwhelmingly grateful that Christ's sacrificial death bridged the chasm between our unrighteousness, and God's uncompromised holiness.

"But God, who is rich in mercy, because of His great love with which He loved us, even when we were dead in [*sin*] trespasses, made us alive together with Christ (*by grace you have been saved*), and raised *us* up together, and made *us* sit together in the heavenly *places* in Christ Jesus, that in the ages to come He might show the exceeding riches of His grace in *His* kindness toward us in Christ Jesus. *For by grace you have been saved* through faith, and that not of yourselves; *it is the gift of God,* not of works, lest anyone should boast." (Ephesians 2:4-9; emphasis added).

The Good News Gospel Truth

The term gospel is derived from the Old English "*god-spell,*" which has the common meaning "*good news,*" or "*glad tidings.*" In a nutshell, the gospel is the good news message of Jesus Christ. Jesus came because God so loved the world that He sent His Son to pay the penalty for our sins. That's part of the good news, but equally important is the "Resurrection."

This is the entire good news gospel;

> "For I delivered to you first of all that which I also received: that Christ died for our sins according to the Scriptures, and that He was buried, and that He rose again the third day according to the Scriptures." (1 Corinthians 15:3-4; NKJV).

Christ resurrected which means He's alive and able to perform all of His abundant promises to believers. The Bible tells us that He is presently in heaven seated at the right-hand side of God the Father waiting until His enemies become His footstool. Furthermore, from that position Christ also intercedes on the behalf of Christians. This intercession is an added spiritual benefit to you for becoming a believer.

> "But this Man, [*Jesus Christ became a Man, to die a Man's death*] after He had offered one sacrifice for sins forever, sat down at the right hand of God, from that time waiting till His enemies are made His footstool. For by one offering He has

perfected forever those who are being sanctified."
(Hebrews 10:12-14; emphasis added).

"Who *is* he who condemns? *It is* Christ who died,
and furthermore is also risen, who is even at the
right hand of God, who also makes intercession
for us." (Romans 8:34)

The resurrection of Christ overwhelmingly serves as His
certificate of authenticity to all His teachings. He traveled through
the door of death, and resurrected to validate His promises and
professions. This can't be said of the claims of Buddha (Buddhism),
Mohammed (Islam), Krishna (Hinduism), or any of the other
host of deceased, human, non-resurrected, false teachers. All the
erroneous teachings they deposited on the living side of death's
door were invalidated when they died and lacked the power to
conquer death itself, as Jesus has done.

One of Christ's most important claims is;

"Jesus said to him, "I am the way, the truth, and the
life. No one comes to the [*heavenly*] Father except
through Me."" (John 14:6; emphasis added).

This is a critical claim considering eternal life can only be
obtained by knowing the heavenly Father, and Christ, whom
He [the Father] sent, according to John 17, listed earlier in this
chapter. Most importantly, the resurrection proves that death has
an Achilles heel. It means that its grip can be loosed from us, but
only by Christ who holds the power over death.

*"O Death, where is your sting? O Hades, where is
your victory?"* The sting of death *is* sin, and the
strength of sin *is* the law. But thanks *be* to God,
who gives us the victory [*over Death and Hades*]
through our Lord Jesus Christ." (1 Corinthian
15:55-57; emphasis added).

How to be Saved – You Must Be Born Again

> "Jesus answered and said to [*Nicodemus*] him, "Most assuredly, I say to you, unless one is born again, he cannot see the kingdom of God.""(John 3:3; emphasis added).

Jesus told Nicodemus, a religious leader of his day, that entrance into the Kingdom of God required being born again. This is a physical impossibility, but a spiritual necessity, and why faith plays a critical role in your salvation. You can't physically witness your new birth; it is a spiritual accomplishment beyond your control that happens upon receiving Christ as your Lord and Savior. God takes full responsibility for your metamorphosis into a new creation at that point.

> "Therefore, if anyone *is* in Christ, *he is* a new creation; old things have passed away; behold, all things have become new." (2 Corinthians 5:17, NKJV).

You must trust God to perform on His promise to escort you through the doors of death into eternity, and to process you into the likeness of Christ. This is the ultimate meaning of being born again, and alongside Christ, is a responsibility undertaken by the third member of the Trinity, the Holy Spirit. Christ holds the power over Death and Hades, but the Holy Spirit is your "*Helper*" that participates in your spiritual processing.

> "I *am* He [*Jesus Christ*] who lives, and was dead, and behold, I am alive forevermore. [*Resurrected*] Amen. And I have the keys of Hades and of Death." (Revelation 1:18; emphasis added).

> "If you love [*Christ*] Me, keep My commandments. And I will pray the Father, and He will give you another Helper [*Holy Spirit*], that He may abide

with you forever— the Spirit of truth, whom the world cannot receive, because it neither sees Him nor knows Him; but you know Him, for He dwells with you and will be in you." (John 14:15-17; emphasis added).

"These things I have spoken to you while being present with you. But the Helper, the Holy Spirit, whom the Father will send in My name, He will teach you all things, and bring to your remembrance all things that I said to you." (John 14:25-26, NKJV)

In order for you to successfully crossover from death to eternal life, *at the appointed time*, God has to work his unique miracle. Christ's resurrection demonstrated that He possesses the power to provide you with everlasting life. Death was not eliminated in the resurrection, it was conquered.

This is why the full gospel involves both God's love and power. His love for us would be of little benefit if it ended with our deaths. His love and power are equally important for our eternal assurance.

Therefore, we are informed in Romans 10, the following:

"But what does it say? *"The word is near you, in your mouth and in your heart"* (that is, the word of faith which we preach): that if you confess with your mouth the Lord Jesus and believe in your heart that God has raised Him from the dead, you will be saved. For with the heart one believes unto righteousness, and with the mouth confession is made unto salvation. For the Scripture says, *"Whoever believes on Him will not be put to shame."* For there is no distinction between Jew and Greek, for the same Lord over all is rich to all who call upon Him. For *"whoever*

calls on the name of the Lord shall be saved.""
(Romans 10:8-13, NKJV).

These Romans passages sum it up for all who seek to be saved through Christ. We must confess that Jesus Christ is Lord, and believe in our hearts that God raised Him from the dead.

The Sinner's Prayer for Salvation

Knowing that confession of Christ as Lord, coupled with a sincere faith that God raised Him from the dead are salvation requirements, the next step is customarily to recite a sinner's prayer in order to officiate one's salvation.

Definition of the Sinner's Prayer

"A sinner's prayer is an evangelical term referring to any prayer of humble repentance spoken or read by individuals who feel convicted of the presence of sin in their life and desire to form or renew a personal relationship with God through his son Jesus Christ. It is not intended as liturgical like a creed or a confiteor. It is intended to be an act of initial conversion to Christianity, and also may be prayed as an act of recommitment for those who are already believers in the faith. The prayer can take on different forms. There is no formula of specific words considered essential, although it usually contains an admission of sin and a petition asking that the Divine (Jesus) enter into the person's life."[64]

Example of the Sinner's Prayer

Below is a sample Sinner's Prayer taken from the Salvation Prayer website. If you are ready to repent from your sins, and to receive Jesus Christ as your personal Lord and Savior, read this prayer will all sincerity of heart to God.

Dear God in heaven, I come to you in the name of Jesus. I acknowledge to You that I am a sinner, and I am sorry for my sins and the life that I have lived; I need your forgiveness.

I believe that your only begotten Son Jesus Christ shed His precious blood on the cross at Calvary and died for my sins, and I am now willing to turn from my sin.

You said in Your Holy Word, Romans 10:9 that if we confess the Lord as our God and believe in our hearts that God raised Jesus from the dead, we shall be saved.

Right now I confess Jesus as the Lord of my soul. With my heart, I believe that God raised Jesus from the dead. This very moment I receive Jesus Christ as my own personal Savior and according to His Word, right now I am saved.

Thank you Jesus for your unlimited grace which has saved me from my sins. I thank you Jesus that your grace never leads to license for sin, but rather it always leads to repentance. Therefore Lord Jesus transform my life so that I may bring glory and honor to you alone and not to myself.

Thank you Jesus for dying for me and giving me eternal life.

Amen.[65]

Congratulations and welcome into the household of God!

Below are the congratulatory words and recommendations also taken from the Salvation Prayer website. If you just prayed the Sinner's Prayer please be sure to read this section for further guidance.

> *"If you just said this prayer and you meant it with all your heart, we believe that you just got saved and are born again. You may ask, "Now that I am saved, what's next?" First of all you need to get into a bible-based church, and study God's Word. Once you have found a church home, you will want to become water-baptized. By accepting Christ you are baptized in the spirit, but it is through water-baptism that you show your obedience to the Lord. Water baptism is a symbol of your salvation from the dead. You were dead but now you live, for the Lord Jesus Christ has redeemed you for a price! The price was His death on the cross. May God Bless You!"*[66]

Remember, being born again is a spiritual phenomenon. You may have felt an emotional response to your commitment to Christ, but don't be concerned if fireworks didn't spark, bands didn't march, sirens didn't sound, or trumpets didn't blast in the background at the time. There will be plenty of ticker-tape for us in heaven, which is where our rewards will be revealed. If you believed and meant what you said, you can be assured God, Who sent His Son to be crucified on our behalf, heard your every word. Even the angels in heaven are rejoicing.

> *"Likewise, I say to you, there is joy in the presence of the angels of God over one sinner who repents."*(Luke 15:10; emphasis added).

Welcome to the family…!

Endnotes

1 J. Barton Payne information was taken on 4/3/19 from this website: https://www.amazon.com/review/R3RRDWI6V8CGMW

2 *The Now Prophecies* devotes 3 chapters to America's future decline and potential prophetic role in Ezekiel 38.

3 Megas and Thlipsis translated from the (New American Standard Hebrew and Greek Dictionaries)

4 Shabua translated from the (New American Standard Hebrew and Greek Dictionaries)

5 Dr. Fruchtenbaum, *The Footsteps of the Messiah (San Antonio: Ariel Publishers, 2004)*, p. 191-192

6 *The Bible Knowledge Commentary: Old Testament by John Walvoord and Roy B. Zuck*

7 *(cf. The Coming Prince by Sir Robert Anderson, Kregel, 1967).*

8 *The Bible Knowledge Commentary: Old Testament by John Walvoord and Roy B. Zuck*

9 Terminal definition taken on 4/5/19 from this website: https://www.merriam-webster.com/dictionary/terminal

10 Abraham's descendants are referenced in Genesis 17:7-8, Exodus 32:13, Luke 1:55 and elsewhere.

11 Dr. Fruchtenbaum, *The Footsteps of the Messiah (San Antonio: Ariel Publishers, 2004)*, p. 177

12 Dr. Fruchtenbaum, *The Footsteps of the Messiah (San Antonio: Ariel Publishers, 2004)*, p. 180-181

13 Egypt as sin is explained at this website: http://evidenceforchristianity.org/what-passages-in-the-new-testament-use-egypt-as-a-symbol-of-sin-and-slavery-to-sin/

14 Boston Globe headline taken from this website on 4/24/19: https://www.bostonglobe.com/lifestyle/travel/2016/03/17/welcome-tel-aviv-gayest-city-earth/y9V15VazXhtSjXVSo9gT9K/story.html

15 Jan Markell quote taken from this article linked here: https://myemail.constantcontact.com/The-Terminal-Generation.html?soid=1101818841456&aid=2VKJGy_6IQ0

16 Isaiah's ministry period was taken on 4/28/19 at this weblink: https://www.encyclopedia.com/philosophy-and-religion/bible/old-testament/isaiah

17 Quoted from the book entitled, *Psalm 83: The Missing Prophecy Revealed, How Israel Becomes the Next Mideast Superpower.* p. 155-156.

18 Ethnos translations taken from the New American Standard Hebrew and Greek Dictionaries under G1484.

19 Pateo translation taken from Strong's Hebrew and Greek Dictionaries under G3961.

20 Tim Drake quote taken on 4/29/19 from this website: https://legatus.org/do-catholics-believe-in-the-rapture/

21 Christian statistics taken on 5/3/19 from this website: https://en.wikipedia.org/wiki/Christian_population_growth

22 Meta tauta Greek translation was taken from the Strong's Exhaustive Concordance of the Bible.

23 Regarding the mystery: Romans 11:25, Ephesians 3:3-6. Regarding the grafting in: Romans 11:17-24

24 *Dr. Rhodes, The End Times In Chronological Order (Harvest House Publishers, 2012),* p. 113-114

25 Dr. Reagan quote taken from the article called "*The Mysterious 144,000.*" It came from this web link: https://christinprophecy.org/articles/the-mysterious-144000/

26 Plague information was taken on 11/4/16 from this website, http://ancienthistory.about.com/od/epidemics/tp/10PlaguesEgypt.htm

27 *Henry M. Morris, The Revelation Record (Tyndale House Publishers, Inc. Wheaton, Illinois),* pages 193-194

28 *Dr. Rhodes, The End Times In Chronological Order (Harvest House Publishers, 2012),* p. 115-116

29 *Tim LaHaye, Revelation Unveiled (Zondervan, 1999),* p. 191

30 Quote taken on 5/16/19 from point #3 at this weblink: https://www.studylight.org/commentaries/hkr/revelation-11.html

31 *nikaoô,* translated from the New American Standard Hebrew and Greek Dictionaries

32 Stephanos definition is from Strong's Concordance. It was taken from this website: http://biblehub.com/greek/4735.htm

33 Dr. Fructhenbaum, *The Footsteps of the Messiah, Ariel Press in San Antonio, 1982,* p. 225.

34 Fruchtenbaum, *The Footsteps of the Messiah,* pg. 226.

35 Fruchtenbaum, *The Footsteps of the Messiah,* pg. 231.

36 Fruchtenbaum, *The Footsteps of the Messiah,* pg. 231.

37 Dr. Mark Hitchcock quote taken 5/23/19 from this website video link: https://www.youtube.com/watch?v=ubrpG8D-oWo

38 Dr. Mark Hitchcock quote taken 5/23/19 from this website video link: https://www.youtube.com/watch?v=ubrpG8D-oWo

39 Hitchcock, *The End of Money: Bible Prophecy and the Coming Economic Collapse,* pg. 33.

40 Hitchcock, *The Second Coming of Babylon,* pg. 176

41 Feiglin quote taken on 6/7/19 from this website: https://www.timesofisrael.com/zehuts-feiglin-says-he-wants-to-build-third-temple-right-away/

42 Sanhedrin Temple Headline and quote taken on 6/8/19 from this website: https://www.breakingisraelnews.com/117830/70-nations-hanukkah-altar-third-temple/

43 Passover sacrifice in 2018 information taken on 6/8/19 from this website: https://www.jpost.com/Israel-News/Lamb-sacrificed-at-foot-of-Temple-Mount-for-first-time-in-modern-history-547187

44   Barnes Notes on the New Testament by Albert Barnes... Revelation 17 commentary section.

45   Pagan Rome and Papal Rome quote taken on 10/6/16 from this website: http://www.reformation.org/pope-constantine.pdf

46   World countries taken on 6/12/19 from this website: https://www.worldometers.info/geography/how-many-countries-are-there-in-the-world/

47   Fruchtenbaum, *The Footsteps of the Messiah*, pg. 231.

48   Mesopotamia information taken on 6/15/19 from this website: https://www.ancient.eu/Mesopotamia/

49   Hitchcock, quote taken from *Middle East Burning*, "The Kings of the East" section.

50   Chuck Missler on the Kings of the East taken from this website: https://www.khouse.org/articles/2005/601/ and Dr. Reagan's comes from this website: https://christinprophecy.org/articles/the-wars-of-the-end-times/

51   China's military personnel taken on 6/15/19 from this website: https://www.globalfirepower.com/country-military-strength-detail.asp?country_id=china#manpower

52   China's military ranking taken on 6/15/19 from this website: https://www.globalfirepower.com/country-military-strength-detail.asp?country_id=china

53   *There's a New World Coming* by Hal Lindsey, pg. 241.

54   Fruchtenbaum outline from *The Footsteps of the Messiah*, pg. 37.

55   Fruchtenbaum outline from *The Footsteps of the Messiah*, pg. 34.

56   Fruchtenbaum outline from *The Footsteps of the Messiah*, pg. 36.

57   For more information on the Club of Rome visit this website: https://en.wikipedia.org/wiki/Club_of_Rome

58   Barnes Notes on the New Testament by Albert Barnes... Revelation 17 commentary section.

59   Arno C. Gaebelein, The Revelation, New York, NY, "Our Hope," 1915, pp. 99, 101,102.

60   Satellite info taken on 6/20/19 from this website: https://en.wikipedia.org/wiki/Satellite

61   Drone definition taken on 6/20/19 from this website: https://www.space.com/29544-what-is-a-drone.html

62   For the Son of God, Jesus Christ, who was preached among you by us—by me, Silvanus, and Timothy—was not Yes and No, but in Him was Yes. (2 Cor. 1:19)

63   Bindi quote taken on 7/19/19 from this website: https://www.hafsite.org/blog/the-purpose-of-the-bindi/

64   Sinner's Prayer quote taken from Wikipedia over the Internet on 8/13/11 at this link: http://en.wikipedia.org/wiki/Sinner's_prayer

65   Sinner's prayer example was copied from the Internet on 8/13/11 at this website link: http://www.salvationprayer.info/prayer.html (slight emphasis was added in this appendix)

66   Quote welcoming those who prayed the sinner's prayer into the family of God copied over the Internet on 8/13/11 at this link: http://www.salvationprayer.info/prayer.html

Order your copies of this entire end times book series at our online bookstore located at www.prophecydepot.com.

The NOW Prophecies

These are the biblical predictions that lack preconditions and could happen NOW! These prophecies include:

- Disaster in Iran

- Destruction of Damascus

- Final Arab-Israeli War – (Psalm 83)

- Toppling of Jordan

- Terrorization of Egypt

- Emergence of the exceedingly great Israeli army

- Expansion of Israel

- Vanishing of the Christians

- Emergence of a GREATER and SAFER Israel

- The Decline of America

The NEXT Prophecies

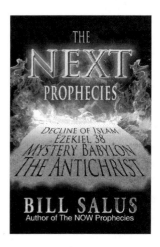

These are the biblical predictions that have minor preconditions and will follow the fulfillment of the NOW Prophecies. These prophecies include:

- Gog of Magog invasion (Ezekiel 38)

- Decline of Islam

- Unrestrained supernatural satanic deception

- Arrival of the Antichrist

- World Wars and global famines and pestilences

- "Mystery Babylon," the Harlot world religion

- Post-Rapture Christian martyrdom

- True content of the False Covenant

- Two phases of the "Overflowing Scourge"

- Start of the third Jewish Temple's construction

Made in the USA
Lexington, KY
26 October 2019